Greatest Stars
of the Opera

Enrico Stinchelli

Greatest Stars of the Opera

The Lives and the Voices of
Two Hundred Golden Years

GREMESE

Performing Arts Series
for Schools and Universities

ACKNOWLEDGEMENTS

We would like to thank the following people for their kind collaboration regarding the photographic material used in the three editions of this book.

Eugene Rizzo and Elena Martini for the beautiful slides by Paul Ronald taken on the set of the opera film *Otello*. The Kaleidos-Roma for the slides of E. Belvedere and A. Rossetti, taken on the set of the opera film *Otello*. Franco Varini (Teatro Comunale of Bologna); Lamberto Scotti (Teatro Comunale of Florence); Giovanni Altavilla (Teatro San Carlo of Naples); Pietro Diliberto (Teatro Massimo of Palermo); Ugo Sandroni (Teatro Regio of Turin); Claudio Gherbitz (Teatro Comunale "Giuseppe Verdi" of Trieste); Carlo Felice Theater of Genoa; Rome Opera House; La Fenice Theater of Venice; Elena Fumagalli (La Scala Theater of Milan); the Hon. Quintavalla (Cultural Councillor of Parma); Vincenzo Raffaele Segreto (Teatro Regio of Parma); Dr. Mariotti (Cultural Councillor of Pesaro); Simona Barabesi (Rossini Opera Festival of Pesaro); and Fondazione Arena di Verona.

Dr. Hans Widrich (Salzburg Festival); Charlotte Bonello (Opéra de Nice), Sydney Opera House Trust; Tokyo Bunka-Kaikan; Louwrens Langevoort (Théatre Royal de la Monnaie of Brussels); Metropolitan Opera House of New York; Louise Sparks (Staatsteater of Pretoria); G. Fiasconaro (Pe Operahuis of Port Elisabeth, South Africa); Valerj Glotov (Kirov Theater of Leningrad); Anja Weigmann (Opera Theater of Nuremberg).

A special thanks to Carlo Marinelli Roscioni for his valuable research; Gunther Zerbes, Ursula Glaser, Ingrid Drosler, Hartwig Bemhard, Giandonato Crico, Ermete Manzoni, Alberto dalla Tomasina, Alfredo Tabocchini, Galliano Passerini, Giovanna Deriu, Sasha Gusov – and all the photographers who have kindly supplied their material.

Another thank you to Carlo Marinelli Roscioni for his valuable research; Jurgen Grand (EMI); Mr. Colombo and Mrs. Marmina (Philips); Franco Guandalini, for the beautiful photos of his wife, the soprano Raina Kabaivanska; Alberto Terrani, for the photos of his wife, the mezzo-soprano Lucia Valentini; to Anton Dermota; Ljuba Welitsch; Katia Ricciarelli; Peter Edelmann; Giuseppe Taddei and all the other artists who have collaborated in achieving this volume.

Photos
As far as possible the Publisher has tried to find the name of the photographers whose photographs are published in this volume, in order to attribute them correctly. However, this research has not always been successful and therefore the Publisher apologizes for any possible errors or omissions. In the event of reprinting the Publisher declares himself ready to make any necessary corrections and to recognize any rights, according to article 70, from law number 633, 1941.

Translated by Hellé Theophilatos (from the original Italian edition published as *Le Stelle della Lirica*.)
Translation integrated and revised by Shula Curto
Jacket design by Studio associato Pardini, Apostoli, Maggi – Rome
Phototypeset by Graphic Art – Rome
Printed and bound by C.S.R. – Rome

First edition published as *Stars of the Opera*
© 1992 GREMESE INTERNATIONAL s.r.l., Rome

New revised second edition
© 1996 GREMESE INTERNATIONAL s.r.l., Rome

New revised third edition
Copyright GREMESE
2002 © E.G.E. s.r.l., Rome

ISBN 88-7301-465-8

Contents

Preface

At first I thought that I would include in *Greatest Stars of the Opera* only a restricted number of illustrious singers: fifteen at most. Choosing them was a problem – for one reason or another singers who had given much to the operatic stage continued to be left out. How can we, after all, define a "great voice"? It is not one that breaks crystal, or reaches ultrasonic high notes with ease, or one that exhibits exceptional lung power and seems never to need to take another breath; nor is it one which flaunts volume and power, hurling itself into audiences' ears. A "great voice" is a soft, malleable instrument; at the same time it is incisive, solid and equal in all the registers, built on hard study and supported by intelligence and sensitivity. It is a voice that manages to communicate, that will always be remembered for the wide range of sensations and emotions it gives the audience. *Vom Herzen möge es wieder zum Herzen gehen*, wrote Beethoven on the score of his *Missa Solemnis*: "from the heart may it reach other hearts". This is the only valid rule to be followed by any true artist.

Everybody who begins to study singing aims at this achievement. However, it is easy to lose one's guidelines or to fall into imitations of previous great singers, or to adopt crowd-pleasing compromises such as enlarged notes, exaggerated acting, excessive *falsetti* or *poitriné* sounds. Thus, mingled one with the other, are singers who evade precise definition: there was "Pippo" Di Stefano whose voice color was one of the most beautiful ever to have been heard, who was adored by the public for his innate amiability and spontaneity, but whose extremely personal singing technique was little appreciated by the critics; or Victoria De Los Angeles, a soprano of exquisite musicality and sensitivity but weak in the high register; Mario Del Monaco's exceptional talent was marred by a questionable style and a sometimes inadmissible exaggeration; and whilst we may hesitate to define the voices of Tito Gobbi, Mirto Picchi, Magda Olivero and Gino Bechi as "beautiful", we cannot deny these singers' interpretative qualities, and in particular the divine Magda's exceptional technique.

The company of the "magnificent fifteen" therefore grew in number to include many other stars, each of whom has in some way contributed to vocal history. This vast selection of names has been organized into various categories according to their voice type (eg. dramatic tenor, *coloratura* soprano, *basso profondo*, etc.), and in chronological order. The entries are, perforce, short, but I have tried to summarize both the best and the worst aspects of each performer, without fear of touching sore spots or troublesome theories. We recommend the appendix to the reader's attention; it contains extra information to complement the text; but above all we suggest you read Alfredo Kraus's Master Class carefully – it will be useful to all singing students and fascinating for all opera lovers.

The Author

Introduction

Acting in Song

Opera was born officially in 1567 during the Carnival at Palazzo Corsi in Florence. However, this event had been preceded by many experiments which had favored its creation. The first musical drama was Jacopo Peri's *Dafne*, with text by Ottavio Rinuccini. They were two of the most enthusiastic and gifted members of a group of people, who, animated by the new spirit of the late Renaissance, would habitually gather at the palace of the Conte de' Bardi. There, the young intellectuals who were part of the *Camerata* of Via de' Benci would discuss the world in general, and especially the dream of renewing music and vocal style. They firmly proposed to return to the simplicity of the ancient Greeks: a single voice was to have supremacy over the polyphonic and contrapuntual tangles that were, by then, out of fashion and in contrast to the widespread humanistic ideals of the time. Vincenzo Galilei, one of the most militant members of the group, wrote: "Why should words be sung by four or five voices so that they become incomprehensible, when the ancients could express their most profound passions with a single voice accompanied only by a lyre? We must renounce counterpoint and return to primitive simplicity". To tell the truth the intellectuals themselves did not know to what "primitive simplicity" they were referring, for few remnants of the Greek tragedies remained. However, thanks to a few significant discoveries they were able to confirm their theories, formulate conclusions, and lay the foundations for the birth of opera, establishing that the monodict style was the only one capable of following the thread of a natural discourse, therefore granting supremacy to soloist singing; melodies were to reflect and idealize the emotions; and, above all, singers were to strive for perfect enunciation so that every listener could understand the text. If we think about it, *recitar cantando* (acting in song) is probably the only real possibility of establishing a bridge from the stage, over the orchestra pit, to the stalls. All too often have we been faced with the almost impossible task of deciphering the incomprehensible sounds emitted by even the most illustrious and acclaimed of singers.

Good acting, a clearly comprehensible rendering of the text but also good singing (including vocal ornaments, the so-called *canto fiorito* which have always helped express the sentiments and emotions of the characters) are the basis for all types of song, from opera to popular music.

The Importance of the Singer

From the days when opera was still in its infancy; from Monteverdi, Vivaldi, Handel, Mozart to the composers of the nineteenth and twentieth centuries, the *conditio sine qua non*, the ace card necessary to make a worldwide public love this "organized madness," is the singer – the clarity of the enunciation, the ease of emission, the agility (in a certain type of repertoire), the variety of phrasing and the beauty of timbre – in one word, his or her *bravura*. These are undeniable facts, despite the

Adelina Patti *(1843-1919).*

Francesco Tamagno *(1850-1905) as Otello.*

claims of some people, and this is why over almost three centuries of operatic history the singer has reigned supreme. Of course, there have been great conductors and great directors who have been acclaimed by the public, but not one of them has ever managed to gather the ovations given to legions of singers – even the less outstanding. From 1600 onwards (but let us not forget what happened in ancient Greece and Rome), singers have been surrounded by immense affection, and even idolization. They have been adored, spoiled, punished fiercely for their defects, over-paid or under-paid (and even paid themselves to be permitted to sing!), loved madly or hated viciously; everything is exaggerated, everything taken to extremes, just as in the plots and the music of so many operas. The singer is the center point of an operatic performance, despite the theory that the conductor fills this role. No matter how displeasing a bad baton might be, a conductor will never be hated or despised as will a singer who "cracks" or suffers some other vocal mishap. Rather, as the history of belcanto teaches us, it is the good singer who manages to save productions that are lacking in conducting and direction. No matter how well the accompaniment of an aria is played, rich in color and shading, with an impeccable performance from every member of the orchestra, applause will only be triggered in the presence of an equally splendid vocal interpretation.

A Witness: the Recording

Having decided that the voice is the most important element in a performance, and mentioning only *en passant* that many awful scores have been saved by good singing (the concept of the singer as co-author of the work lasted well into the nineteenth century), we come to the most pressing problem, as far as we are concerned. We have taken into consideration only the "stars" of the twentieth century on, leaving untouched nearly two centuries of operatic history. Why?

First of all because, from Caruso on, we can judge more directly all the most important operatic stars thanks to the recordings they have left us. Personally I favor records and consider them a most important method of propagation, which, if listened to correctly, enable us to identify precise aspects of an artist (such as vocal technique and musicality), the interpretative traditions of the time, and even a social and historical reality, which would otherwise rely only on dusty memories or biased writings. But the record is there: it may camouflage a timbre, almost hiding it, make it opaque, or sometimes lighten it; a very old record can even alter the intonation, but none can ever stop a strong stylistic and technical personality from emerging. For instance, it may be said that Tamagno's voice was different when heard in the theater, or that his recordings do not do him justice; but

Mario Ancona *(1860-1931)*.

Enrico Caruso *(1873-1921) in* Aida.

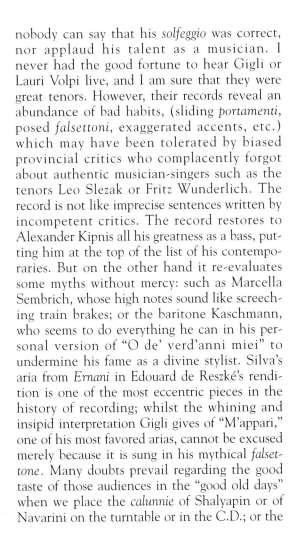

nobody can say that his *solfeggio* was correct, nor applaud his talent as a musician. I never had the good fortune to hear Gigli or Lauri Volpi live, and I am sure that they were great tenors. However, their records reveal an abundance of bad habits, (sliding *portamenti*, posed *falsettoni*, exaggerated accents, etc.) which may have been tolerated by biased provincial critics who complacently forgot about authentic musician-singers such as the tenors Leo Slezak or Fritz Wunderlich. The record is not like imprecise sentences written by incompetent critics. The record restores to Alexander Kipnis all his greatness as a bass, putting him at the top of the list of his contemporaries. But on the other hand it re-evaluates some myths without mercy: such as Marcella Sembrich, whose high notes sound like screeching train brakes; or the baritone Kaschmann, who seems to do everything he can in his personal version of "O de' verd'anni miei" to undermine his fame as a divine stylist. Silva's aria from *Ernani* in Edouard de Reszké's rendition is one of the most eccentric pieces in the history of recording; whilst the whining and insipid interpretation Gigli gives of "M'appari," one of his most favored arias, cannot be excused merely because it is sung in his mythical *falsettone*. Many doubts prevail regarding the good taste of those audiences in the "good old days" when we place the *calunnie* of Shalyapin or of Navarini on the turntable or in the C.D.; or the

Leo Slezak *(1873-1946)*.

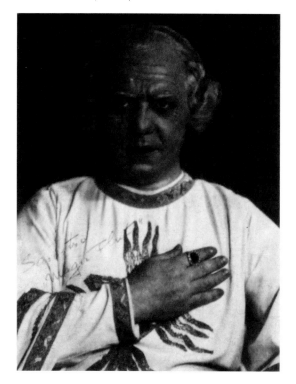

Alexander Kipnis *(1891-1978) in* The Magic Flute.

Marcella Sambrich *(1858-1935) in* Il Barbiere di Siviglia.

serenades of Battistini (but his famous "Eri tu" is no joke either) from *Don Giovanni*; the arias from *I Puritani* with De Lucia or Hipólito Lázaro; Martinelli's *Otello*; or the "Ho-jo-to-ho!" of Litvinne; the "Ritorna vincitor" of Giannina Russ; and the acrobatics – let us call them that – of the contralto Guerrina Fabbri battling with the melismas of Arsace. The list is

long. Thanks to records, the sensitive listener and, above all, the critic who has some idea of singing technique (*rara avis*) can conceive what enormous progress the singer has made towards being a musician and not just a "sound machine". Amongst the singers of the end of the nineteenth century there are none who can compare with such as artists as Gedda, Fischer-

Eduard de Reszké *(1853-1917) in* Faust.

Fernando De Lucia *(1860-1925).*

Hans Hotter *(1909) in* Salome.

Bidù Sayao *(1902) in* La Traviata.

Dieskau, Kipnis, Schipa, Hotter, Wunderlich, Taddei, Ludwig, Schwarzkopf, Olivero, Freni, Kraus, Tebaldi, Callas, Simionato, Stignani, Lemnitz, Ramey, Horne, or Scotto, in other words artists who have put their voices, beautiful or ugly as they may be, at the service of the composer. If by some miracle, there were recordings from the seventeenth and, especially,

Ebe Stignani *(1904-1974) in* Cavalleria Rusticana.

the eighteenth centuries, we would surely hear some good ones! And if we are allowed to remember those "first performers" with a kind of decaying nostalgia, with no documentation on which to base our judgment aside from the scribblings of certain "voice-ologists", as unreliable then as now, it is equally acceptable that we be allowed to doubt the excellence of many famed performers, basing our judgment on the writings of such luminaries as Stendhal, Berlioz, Schumann, Giulio Ricordi, Boito, and other great *chroniqueurs*.

Golden Voices, Brazen Faces

How many clichés, how many lies, how many useless nasty comments have we read or heard from critics against this or that singer. One of the most shocking stances is that taken against the "fabulous nineteen-fifties". Quite the contrary, that period was the last great flowering of voices from the revolutionary advent of Caruso onwards. Just glancing through the theater annals of those years we are astounded: a wide repertory to satisfy all tastes, in every theater, even the provincial ones; excellent protagonists, even the doubles; the possibility of creating at least ten different casts for operas such as *Trovatore, Norma, Rigoletto, Traviata* or *Andrea Chénier*, for which today we cannot even find one cast; widespread popular enthusiasm; great rivalry; memorable performances; accounts

PARALLEL CAREERS

Singer	Year of Debut	Year of Withdrawal
Angelica Catalani (1780-1849). Endowed with a flexible and acrobatic voice, which reached up to high E flat, she was musically unprepared, unable to perform Mozart's accompanied recitatives correctly	1797 (in *Lodoiska* by Mayr at Venice)	About 1830 (however already in 1824 the London and Berlin public protested against her precarious vocal condition)
Renata Scotto (1933). Her repertoire goes from *Lucia* to *Tosca* and includes the most complicated parts for coloratura soprano and *lirico spinto* soprano	She sang "Stride la vampa" in public in 1948, and in 1952 made her theater debut singing *Traviata* at Savona	Still active after a fifty-year-long career
Isabella Colbran (1785-1845). Stendhal praised her beauty and her acting, but judged her singing off-key and her method deplorable. Her husband, Rossini, used to arrange parts to suit her	1806 (?). Madrid	About 1824 (according to Stendhal her decline was already clear in 1816, when many in the audience strongly protested against her singing)
Leyla Gencer (1927). She has sung the rare Donizetti roles and Santuzza, Charlotte and Butterfly, Violetta and Suor Angelica, Donna Anna and Gilda, from Monteverdi to Verism	1950 (as Santuzza in *Cavalleria* at Ankara)	1985 (last stage performance with a little opera by Gnecco at La Fenice, Venice). Subsequent appearances in recital only
Giuditta Pasta (1797-1865). Right from her debut there was talk of an opaque timbre and a precarious intonation. In 1841 Mendelssohn wrote of the "catastrophic condition of her voice" and other "serious problems of intonation"	1815 (a small part at La Scala)	1841 (she decided to retire after a disastrous tour of Poland and Russia, although her vocal condition was already badly compromised in 1834)
Joan Sutherland (1926). Starting from coloratura roles she gradually included in her repertoire *Aida, Ballo in Maschera, Adriana Lecouvreur*, etc., ranging from Handel to Tippett and Bononcini	1952 (as the First Lady in *The Magic Flute*)	1990 (as Marguerite in *Les Huguenots* in Sydney)

which attest to the vitality and brilliance of opera in that period.

The *divi* transmitted emotions which justified the title, surrounded by that magic aura which lifts the singer above the level of show-business.

Now some people, surely the most singularly folkloristic in the opera world, insist that the nineteen-fifties were a sort of Pandora's box, the apex of bad singing, especially when compared with the "glorious" period that ranges from the first half of the seventeenth century until about 1830. We believe such theories to be not only gratuitous, but quite unsupported by any satisfactory proof. If it is true that the benefits of a good vocal preparation and continual practice will accompany a singer throughout life, providing protection from precocious decline and vocal mishaps, then a comparison between some of the much-maligned stars of the fifties and their mythicized colleagues of one hundred and twenty years earlier would be very interesting.

How many tenors worthy of that name could have boasted a vocal longevity comparable to that of Schipa, Lauri Volpi, Gigli or Kraus? Isn't Del Monaco worth more than Donzelli, the first to perform Pollione, who had to lower the *concertato* of Donizetti's *Parisina* because he had no high notes? And we must remember that orchestras at the beginning of the nineteenth century were much smaller than today's. Moreover, the contemporary listener, deafened by record players, radio and television all at full blast, demands greater sonority in the singer. This cannot be denied.

From Caruso onwards, singers have begun to project their voices better, to abandon the constant use of falsetto and to search for a more consistent color. They have learned to sustain sound with the help of a new method of breathing which is radically opposed to the old method used by the *castrati* (who did not take full advantage of the diaphragm muscle since they pulled the stomach inwards during exhalation). Without wishing to over-generalize or indulge in too many technical explanations, if we consider the evolution in singing which has occurred since the end of the eighteen hundreds until today, we realize what conquests both men and women have made in the field of operatic interpretation. However, it is true that great talents have been lacking, perhaps because of the excessive publicity given to certain far from exemplary exponents. It is also true, alas, that good singing teachers are becoming a rare species, and that there is an absurd proliferation (especially in Italy, strangely enough) of singing "gurus" or "witch doctors"; some are unashamedly active during *en plein-air* perfection and master classes, while others operate within the darkness of their home dens. A country that is incapable of guaranteeing a sound vocal study in its conservatoriums or musical academies is forced to tolerate a large amount of private initiative, which, of course, eludes control and leaves room for fraudulent practice. In such conditions it is impossible to expect the birth of new opera stars.

Enrico Stinchelli

Leonard Warren *(1911-1960),* **Jussi Björling** *(1907-1960),* *and* **Zinka Milanov** *(1906-1989) in the recording studio.*

Enrico Caruso *in* Carmen.

The Tenors

The Tenor Voice:
Range and Emission

The tenor is the highest of the male voices and usually ranges from c to c´´, with the most easily executed octave extending from g to g´. The type of emission used is that of chest voice for the lower and middle notes and head voice for the high notes. It is thus defined as "mixed emission". The joining of these two registers, or the *passaggio*, occurs between e´ flat and f´ sharp. Of course, this *passaggio* must never be heard in a well-trained voice, despite the fact that it is cultivated by many incompetent singing teachers. Worse still are the attempts to recreate it artificially, resulting in those awful "vomiting" sounds, hiccups, strangled notes, darkenings, and innumerable other unnatural voice placements.

Tenors in the *Verismo* Repertory

The dawning of the *Verismo* style occurred towards the end of the nineteenth century and coincided exactly with the decline of the Belcanto School. Verdi's compositions represent the last contribution of genius to Grand Opera but also, unwittingly, the introduction of veristic elements into lyric drama. The mythical characters disappeared, as did their tales of idealized love. The old arias were transformed into a continuous, uninterrupted musical discourse. The naturalistic opera of the *Giovane Scuola* (Young School) in Italy (Puccini, Leoncavallo, Mascagni, Cilea and Giordano) proposed a type of drama inspired by what was "real" (*il vero*), the harsh truth and the use of an immediate and passionate style in emotional passages. These concepts are all well demonstrated in the prologue to Leoncavallo's *Pagliacci* (1892). "L'autore ha cercato di pingervi uno squarcio di vita. Egli ha per massima sol che l'artista è un uom, e che per gli uomini scrivere ei deve, ed al Vero ispirarsi". (The author/composer has tried instead to depict a segment of life. His only belief is that the artist is a man, and that he must write for men alone, and be inspired by what is real).

Instead of trills and *roulades* which were now considered useless, screams ("A te la mala Pasqua!," *Cavalleria Rusticana*), insults ("Sgualdrina," *Tabarro*), desperate weeping ("Mario, Mario," finale of *Tosca*), laughter ("Nemico della patria," *Andrea Chénier*) and even the spoken word ("Che vuol dire...", finale of *La Bohème*) were preferred. Everyday language was imitated. Little did it matter if these forms were used in a conventional way, or as tearjerkers; although they were preferably inserted into a popular context, a sort of plebeian tragedy.

Of course, the tenor vocal line was shaken up, even if the change was slow and gradual. Everything had to be adapted to the fashion and taste of the time and the changing social conditions. Two different schools arose. One consisted of the *tenori di forza*, who had strong, robust voices with intense color and who were able to confront both Verdi's compositions and those of the *Giovane Scuola* and emerge unscathed. The other was that of the *tenori di grazia*, who were dedicated to a more virtuoso repertory and in a higher range. Unfortunately, the latter group were frequently inclined to use falsetto and to resort to some highly questionable technical solutions.

Leaders of a New Line:
Caruso, De Lucia and Bonci

In *verismo* opera the tenor is still the protagonist, though no longer in terms of stylized singing, with its elegiac arias culminating in stratospheric high notes. In *verismo* he has become the incarnation of the passionate male, all blood and guts, hairy-chested, just like the clichés of the typical southern Italian male. His voice tends to be dark and widened in the central register: the so-called "Mediterranean" sound. He is not at all inclined to flowery, delicate singing or showy high notes.

We must remember that the difficult transition from the eighteen hundreds to the following century was characterized by an increased voice volume due in part to the use of larger, louder orchestras, a factor imposed by the new needs of the late-romantic compositions.

Together with **Emmy Destinn** (in the photo), and the baritone Amato, **Caruso**, under the baton of Toscanini, took part in the first historical performance of The Girl of the Golden West in New York in 1910. His rendering of the "good" outlaw, Dick Johnson, remains unequalled.

The great contralto **Gabriella Besanzoni** offers a refreshing drink to **Enrico Caruso**, her friend and partner in so many Carmens.

A victorious Radames born at the foot of Vesuvius, **Enrico Caruso**. He sang in his native city during the 1901-1902 season in both Manon and Elisir d'Amore. Despite being in fine form he did not menage to equal the success of his rival De Lucia, and had to undergo humiliating attacks from the Neapolitan critics – he who was as Neapolitan as pizza, tomato sauce and spaghetti! Naples would not see him again until shortly before his death when, in 1921, suffering from emphysema, he made his return.

The vanguard of the twentieth century tenors and the one who has remained a point of reference for a great many singers is Enrico Caruso, whose technique may be compared with the refined and ancient art used by Fernando De Lucia and Alessandro Bonci.

Enrico Caruso (Naples 1873 – 1921) described his own voice as similar to a cello. In fact his sweeping use of breath, his perfect legato and his velvety timbre made his voice resemble this string instrument more than any other tenor voice known until then.

After having completed his studies, albeit somewhat patchy due to his poor financial situation, Caruso made his debut in March 1895, in Morelli's *L'Amico Francesco*, at the Teatro Nuovo of Naples. From then until 1906-7 he was admired as a *tenore di grazia* with exceptional gifts. His Duca di Mantova, his Nadir, Nemorino, Des Grieux in Massenet's *Manon*, and his Faust were amazing for his refined phrasing, his perfect breathing technique, but above all for the exceptional natural beauty of his voice. It was rich with harmonics and brilliant in the first high notes. However from b´ flat onwards he had to use a *falsettone*, or, if necessary, lower the aria key. (This happened in Enzo's aria in *La Gioconda*, and, with Puccini's approval, in Rodolfo's aria in *La Bohème*).

The sensual bronzed color of his voice and the passion he put into his interpretations made him synonymous with the *verismo* tenor. During his American career (from 1903-4 until 1920) his myth grew, thanks to his memorable performances in *Carmen*, *Pagliacci*, *Bohème*, *Tosca*, *Manon Lescaut* and, especially, *La Fanciulla del West* of which he was the first interpreter at the Metropolitan Opera in New York in 1910.

Caruso sang more than six hundred times at the Metropolitan in a repertory totaling some forty different operas (amongst these the first American performances of *Armide* and *La Forza del Destino*).

After a temporary loss of voice during the 1908-9 season, his timbre became even more baritone-like, and more powerful, and his interpretations even more fascinating. In the theater (and also on recordings) he sang "Vecchia zimarra" hidden behind the scenery whilst the indisposed bass had only to mime the words of his own aria.

Between 1902 and 1920 this great tenor made more than two hundred records, earning dizzying sums of money. His was the first truly phonogenic voice and was immediately exploited by the newly established recording industry.

Caruso died of a lung abscess, which, on January 24, 1921, had forced him to interrupt a performance of *L'Ebrea* at the Metropolitan.

De Lucia *as Turiddu. This role was really very far from his natural belcanto repertory; but he performed it often and with great success.*

In comparison with Caruso's rich voice and passion, **Fernando De Lucia** (Naples 1860 – Naples 1925) exhibited a stylized art which seemed almost insipid with its exaggerated taste for *sfumature*, *diminuendi* and *filature*. It sounded as if he was simply playing with his voice in a fanciful game. He applied these same formulas to both repertories: that of the *tenore di grazia* (*Faust*, *Elisir d'Amore*, *Sonnambula*, *Rigoletto*, *The Pearl Fishers*) and that of the *verismo* school in which he specialized after 1891. He was the first to interpret *L'Amico Fritz*, *I Rantzau*, *Silvano* and *Iris*, all by Mascagni; and he often sang *Tosca*, *Cavalleria Rusticana*, *Fedora*, *Bohème* and *Carmen*.

There is nothing surprising in De Lucia's choice of repertory; it was customary at that time for tenors to sing both *Barbiere* and *Cavalleria*; the *verismo* tenor is really only an invention of the last fifty or so years. The first singers to perform the operas of the *Giovane Scuola* were actually a mixture, possessing the stylistic prerogatives inherited directly from belcanto and perfectly adaptable to the new works.

Certainly, the *rallentandi* and *melismi* used by De Lucia surpassed any artistic licence. Lauri Volpi in his book *Voci Parallele* recalls how De Lucia would presumptuously change the words at the end of the aria "Recondita armonia" from *Tosca*. (He would not say "Tosca sei tu", but rather "Tosca sei te," thus rendering the sentence grammatically incorrect). He did this to achieve the increased resonance provided by the "e" vowel compared with that given by the "u" vowel. However, the Neapolitan tenor possessed a varied and graceful phrasing manner and a soft, velvety timbre that became irresistible in moments of ecstatic abandon, even if hampered somewhat by an accentuated *vibrato stretto* (narrow vibration) probably due to a lack of sustainment.

Alessandro Bonci (Cesena, Emilia-Romagna 1870 – Viserba, Emilia-Romagna 1940) was another of Caruso's rivals from the old-style, delicate singing school. Bonci made his debut in January, 1896, as Fenton in Verdi's *Falstaff*, and gave his farewell performance in the *Requiem* by that same composer in 1927. Bonci shared with De Lucia a pure timbre, a noticeable *vibrato stretto* and a very refined technique, and although he had a greater range than De Lucia, reaching up to high c´´, his *verismo* repertory was more limited.

He preferred singing *Rigoletto, Sonnambula, Puritani, Faust,* Massenet's *Manon, Elisir d'Amore, Don Giovanni, Barbiere, Lucia di Lammermoor* and, his favorite, *Un Ballo in Maschera.* Although he did not possess an authentic Verdi incisiveness, he managed all the same to triumph in this role because of his elegant style and his famous little laugh in the quintet "È scherzo od è follia," a variation that Verdi himself much appreciated in May 1898.

Tenors of the Twentieth Century

Before the advent of *verismo* it was most important for all singers, and not only tenors, to be able to range smoothly over all the registers, from the low to the medium to the high. Composers would suit each opera to the vocal characteristics of each singer, just as a tailor adapts clothing to the personal measurements of his clients. Advantage was taken of the best qualities of each singer and during performances protagonists would often add even more ornamentation, such as complicated *cadenze*, or changing the very arias for others they preferred. They thus contributed considerably to the final outcome of the performance and the ultimate success of the work and its composer, who accepted these liberties with little ado. Even Verdi asked the expert Donizetti to write some extra *cadenze* and variations for him, to add to several repeat performances of *Ernani.*

The naturalistic or *verismo* theater ended all this. Here it was the performer, now limited in his vocality, who chose the opera and composer best suited to his characteristics, be it Rossini (in declining popularity), Donizetti, Verdi or Mascagni. This is the origin of the classification of voice types currently used, such as lyric, dramatic, etc., categories which are specific and restricted.

We have already said that *verismo* required large voices of medium extension, but it especially needed effective actors: dynamic, passionate, and even exaggerated. And so vocal technique began to take second place to theatrics. Little by little the last masters of belcanto were disappearing, replaced by the verist performers. In the same manner the last exponents of the nineteenth century gave way to the artists who followed Caruso and who were, more often than not, poor imitations or bad copies of the original.

The *verismo* technique had no need for voices that were extended or extremely agile. The verist tradition required shouts, sobs and cries, and this contributed to the advent of singers who were only interested in declaiming at full voice with little or no mercy for the listener. Even today some of them continue to exert a negative influence, thanks especially to the ever-expanding record industry.

All the same, the verist school of singing had one great value: it expressed the principles of a technique of voice production based on the homogeneity of the entire range and on the sustainment of every note, thus ridding the art of the ostentatious mannerisms which, at the end of the nineteenth century, had reached the absolute limits of tolerance. When listened to today, some performances given by the so-called "belcantisti," from De Lucia to Battistini, from Patti to Marcella Sembrich, are simply comical.

The change from a concept which had regarded the singer as co-author of an opera (1600-1850) to one according to which the opera modeled the singer, created the twentieth century separation of the tenor voice into various categories.

The light or light lyric tenor, whose voice often lacks color and who frequently resorts to falsetto, was adapted to roles once entrusted to the *tenore di grazia*; the lyric tenor, who was formerly defined as of "mixed character," took on a wider repertory ranging from the later Verdi (*Traviata, Rigoletto*) to some of the verist works (*La Bohème, Butterfly,* etc.); the *tenore lirico spinto*, formerly the *tenore di forza*, was assigned the more complicated verist roles (*Andrea Chénier,* Johnson in *Fanciulla del West,* Folco in *Isabeau,* Calaf in *Turandot*); and the dramatic tenor, the classic Wagnerian *Heldentenor*, was used to interpret roles such as *Otello* or Samson in Saint-Saëns' *Samson and Delilah.*

LIGHT LYRIC AND LYRIC TENORS OF THE TWENTIETH CENTURY

Giuseppe Anselmi (Nicolosi, Catania 1876 – Zoagli, Genoa 1929) came from the same mould as Bonci and De Lucia. Elegant and refined, he sang as a *tenore di grazia* from 1896 to 1916. Because of his vocal ductility and purity, and noble appearance, he was a favorite in operas such as *Rigoletto, Manon, Barbiere, Lucia, Werther* and *Tosca*. He obtained great success in London, Buenos Aires, Madrid and St. Petersburg, as well as in all the major Italian theaters.

He may be criticized only for an excessively affected pronunciation in declarations of love or, for that matter, any languid phrase, and an excessive use of embellishments in the Liberty style. These defects are easily heard in any of his recordings but Anselmi was, after all, only following the fashions of his time and he was able to do so because he possessed an extraordinary voice.

Another example of vocal and physical elegance was the tenor **Edoardo Garbin** (Padua 1865 – Brescia 1943), the first Fenton in Verdi's

*A group photo for Leoncavallo's Zazà. From the left: the tenor **Edoardo Garbin**, first Fenton in Falstaff at La Scala (1893), was a refined singer and actor, who, together with his wife, the soprano **Adelina Stehle**, was frequently applauded. To his left the soprano **Rosina Storchio**, Leoncavallo, and, with top hat, the baritone **Mario Sammarco**.*

*Lensky's "Farewell to Life" sung by **Leonid Sobinov** greatly moved audiences. It is rare to find a tenor who responds with such sensitivity to the plot of Tchaikovsky's opera Eugene Onegin. (Archives of the Kirov Theater, Leningrad, 1910)*

Falstaff. He was gifted with a light and very controlled emission, and executed the high registers and *mezzavoce* with confidence. Due to his talent Garbin was also an excellent verist, especially in Puccini roles, being acclaimed above all in *Adriana Lecouvreur* and *Fedora*.

Lucien Muratore (Marseille 1876 – Paris 1954) is to be remembered as a historic performer of French lyric roles, from Gounod to Massenet. Formerly an actor, he sang frequently in French and American opera theaters between 1902 and 1936 and was the first interpreter of over thirty new roles.

Thanks to his lively intelligence, he knew how to exploit his vocal and interpretative gifts to the utmost, wisely controlling a voice that was, by nature, deprived of any special tone-color. In 1913 he married the famous Lina Cavalieri, with whom he made several films.

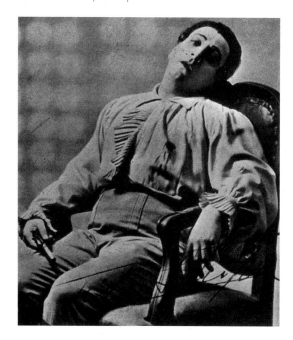

*Werther's suicide – **Schipa** was one of the best performers of the part in Massenet's opera. It allowed him to show all his poetry, elegiac abandon, and wonderful vocal nuances. However, during the second half of his career he would always lower the aria "Pourquoi me réveiller" by a semi-tone.*

Leonid Sobinov (Jaroslav 1872 – Riga 1934) triumphed in Russia. Unforgettable as Lensky in *Eugene Onegin*, he studied in Moscow and made his debut in 1894. He sang mostly in St. Petersburg in a very wide repertory (Gounod's *Roméo et Juliette, Lohengrin, Orfeo, Werther, Traviata, Fra Diavolo, Barbiere, Don Pasquale*, etc.). He also performed in Italy (La Scala: 1904, 1906, 1911) and in France, retiring in 1924.

Sobinov possessed a beautiful voice color and a natural gentleness which made him perfect for melancholic roles, those of sensitive characters destined for a tragic end. He was also elegant, refined, handsome, and had an excellent cultural background.

John MacCormack (Athlone, Eire 1884 – Dublin 1945) was a rival of Bonci, De Lucia and Anselmi for polished sound, vocal consistency, facility with which he reached high notes, moderation and varied phrasing. However, he was hindered by his corpulence, which made him quite ill-suited to roles such as Rodolfo, Edgardo or Pinkerton. Tormented by a "fat man" complex, MacCormack retired early from the stage in 1920 and dedicated his talent exclusively to concert performances.

He had twenty-one roles in his repertory that ranged from lighter parts (*Don Giovanni, Sonnambula, Faust, Rigoletto*) to some of the verist repertory (*Cavalleria, Pagliacci, Butterfly, Bohème*). He made his debut in 1906 (*L'Amico*

Fritz) at Savona, then at Covent Garden (*Cavalleria Rusticana*). From 1909 on he collaborated with the opera companies of Boston, Philadelphia, Chicago and New York.

He received the title of "Conte Palatino" from Pope Pius XI for his worthy activities in the sphere of sacred music in 1924. His interpretation of Gounod's "Ave Maria", recorded with the accompaniment of Fritz Kreisler on the violin, has remained a myth.

The great **Tito Schipa** (Lecce, Puglia 1888 – New York 1965) sang from 1910 (he made his debut in *Traviata* at Vercelli) until 1960, when he withdrew from the stage after a final triumphant series of concerts.

The secret of his vocal longevity can be found in his amazing technique and the particular formation of his facial cavities, which allowed a positioning completely in the "mask." Schipa managed to make an almost unlimited use of his voice which was, in actual fact, neither beautiful nor extended. He passed easily from a *fortissimo* to a *filato* and vice-versa; he could attack or sing the most difficult passages in *mezzavoce* ("Parmi veder le lagrime," for example, from *Rigoletto*); he colored every aria poetically, reaching the

Tito Schipa *in one of his last concerts. (Archive of La Fenice Theater, Venice)*

extreme apex of his expressive possibilities in the part of *Werther*.

He enjoyed world-wide appreciation for his interpretations of *Bohème, Rigoletto, Manon, Barbiere, Elisir, Don Pasquale, Lucia, Don Giovanni, Sonnambula, Arlesiana* and *Tosca*, all roles characterized by the use of secure technique and imagination, the two ingredients of true belcanto.

Schipa also sang at Chicago (1919-1932), at the Metropolitan Opera (1932-35, 1940-41), and at San Francisco from 1924 onwards.

Beniamino Gigli (Recanati, Marche 1890 – Rome 1957) enjoyed immense popularity, perhaps inferior only to that of Caruso. After his beginnings as a choir boy and his studies at the Santa Cecilia Conservatorium in Rome, he won the competition held by Maestro Cleofonte Campanini at Parma for young singers, after which he debuted at Rovigo in *La Gioconda* (October 14, 1914). He had been well launched and in only a few years time he was in demand by all the major companies worldwide. From 1920 until 1932 he was very active at the Metropolitan of New York, where he had taken

The Irish tenor **John MacCormack**, in the title role of Gounod's Faust. One of the great names in the history of recordings.

Beniamino Gigli in his costume for the role of Enzo Grimaldo in La Gioconda. The warmth of his mezzavoce and the penetrating timbre in the aria "Cielo e mar" are amongst the best things left by Gigli on record.

Caruso's place. After this he returned to Europe, where he was already well known, and continued his career until 1955 with a repertory so large that nobody has ever been able to rival it. In fact, Gigli possessed a vocal apparatus that could be adapted to any operatic part. It was warm and velvety in tone, equal in all registers, reaching past c´´, with a perfect legato and an enchanting *mezzavoce*.

He performed at Covent Garden in 1930-31, 1938-39, and also in 1946, when he sang both Canio and Turiddu in the same evening.

Between 1920 and 1940, he sang Faust, Nemorino, Canio, Turiddu, Chénier, Rodolfo, Riccardo, that is, from Donizetti and even Bellini (*Sonnambula, Pirata,* and *Norma* at Catania in 1945) to Verdi, Puccini, Giordano, Mascagni, Cilea, Wagner (*Lohengrin*), as well as the French lyric authors, all splendidly.

This was a huge repertory that clearly demonstrates his exceptional talent. One of the last costume appearances of this great tenor was in *Pagliacci* at La Fenice, Venice, on February 14, 1954. It was a triumphant evening for a singer who was almost sixty-four years old.

Gigli's vocal longevity, as that of all great artists, was due to a solid technique based on correct respiration and a high resonance position in the "mask". Gigli knew how to use mixed sound (that resonates both in chest and head) with special effectiveness. With a minimum of effort he could produce high notes which were both ringing and robust. The last phase of Gigli's career was damaged by certain verist exaggerations such as sobs (the ones after "No, pazzo son" from *Manon Lescaut* are famous) and inconsiderate yells (like those after the "Improvviso" of *Chénier*, or Cavaradossi's "Farewell to Life"). In contrast he was often insipid in Neapolitan songs or popular ditties which he so often exhibited in concerts and on record. Perhaps it is the price one pays to gain international popularity and perpetuate one's own myth, particularly in America. Despite a somewhat graceless figure and lack of acting talent, Gigli made a number of films.

No, this is not a corpulent Douglas Fairbanks in "The Adventures of Sinbad the Sailor," but **Ferruccio Tagliavini** *in the "Friendship" duet from* The Pearl Fishers. *This is the performance of 19 February 1952, together with the baritone Tagliabue. (Historic Archives of the Rome Opera Theater)*

The 1956-1957 season of the Rome Opera was opened with Mascagni's Iris on December 26. Gavazzeni was conducting, Wallman directing, and **Giuseppe Di Stefano** *was singing with Petrella and Christoff (Photo: Oscar Savio. Historic Archives of the Rome Opera Theater).*

In the Firmament of the Great, Some Stars Shine Brighter

As a *tenore di grazia* **Dino Borgioli** (Florence 1891 – 1960) would today have no rivals, whereas in his time he had many, and worthy ones at that.

He made his debut in *La Favorita* at Milan in 1917, and from then on gained world-wide acclaim, particularly in England. He performed operas by Bellini, Donizetti and Rossini, without mannerisms and with a well-formed and technically sound voice.

Jussi (Johan) Björling (Stora Tuna 1911 – Siar Oe, Stockholm 1960), an idol at the Met and Covent Garden, he boasted one of the finest timbres ever heard in the twentieth century.

Björling had a superbly refined technique and penetrating high notes, while his emission was measured and noble. He possessed a vocal flexibility which could manage the finest shadings of sound yet launch unhesitatingly into the fullest and richest dramatic passages. And he could produce both a measured Don Ottavio (Mozart) and an exuberant Des Grieux (Puccini), at the same time carrying on a busy Lieder repertoire.

Fortunately, Björling has left us a part of his musical heritage on record, among which of particular interest are the complete opera recordings of *Trovatore*, *Bohème*, *Turandot*, *Manon Lescaut*, *Rigoletto*, and *Ballo in Maschera*. He also participated in many highly successful "live" recordings, one of the best being a *Roméo et Juliette* (Gounod), recorded at the Met, with Bidú Sayao as his partner.

To collect Gigli's heritage, there came a small and amiable Italian tenor, **Ferruccio Tagliavini** (Barco, Reggio Emilia 1913 – Reggio Emilia 1995), who made his debut at Florence in *La Bohème* in 1938. There were many similarities with Gigli: the lovely color of his voice, the pure *falsettone*, the clear enunciation, the passionate phrasing, and, unfortunately, also some of his faults, such as the well-known "hiccups" and the unnecessary *acciaccature*.

Until the mid-fifties Tagliavini was one of the best performers of the *Pearl Fishers*, *L'Amico Fritz*, *Arlesiana*, *Werther*, *Manon*, *Lucia*, and, above all, he was an unforgettable Nemorino. Later, a choice of unsuitable repertory (*Tosca*, *Fedora*, *Ballo in Maschera*) hardened his voice and he lost polish and roundness in the *passaggio*.

Tagliavini sang regularly at the Metropolitan Opera between 1941 and 1954, and at Covent Garden in 1950 and 1955-56, touring with La Scala.

Of the great *tenori di grazia* of the forties and fifties, **Cesare Valletti** (Rome 1922 – Milan 2000) is to be remembered as perhaps the most worthy follower of Tito Schipa. His timbre was clear and limpid, extended up to b´, warm and caressing in the *mezzavoce*. Valletti made a varied and imaginative use of shadings, and gave just the right coloring to every phrase, at the same time pleasingly modulating his voice. From 1947 until 1962 he was one of the best singers of Werther, Elvino, Edgardo, Nemorino, Des Grieux (in Massenet's M*anon*), Don Ottavio, Almaviva in Rossini's *Barbiere* and Alfredo (*Traviata*). However, towards the end of the nineteen-fifties the first signs of decline began to appear. His high notes became forced, his emission open and his voice opaque and veiled. Perhaps Valletti's stay at the Metropolitan between 1953 and 1960 accelerated the fading of his star.

Giuseppe "Pippo" Di Stefano (Motta S. Anastasia, Catania 1921) has always declared with extreme honesty that he was never subjugated to singing technique but was guided by his instinct. He always preferred generous emotional participation and a psychological characterization of his roles to the purely vocal aspect. This put at risk his own vocal integrity, which he finally sacrificed. Such, however, was the price to be paid for the truly revolutionary contribution made by Di Stefano to the spread of opera in the twentieth century. He had the ability to emotionally engage not only the experts but the entire audience in his performance by

The Swedish tenor **Jussi Bjorling**, in the title role of Gounod's Faust. He was admired in Verdi and Puccini as well as in French music.

reversing the usual technique/instinct values and giving first place to the poetic text through his clear enunciation and phrasing. A rare gift indeed.

We must not forget that in his early days, at least until 1952-53, Di Stefano, who made his debut at Reggio Emilia in 1946 in *Manon*, was confident in the most arduous belcanto repertory: from *Puritani* to *Barbiere*, from *Favorita* to *Sonnambula*, displaying high notes, with perfect

Di Stefano sang Andrea Chenier more than once, even though the part was not suited to his purely lyrical voice. The best results were to be heard in the two arias: "Un dì all'azzurro spazio" and "Come un bel dì di maggio." (Photo: Oscar Savio. Historic Archives of the Rome Opera Theater)

filati in the most difficult phrases (the "Dream" in *Manon* and the incredible high c˝ in *diminuendo* in the New York *Faust*) as well as a velvet sound of incomparable beauty.

Usually the reason for Di Stefano's early decline is attributed to his particular technique of "open singing". We suggest these are comments by people who know little about singing. The truth is that the Sicilian had a great technique based on word articulation and on the purity and height of his sound, unmarred by horrible darkenings or "coverings." Problems occurred as soon as "Pippo" moved away from his natural repertory to explore roles that were not suited to his particular talent, operas such as *Iris*, *Forza del Destino*, *Turandot* and even *Aida* and *Otello*. There was a progressive and inexhorable decline: the *mezzavoce* became falsetto, the high notes became harsh and nasal; he lost the ability to respect dynamic signs and sang everything in full voice, helped, it is true, by a beautiful timbre, but which in the end became monotonous and forced.

However, the public adored Di Stefano and even during his worst moments it rewarded the Sicilian tenor for his amiability and generosity. During the seventies he participated in performances of little known operas and specialized in operetta.

Alfredo Kraus (Las Palmas 1927 – Madrid

1999) happily wed the Italian school of Pertile and Schipa with the great Spanish tradition exemplified by Fleta. For forty years (starting in a *Rigoletto* at Cairo in January, 1956) he performed in a restricted number of operas that were all perfectly suited to his means: *Rigoletto*, *Traviata*, *Werther*, *Manon*, *Faust*, *Lucia*, *La Fille du Régiment*, *La Favorita*, *Don Pasquale* and *Elisir*.

With intelligent and persistent study he formed a voice that was incredibly smooth and flexible. He began with a modest vocal color and an inconspicuous volume, but a highly calculated breathing technique allowed him to perform *smorzature* or *rinforzandi* whenever he wished. The wonderful *messa di voce* at the end of the aria "Pour me rapprocher de Marie" from *La Fille du Régiment* is an example. He could make his breath last forever, as in the duet from *Lucia*, "Verranno a te...", or the endless "Ah! Manon" from the end of the "Dream Scene" (Massenet's *Manon*), and he had an extension that reached e˝ flat at full voice.

Kraus was a true gentleman in both life and art. He was always extremely elegant, well-mannered, and self-controlled. Thanks to a perfect technique and a boundless love for his profession, he sang almost until his dying day, exhibiting his famous high notes and captivating audiences with his perfectly calibrated phrasing, full

*The young partner of the beautiful **Virginia Zeani** is **Alfredo Kraus** in a 1960 Traviata. All the most important post-war Violettas have enjoyed singing with this exceptional Alfredo. (Photo: F Villani. Historic Archives of the Teatro Comunale dI Bologna)*

*"Libiamo, libiamo nei lieti calici…" sings **Kraus** in an impeccable dinner suit, whilst being observed by the soprano **Adriana Maliponte** and the noble guests present at the first act party of La Traviata. (Photographic Archives of the Pretoria Opera Theater, 1981)*

*In a role that has become identified with his name **Alfredo Kraus** as the Duke of Mantua in Rigoletto.*

of subtle nuances, and his respect for dynamic signs. In the spring of 1999, Spanish audiences again had occasion to acclaim their countryman after a memorable concert in Madrid, before cancer robbed him of his art and of his very life. His voice lives on in a number of recordings, although the international record industry was late in discovering one of the greatest tenors of the twentieth century.

Luciano Pavarotti (Modena 1935) studied with Arrigo Pola and made his debut in 1961 at Reggio Emilia in *La Bohème*. As seems evident from the recording of that first evening, he was destined to a Bellini or Donizetti repertory with an occasional escapade into Verdi (*Luisa Miller*, *Rigoletto*) or Puccini (*Butterfly*, *Bohème*, *Turandot*). His voice is light and clear, almost contralto in the high notes which are ringing, penetrating and extending past high d″. His diction and legato are impeccable. These are characteristics of the old *tenore di grazia* and it is not a coincidence that, together with Alfredo Kraus, this tenor from Modena proved one of the best interpreters of operas such as *Puritani*, *Favorita*, *Fille du Régiment*, *Lucia* and *Rigoletto* from 1962 until 1975, forming, during this period, a wonderful partnership with Joan Sutherland.

Pavarotti first sang at Covent Garden in 1963 in the role of Rodolfo, and then went on to sing *Sonnambula*, *Traviata*, *Rigoletto* and *Lucia*. In 1964 he sang Idamante in *Idomeneo* (Mozart) at Glyndebourne; with Joan Sutherland and Richard Bonynge, he made a successful tour of Australia. Since 1968 he has sung regularly at the Metropolitan in New York.

With the increase of his popularity in the United States, Pavarotti has allowed himself be exploited by the show-business industry. By participating in any and every type of musical exhibition in town squares, parks, sporting stadiums, etc., and in television and recording studios, he has passed himself off as the typical Italian tenor export. In 1990 he was the symbol of Italy in the World Cup Soccer Championship, singing everywhere, often with rather dubious artistic results. In fact, the dictates of the market have gradually forced Pavarotti to abandon his natural belcanto repertory in favor of more lucrative engagements such as *Tosca*, *Trovatore*, *Gioconda* and *Aida*. He has given good performances in these roles, thanks to the beauty of his voice and his solid technique; but it is clear that he was more at ease in the parts of Nemorino, the Duke of Mantua, Rodolfo in both *La Bohème* and *Luisa*

A gala at the San Carlo of Naples, 1973. **Pavarotti** *has always been characterized by the great variety of his repertoire in concerts. He covers Bononcini, Scarlatti, Gluck, Mozart, Donizetti, Verdi, Tosti, Liszt, Massenet and Puccini. One of his favorite encores is "Nessun Dorma" (Turandot). Another is "Una furtiva lagrima" from Donizetti's Elisir d'Amore. (Photo: Troncone. Archives of the San Carlo Theater, Naples)*

*The ideal Verdi part for **Pavarotti** is Riccardo in Ballo in Maschera. In this photo we see the final death scene. To the left is the soprano **Maria Chiara**. (Photo: Marchiori. Archives of the Teatro Comunale of Florence)*

*Naples, April 24, 1973: Caruso's home town commemorates him one hundred years after his birth. A galaxy of illustrious tenors participates. From the left **Mario Del Monaco**, Maestro De Fabritiis, **Alain Vanzo**, **Luciano Pavarotti**, **Vladimir Atlantov**, and **Ferruccio Tagliavini**. (Historic Archives of the San Carlo Opera Theater, Naples. Photo: Troncone)*

Miller, and Riccardo in *Ballo in Maschera*. His corpulence has imposed some understandable limits to his appearance in the French *lyrique* repertory of which he would have been an ideal interpreter (Romeo, Werther, Des Grieux).

Following the explosive successs of "The Three Tenors" concert at Caracalla in 1990, Pavarotti's fame has grown even more, permitting him to reach hitherto unforeseen heights and earn huge sums of money for each appearance. Pavarotti has thus overstepped the bounds of "serious" music, with its artistic and financial limits, to launch into the multifarious world of rock. The so-called "Pavarotti International", a mega-concert organized annually *en plein air* at Modena, may well be a spectacular event, but it is also one of debatable taste, a potpourri of rock and opera. In recent years he has virtually become his own trade mark, he has sung in a duet with the popular Italian rap star Jovanotti and with the Spice Girls, he has presented the Sanremo Song Contest and filled the pages of sentimental magazines with his romance with his former secretary Nicoletta Mantovani.

Not surprisingly, he has gradually withdrawn from the opera scene, despite a voice that is still of good quality, as was evident from his appearances during the nineteen-nineties (*Andrea Chénier* at Vienna and the Met, *Tosca, Elisir d'Amore, Ballo in Maschera*). Following the unfortunate vocal "cracks" during the performance of the *Fille du Régiment* at the Metropolitan in 1995 (what on earth made him agree to take part in the first place?) and the disastrous "first" night of *Don Carlos* at La Scala in 1993, Pavarotti has limited his appearances to operas such as *Tosca* and *Elisir d'Amore*, staged mainly at the New York Metropolitan. More recently, he sang in the Rome staging of *Tosca*, on January 14 , 2000, directed by Placido Domingo, and in the triumphal *Tosca* at Covent Garden in 2002.

Veriano Luchetti (Tuscania, Viterbo 1937) has built himself a sturdy reputation in the lyric tenor category over the years, and is one of the most complete artists. It was a hard-won battle, since Luchetti began his career towards the second half of the sixties, his first big success being in Meyerbeer's *Africana*. It was a time when the operatic circuit was still crowded with old glories; and at the same time Pavarotti, Domingo and Carreras were emerging to become immediate public favorites.

Luchetti, however, had all the qualities to equal and, occasionally, to surpass his illustrious colleagues. His voice has always been very flexible and smooth in all the three registers, with a moderately pleasant tone-color, but with an extended range, an authentic *mezzavoce*, and a perfectly placed sound. His is the ideal voice for Pinkerton, Edgardo, Rodolfo, the Duke of Mantua, but also adaptable to more dramatic roles such as Don Alvaro, Don José, or Arrigo (*Vespri Siciliani*). Luchetti has specialized in parts generally neglected by the superstars, such as Foresto in *Attila*, Macduff in *Macbeth* and Gabriele Adorno in *Simon Boccanegra*, offering outstanding performances in these roles all over the globe.

There are two important Spanish tenors who could have had long and memorable careers, had they had not fallen victim to a mistaken repertory and faulty technique. **José Carreras** (Barcelona 1946) was a fantastic lyric tenor until the second half of the nineteen-seventies: a very brief period of vocal glory indeed. During this time he was able to perform triumphantly

*It was the 1982-83 season, and after an absence from the stage which had lasted almost two years, **Jaime Aragall** returns to perform the part of Mario Cavaradossi at the San Carlo. He is not at his best; but the audience is happy to be able to once again applaud the Spanish tenor. (Archives of the San Carlo Opera Theater of Naples. Photo: Troncone)*

in *Lucrezia Borgia* (Barcelona 1971), *Butterfly* (New York 1972), *Rigoletto* (Vienna 1975), *Don Carlos* (Salzburg 1976) and in other operas such as *Traviata*, *Lombardi* and *Bohème*, singing with unequalled charm. His silken tone and clear enunciation seemed, miraculously, to reincarnate the great Giuseppe Di Stefano. In fact, Carreras has never denied his admiration for Di Stefano, and has always said he is proud of such a comparison. The same gifts but perhaps also the same defects. The choice of a harsh repertory (*Tosca*, *Aida*, *Forza del Destino*, *Andrea Chénier*, *Trovatore*, *Turandot*) has produced an even more drastic decline than that of his predecessor. It was already noticeable in the Salzburg *Aida*, 1979, directed by von Karajan. Carreras' voice was compromised by hard sounds, *falsetti*, a defective legato and throat 'pushing'. The 1986 *Don Carlos* (Salzburg) mercilessly showed the accentuation of these faults.

In July of 1987, during the shooting of Comencini's opera-film *La Bohème*, Carreras was taken ill with a serious form of leukaemia. Both his life and his career were at risk, but thanks to efficient treatment and the affectionate moral support of opera lovers the world over he has returned to singing, first only in concerts, then in a victorious *Carmen* in Vienna in 1990 and since then in many operas all over the world.

Jaime Aragall (Barcelona 1939), more than a victim of his voice, is a victim of his nerves. Mother Nature has endowed him with a seductive, almost voluptuous timbre, and good high notes, especially when emitted with due calm and concentration. The only real enemy of this singer is his character. In Vienna a few years ago he interrupted a performance of *Tosca* announcing his withdrawal from the stage. It was an evening full of shock and distress for his numerous fans at the Staatsoper. The tenor sang "E lucean le stelle" with his voice broken by weeping. He seemed a mere shadow of himself.

Two years later, however, he returned to the stage interpreting with renewed enthusiasm *Ballo in Maschera*, *Don Carlos* and *Tosca*, finding occasional bursts of his former glory. The role of the Spanish Infante is the one that most suits Aragall, vocally and psychologically. Alas, he tends to sing loudly throughout, with no shadings or *mezzevoci* and this often makes his interpretative style monotonous and inelegant. During his early career years, Aragall was an excellent Donizetti tenor, frequently singing with Montserrat Caballé.

Another of the more recent lyric tenors is **Dano Raffanti** (Capannori, Lucca 1948) who was an excellent Nemorino, Duca di Mantova and a noteworthy Rossini tenor. He has rare vocal color and penetrating high notes but is

José Carreras *in the version of* Carmen *staged at the Verona Arena in 1999. Thanks to excellent medical care and the moral support of fans the world over, this tenor from Catalonia made a triumphant come-back after having been taken seriously ill with leukaemia in 1987. (Fondazione Arena di Verona. Photo: Gianfranco Fainello)*

too emotional and inconsistent, and this has often led to negative results.

The American **Neil Shicoff** (New York 1949) is also gifted with worthy vocal qualities. He is in demand in the major theaters as Faust, the Duca di Mantova and Rodolfo. Meanwhile, the Puccini roles and early Verdi parts are successfully upheld in the United States by **Giuliano Ciannella** (Bologna 1940). He personally knew, and was appreciated by the old Lauri Volpi. The Argentinian **Luis Lima** (Cordoba 1948), after having debuted as Turiddu in 1974 at Lisbon, has changed to a repertory more suited to his means (*Traviata*, *Don Carlos*, *Faust*, *Bohème*, *Lucia* and *Butterfly*). He has revealed such good qualities as clear enunciation and a pleasant vocal color. **Alberto Cupido** (Portofino, Genoa 1950) is also endowed with a strong, ringing voice of clear color, suited to both the Donizetti belcanto (*Lucia*, *Maria de Rudenz*, *Favorita*) and the lyric and *lirico-spinto* repertory (he gave admirable performances in Mascagni's *Cena delle Beffe*, as Calef in *Turandot* and Mario in *Tosca*). Interesting newcomers of the latest generation include the American **Richard**

Andrea Bocelli and *Cecilia Gasdia* in L'Amico Fritz directed by Steven Mercurio at the Verona Arena in 2001. Bocelli is the most controversial tenor of the moment, a singer you either love or hate, having turned to opera after beginning his singing career in the world of pop music. (Fondazione Arena di Verona. Photo: Gianfranco Fainello)

Leech (Binghamton, New York 1956), front-ranking artist of the Met's classical tenor repertory (*Tosca, Ballo in Maschera, Faust, Rigoletto*), thanks to a pleasant timbre and confident technique; the French singer **Roberto Alagna** (Marseille 1963), who made his name in *Traviata* and *Rigoletto* at La Scala and has also gone on to make several recordings (he is renowned for his kitsch record sleeves in which he appears together with his wife, the soprano Angela Gheorghiu). He has a naturally powerful voice and is not above including in his performance certain new age "eccentricities" (for instance, in *Elisir d'Amore* he sang the duet with Adina doubled over, head down and added variations and embellishments to the famous "Furtiva lagrima"). Recently, he has tackled more dramatic roles, such as Manrico in *Trovatore* (Florence 2001), Canio in *Pagliacci*, Mario in *Tosca* and *Don Carlos*, which were favorably greeted by the public and the critics alike.

The nineties saw the advent of another interesting singer, a tenor named **Marcello Alvarez**, who recently triumphed in *Rigoletto* (which he also performed at the Verona Arena in 1998),

Traviata, Faust, Puritani, Werther and *Manon*. His emission and technical prowess are reminiscent of the great Kraus. Further talented newcomers in Italy, but who have also already made names for themselves abroad, are **Marcello Giordani, Giuseppe Filianoti** (Reggio Calabria 1974), Alfredo Kraus's last pupil, **Salvatore Licitra** (Berna 1968), who made a splendid debut at the Verona Arena in *Ballo in Maschera* in 1998 for which he was hailed a "new Pavarotti" (less impressive were his performances in *Forza del Destino* and *Tosca* at La Scala in 1999 and 2000, though it must be added that this was mainly due to the predominance of Maestro Muti's orchestra), **Cesare Catani** and **Maurizio Graziani**, both of whom are capable of a wide repertory; Graziani in particular frequently performs in dramatic roles (*Aida, Forza del Destino, Manon Lascaut, Turandot*). A special mention goes to the Sicilian tenor **Vincenzo La Scola** (Palermo 1960), who by the wise administration of his natural abilities, has encountered few problems in skipping from light opera to more dramatic roles (even *Aida, Simon Boccanegra, Tosca*). His voice is very pleasing, with an impressive extension; moreover, his attractive manner and natural spontaneity have assured him a prominent place on the contemporary opera scene. Germany's **Marcus Haddock** (1957) has achieved notoriety thanks to his excellent musical qualities and, it may be added, to his good looks, while his spontaneously flamboyant timbre is reminiscent of Carreras. He was enthusiastically applauded for his *Rondine* in Bonn and *Werther* in Brussels in 1999, and has made numerous appearances in America. Performing above all in the United States is **Jerry Hadley** (1957), who made a spectacular debut in the *Bohème* directed by Bernstein in Rome, which also marked Bernstein's return to Puccini's operas. Endowed with a clear and extensive voice, Hadley has sung many lyrical roles, some with less success than others but always at top level, and specializing in operetta and the American musical.

Mario Malagnini (Salò, Brescia 1958) began his career as a dramatic tenor but then wisely turned to a repertory better suited to his natural vocal abilities: *Traviata, Rigoletto, Bohème, Carmen, Madama Butterfly*. Malagnini's ringing, well-emitted voice is ideally suited to the role of Don José, while his physical appearance makes him perfect for the role in *Tosca*.

The Bocelli Phenomenon

The biggest news of the new millennium is the controversial tenor from Pisa **Andrea**

Andrea Bocelli with **Zubin Mehta.**
*Famous conductors such as Mehta and
Lorin Maazel have vigorously defended
this Tuscan tenor from his critics.
(Photo: Sasha Gosov)*

*A photo of **Salvatore
Licitra** and **Fiorenza
Cedolins** in* Il Trovatore
*directed by Franco
Zeffirelli at the Verona
Arena in 2001. Licitra has
made a name for himself
among the singers of the
latest generation thanks to
his smooth, well-extended
voice. (Fondazione Arena
di Verona.
Photo: Gainfranco Fainello)*

Marcelo Alvarez *and* ***Ivna Mula*** *in La Traviata (Verona Arena, 2001). Alvarez is gifted with an emission and technical prowess reminiscent of the great Alfredo Kraus. (Fondazione Arena di Verona. Photo: Gianfranco Fainello)*

Bocelli (1958), an artist you either love or hate! He is cultured, tenacious and will stop at nothing to achieve his goals. Thus, he has succeeded in one of the toughest tasks, combining his initial successes in the field of light music (he won a Sanremo Song Contest) with equal accomplishments in the more complex field of opera. A pupil of Maestro Bettarini at Prato, former teacher of Corelli and Bastianini, then of Corelli himself, Andrea Bocelli is the one and only true novelty of the pachydermous world of contemporary opera. Launched by Zucchero and Pavarotti, topping the hit parade in many countries of the world, he could easily have stayed where he was, engaged in an endless series of concert performances and turning out records one after the other, with none of the ups and downs the opera singer has to face. But not Andrea Bocelli. He stubbornly undertook singing lessons and made his debut as Macduff in *Macbeth* and then in *Bohème* (Cagliari 1998), this time with the TV cameras of half the world pointing in his direction. Recordings of *Tosca*,

Trovatore and *Aida* have already been released, conducted by such illustrious names as Mehta and Maazel, both of whom have vigorously defended Bocelli from his critics. In 1999 his debut in *Werther* at Detroit was mercilessly attacked by the majority of the press. He was accused of having a small voice, lacking in the high registers; yet audiences are on his side. For the first time theaters are filled with people who would look equally at home at a rock concert; for the first time TV programs world-wide speak the language of opera; for the first time young people have begun to show an interest in a form of melodrama hitherto deemed fit only for the museum. Bocelli, with his unmistakable, velvety timbre, has unwittingly performed a miracle: that of giving a new lease of life to a type of music which seemed, after a slow but inexorable decline, to be a relic of the past. A miracle as great as that he has achieved on stage, performing as well, if not better than many of his colleagues, despite the grave handicap of his blindness.

THE LIGHT TENORS:
AN ENDANGERED SPECIES

The light tenors, or *lirico-leggero*, often tend to be a parody of the former *tenori di grazia*. Their voices are exiguous, colorless, insipid; and they make frequent use of falsetto, with squealing high notes and difficulty in any forceful coloratura passages (the true Rossini coloratura). They are the heirs (or imitators) of the ill-equipped tenors who proliferated in the era of Bonci and De Lucia (but descended from the previous century), who made use of a clavicular breathing technique resulting in an inconsistent sound and false coloring.

Because of these truly bad qualities light tenors were summoned to sing the comic operas of the eighteenth century but also Handel, Rossini, Bellini, Donizetti and sometimes Verdi. We will mention only the best, those who, in the twentieth century, left favorable memories of their peak years. **Luis Alva** (Lima 1927) sang for more than thirty years. He was the protagonist of many revivals and also gave a number of famous performances of Nemorino and Almaviva.

Alvino Misciano (Narni, Terni 1915 – Milan 1997) was active in a very wide repertory and participated in many eighteenth century revivals. **Nicola Monti** (Milan 1920 – Fidenza, Parma 1993) was an undoubtedly stylish performer, often applauded as Elvino in *La Sonnambula* and Paolino in *Il Matrimonio Segreto*. **Luigi Infantino** (Regalbuto, Enna 1921 – Rome 1991) was initially hailed as a promising light lyric tenor for a general repertory; but, after his voice had degenerated at an early stage, he was relegated to first performances or revivals of forgotten operas.

Of a different caliber was **Agostino Lazzari** (Genoa 1919 – 1981), whose voice was endowed with a more substantial timbre and a broader technical base. Lazzari was an excellent Almaviva, Don Ramiro (in *Cenerentola*), Hoffmann, Nemorino and Werther, as well as being a specialist in operetta and contemporary opera. The same can be said of **Pietro Bottazzo** (Mestrino, Padua 1936 – Vicenza 1999), a tenor with a clear, well-prepared, agile voice which extended into the *falsettone*, to whom goes the merit of having brought Rossini back into his true dimension during the sixties and seventies. He participated in many recordings for the RAI (Italian Television and Radio).

Less a singer of Rossini than of the French *lyrique* repertory (*Lakmé, Mireille, Mignon*), **Alain Vanzo** (Montecarlo 1928 – Gournay-sur-Marne 2002) was a very refined and agile singer, well able to use falsetto in the highest parts of the score. The many records he made bare witness to his stylistic prowess and vocal elegance. Vanzo was perhaps the last representative of repute of the French school, whose most eminent protagonist was Thill.

A recent newcomer to the scene is Rome-born **Giuseppe Sabbatini** (1958), former double-bass player of the disbanded Orchestra di Roma of the RAI, who sings a classical light repertory (*Rigoletto, Favorita, Puritani, Werther, Faust, Figlia del reggimento*). His voice does not possess a particularly impressive color, while his emission tends to be nasal, even petulant at times, but thanks to his musical precision and a wide range of tone-color, Sabbatini enjoys considerable success. Another Italian, **Pietro Ballo** (Palermo 1952), has made regular stage appearances since the nineteen-eighties, in a repertory including *Rigoletto, Elisir d'Amore, Gianni Schicchi, Amico Fritz* and *Faust*. His vocal color is attractive, technique confident and he reaches the high notes with ease. His performance is, however, unexceptional, likewise his style.

The tenors **Aquiles Machado** (Barquisimeto, Venezuela 1971) and **José Sempere** (Crevillenta, Spain 1955) have interesting voices but an unimpressive stage manner. However, the current rarity of authentic "espada" tenors, that is to say capable of reaching incredible high notes, makes both these singers indispensable for operas requiring full voice extension.

Fuller and mellower is the voice of **Ramon Vargas** (Mexico City 1959), who tackles both Rossini's *Almaviva* and Nemorino in *Elisir d'Amore* with equal mastery and who is admired in theaters world-wide for his confidence and ability to communicate.

The Great Mozart Tenors of the Twentieth Century

Many of the best Mozart singers and those of the German lyric repertory of the twentieth century can be found amongst the lyric, dramatic and occasionally even amongst the Wagnerian tenors: Roswänge, MacCormack, Schipa, Gigli, Kraus. However, a few important names should

Ramon Vargas *captured off-stage during a performance of* Il Barbiere di Siviglia *(Verona Arena, 2001). This Mexican tenor is renowned for his confidence and powers of expression. (Fondazione Arena di Verona. Photo: Gianfrance Fainello)*

be mentioned, starting with **Herman Jadlowker** (Riga 1877 – Tel Aviv 1953). A tenor with a dark, almost baritone-like timbre, outstanding in fast vocalizing and trills, he was a great interpreter of *Idomeneo*. His execution of the bravura aria "Fuor del mar" is unsurpassable. He also sang many other dramatic works, from Verdi to Wagner. Another Mozartian great in the twenties and thirties was the Hungarian **Koloman Patacky** (Alsö Neudra 1896 – Hollywood 1964) whose voice was sweet and seductive and emission ethereal. He was a skilled artisan of expressive nuance. For instance, his remarkably pure high B flat "in morendo" ("dying") at the end of *Celeste Aida*. He was an exceptional Florestan, Tamino and Don Ottavio.

Richard Tauber (Linz 1891 – London 1948) was also a great Mozart singer. His robust, sensual voice was well-suited to this repertory, a voice he could soften and sweeten at will, as demonstrated in his performances of Don Ottavio, Tamino and Belmonte, between 1913, when he started his career, and 1947, when he retired permanently after his last performance as Don Ottavio at Covent Garden.

Anton Dermota (Kropa, Slovenia 1910 – Vienna 1989) belongs to the last great generation of Mozart singers. From 1936, the year of his debut in *Traviata*, until his retirement in January 1982, singing Tamino at the Vienna Staatsoper, he was Mozart's knight in shining armor. He executed a style of phrasing that belongs entirely to the Italian belcanto tradition, the tradition from which Mozart drew inspiration when he wrote his operas: singing while breathing, a light and mellow emission, imagination and style.

He was accompanied by all the greatest conductors of the twentieth century. Dermota offered a perfect interpretation, without ostentation, of Don Ottavio, Belmonte, Ferrando, and, above all, Tamino. Even in his last performance of this role, at the sprightly age of seventy-two, Dermota gave an exemplary lesson.

Fritz Wunderlich (Kusel 1930 – Heidelberg 1966) sang his last opera as Tamino (*The Magic Flute*) during early September 1966 at the Edinburgh Festival. Soon after, a tragic accident in Germany was to interrupt his brilliant career, a career which had begun as Tamino in 1954 at Fribourg, Switzerland. Thus the most beautiful tenor voice ever heard in Germany, and one of the most impressive voices of the twentieth century, disappeared from the stage, an immaculate voice, warm and sensual in the center, with fluid emission and radiant high notes. It was a miraculous combination of the best qualities of Björling and those of Di Stefano. Wunderlich was superb in Mozart, in contemporary German and Austrian works, in Handel oratorios, in the Masses of Bach, Haydn and Beethoven, in the leideristic repertoire and in operetta, of which he was universally crowned king. But he was also an unforgettable Lensky and a passionate Alfredo, not to mention Count Almaviva, whom he at last succeeded in liberating from the unbearable *falsetti* of so many dandies.

Wunderlich, who was a qualified French horn player, was above all a musician who succeeded in eliminating from his singing all the bad habits of his predecessors, such as excessive *portamenti* and *solfeggio* inaccuracies.

With **Nicolaij Gedda** (Stockholm 1925) we come to the end of the era of great Mozart singers. He was capable of singing in all languages in an extremely wide repertory, had a long-lasting career (true of all real singers) and was stylistically perfect. In Italy, at the Maggio Musicale in Florence in 1980, he created a superbly intense and melancholic Lensky, rich in different shadings and details; while his Lieder concerts are works of art in the use of vocal fantasy and style. And as in the case of Wunderlich, Gedda's musical capacity and preparation are superb.

The Rossini Renaissance and the Search for the *Tenore Contraltino*

During the last twenty years we have been witness to the triumphant return of Rossini to the operatic stage. This was thanks to the Rossini Opera Festival of Pesaro and to the critical studies sponsored by its Foundation (accompanied by the release of all of Rossini's

April 1986. Time does not seem to pass for one of the most intelligent and refined tenors of our time: **Nicolai Gedda** *receives well-deserved applause during a concert at the San Carlo. (Historic Archives of the San Carlo Opera Theater of Naples)*

operas on record in their new philological form). Among the younger generation a new interest has risen regarding long-gone ways of performing: florid singing, variations, decorative fantasy.

It has been particularly difficult to find an authentic Rossini tenor, someone who could perform accurately in complex roles, ranging from Almaviva to Otello, from Ramiro to Giacomo V (*Donna del Lago*), from Argirio (*Tancredi*) to Arnoldo. However, there is a substantial group of singers willing to try and some have proved their value, not only at Pesaro but in theaters engaged in the Rossini Renaissance all over the world. These newcomers include **Ernesto Palacio** (Lima 1946) and **Francisco Araiza** (Mexico City 1950); both are discreet *virtuosi* although with precise limits. Palacio, who retired in 1999, was a disciplined and elegant tenor, whose qualities were nonetheless underestimated, despite his numerous stage appearances and record releases. Particularly memorable were his performances as Almaviva together with the great Marilyn Horne at the Sferisterio in Macerata and as Lindoro in *L'Italiana in Algeri* recorded for Erato.

The singing career of Araiza can be divided into two phases. The first he dedicated to Mozart and Rossini, with excellent results as Tamino, Don Ottavio, Ramiro in *La Cenerentola*, with frequent excursions into Lieder music, especially German Lieder. Then came the Kafka metamorphosis, which has led Araiza to gradually introduce into his repertory operas such as *Faust*, *Bohème* and even *Lohengrin* and *Forza del Destino*, which have certainly put a strain on his vocal capacity. In these dramatic roles Araiza has given less than memorable performances; his voice often sounds hard and forced, with poor intonation. However, he is a true professional, with a pleasing stage manner and has released a large number of records.

Dalmacio González (Olot 1946) possesses a small but very high voice, especially suited to roles such as Argirio and Lindoro in *L'Italiana in Algeri*. The same may be said of **Raoul Gimenez** (Mataró, Barcelona 1940), less confident perhaps than Gonzales and with a narrower vocal range, but similarly engaged in the Rossini repertory and belcanto in general.

Particularly attractive is the voice of **Luca Canonici** (Montevarchi, Arezzo 1960), launched internationally by the film–opera *La Bohème* directed by Luigi Comencini in which he sang the part of Rodolfo, stepping in for Carreras who had been taken ill. Canonici has a voice of limited volume but exquisite timbre and succeeds in achieving a particularly clear enunciation. In exploiting this "easy" voice, he has tended to neglect technique, which has prevented him from extending his repertory and thus his success. For the moment he is an excellent Nemorino, or Ernesto in *Don Pasquale*, and he also sings operetta.

During the nineteen-eighties, at the height of the Rossini renaissance, two names emerged together, **Rockwell Blake** (Plattsburgh 1951) and **Chris Merritt** (Oklahoma City 1952), one thin, the other fat, a sort of operatic version of Laurel and Hardy. Both are able to sustain *messe di voce*, trills, and full-bodied *falsettoni*. Of the two, Blake is the one who has studied more and with better results. Naturally gifted with an unexceptional voice, he has succeeded nonetheless in constructing a solid technique. With a correct breath measurement he has been able to achieve incredible speed and agility in vocalized passages and can easily overcome the almost unsurmountable difficulties encountered in *Zelmira, Otello, Ermione, Armida, Donna del Lago* and Rossini's *Elisabetta Regina d'Inghilterra*. Merritt's case is quite the opposite. He has great natural gifts: a dark color in the middle register, a high register reaching up to e′′ (in *falsettone rinforzato*); but these enviable qualities lack the

support of adequate technique, and equality of sound between the registers has always been lacking. These defects can be well hidden in Rossini operas, but they are, alas, blatantly evident in the Romantic repertory and in Verdi roles.

The fortunes of the Blake-Merritt duo lasted less than a decade and the critics who had announced a miracle were forced to admit they had been a shade too hasty in their judgment. Merritt's decline was particularly drastic, especially after his disastrous performances at La Scala with Muti (*William Tell* and the ridiculous *Vespri Siciliani* in 1989), which were followed by equally disastrous recitals of *Trovatore* in minor American theaters.

Other interesting American singers of Rossini opera are: **Bruce Ford** (Lubbock 1956), **Paul-Austin Kelly** (Kingston, New York 1960), **Gregory Kunde** (Kunkakee 1954) and **Charles Workman.** Kelly and Workman both have high-pitched, asexual voices, while Ford and Kunde especially have a much deeper tone-color. Kunde is well able to sing not only Rossini but also Bellini (*Sonnambula* and *Puritani*) and the French repertory (he has given

Rockwell Blake *as Lindoro in* L'Italiana in Algeri, *one of his favorite roles.*
(Photo: A.B. Williamson)

excellent performances in Massenet's *Manon* and Gounod's *Faust*).

The Celletti School: Apocalypse Now

The Rossini revival, like all fads, was bound to produce fallen angels, ill-fated creations and grotesque exaggerations. These are summed up in two singers of the "Celletti School", so called after Rodolfo Celletti, exegete and singing teacher, who was for several years the art director of the Festival of Valle d'Istria of Martina Franca. The two singers in question are **William Matteuzzi** (Bologna 1957) and **Giuseppe Morino** (Assisi, Perugia 1950).

They are typical examples of the theoretical tenor, guinea pigs to be subjected to all manner of dangerous experiments, robots invented according to a stock of theories derived from ancient treatises, antediluvian texts and concepts on the threshold of the paranormal. Matteuzzi has become famous for his stratospheric use of falsettone, which in almost every opera he pushes to high f´´. His variations and cadences (in *Cenerentola*, *Barbiere*, *Conte Ory*, *Italiana in Algeri*, *Ricciardo e Zoraide*, and even in *Fille du Régiment* and *Puritani*) have on a number of occasions gone beyond accettable limits, crossed the line, sounding more like a cat who has had his tail trodden on, or a crying baby, than a romantic opera hero. Morino's case is even more astonishing. Captured by talent scout Celletti from the Duomo of Assisi, subjected to a vocal full immersion along the lines of the cas-

trati, he emerged to sound just like a tremulous old 78 record. Morini's voice is one of the most graceless in the history of opera singing, and as if this were not enough, he also has a totally unsuitable physique. And yet he sang, before the inevitable decline set in and he had trouble with the law, even at La Scala (*Fetonte*, *Lucia di Lammermoor*, *Alceste*). Powerful agents and deaf art directors are the only possible explanation.

A Promise Kept: Juan-Diego Florez

Once the philological enthusiasm for Rossini had died down, fortunately, given the extremes to which it had been taken, the scene was at last taken over by a tenor endowed with both a graceful elegance and incredible technical prowess. **Juan-Diego Florez** (Lima 1973) was a pupil of Ernesto Palacio. At Pesaro, in 1997, at only twenty-two years of age, he successfully performed one of the most difficult of Rossini's operas, *Matilde di Shaban*. Since then, his rise to fame has been continuous, taking him to some of the world's most important theaters to sing operas of unquestionable complexity (*Semiramide* at Vienna, *Conte Ory* at the Maggio Fiorentino, *Barbiere di Siviglia* at La Scala). Florez's voice has excellent tone-color over its entire range, and can rise to high D without effort. He has an elegant style and perfect breath control, enabling him to achieve impeccable legato and intonation. Moreover, his attractive appearance and youthful freshness make him a captivating figure on stage.

THE DRAMATIC AND *LIRICO-SPINTO* TENORS OF THE ITALIAN REPERTORY DURING THE LAST CENTURY

One of Caruso's earliest followers at the beginning of the twentieth century was **Giovanni Zenatello** (Verona 1876 – New York 1949), another singer who began his career as a baritone but soon became a tenor. His initial studies gave his voice a rich color, resonant in the middle and lower registers, with smooth emission, but which could also reach the high register with ease. During the first twenty years of the twentieth century he was much in demand as Otello, Don José, Canio, Des Grieux in Puccini's *Manon Lescaut*, Riccardo in *Ballo in Maschera*, and, above all, as Radames. It was he who sang this part in the version of *Aida* which opened the summer festival at the Verona Arena (August 1913). Zenatello became the

The great **Miguel Fleta** in the fourth act of Bizet's Carmen. Few have been able to equal his rendering of "The Flower Song." (Photo from EMI Archives, 1929)

mentor of this project and would personally organize the performances.

A great verist performer was **Piero Schiavazzi** (Cagliari 1875 – Rome 1949) who, between 1899 and 1924, was engaged in operas such as *Cavalleria, Iris, Conchita* by Zandonai and *Fedora*, though he was also a good interpreter of the *tenore di grazia* repertory (*Lucia, Rigoletto*). Alas, after 1911 his voice became strained due to excessive work and a rather unconventional singing technique.

Bernardo De Muro (Tempio Pausania, Sassari 1881 – Rome 1955) was amazing for his length of breath, his sonority and volume as well as his polished and forceful high notes. These skills derived from a solid breathing technique – his diaphragm muscles were made of iron – and from Mother Nature, who had seen fit to give such a voice to this stocky little tenor from Sardinia. However, he was known to abuse his abilities and committed artistic licenses frequently. His interminable high note on the phrase "Sacerdote, io resto a te" from the third act finale of *Aida* has remained famous to this day. He would hold the note while walking all the way from the back of the stage to the very front edge where he would consign his sword to a spectator in one of the front seats. It was a gesture of defiance and spite towards Ramfis, but above all a demonstration of super-human lung power.

The risky *tessiture*, the exaggerated *corone* and the vocal athletics performed in *Cavalleria, Pagliacci, Andrea Chénier, Iris, Fanciulla del West, Trovatore* and *Isabeau* (which was De Muro's favorite opera) helped accelerate the decline of his voice around the mid-twenties. However, his retirement from the stage took place in 1938 at Rome with a last amazing interpretation of Falco in *Isabeau*.

Fleta, Cortis, Lázaro: Three Spanish Aces

Miguel Fleta (Albalate del Cinca 1897 – La Coruña 1938) began his cereer in 1919 at Trieste in *Francesca da Rimini* and was immediately classified as the typical *tenore espada*. With a warm, sensual timbre soaring to explosive high notes, he was capable of reinforcing or diminishing the volume of sound at any height, as in *Tosca, Aida, Carmen* and *Turandot*. Fleta was, in fact, the first performer of *Turandot* at La Scala in 1926 under the baton of Arturo Toscanini.

Notwithstanding his excellent technique, the Spanish tenor was the victim of a premature decline. Only a decade after his first appearance his voice already presented signs of tiredness and strain, with dangerous inequalities and, towards the end of the thirties, it wobbled uncontrollably. In *Voci Parallele* Lauri Volpi expresses the great regret and sincere compassion he felt when he was among the audience at Fleta's last appearance in *Christus*, a work by a young Spanish composer.

Antonio Cortis (Altea 1891 – Denia, Valencia 1952) sang from 1919 until 1937 and was applauded in all the major Italian and Spanish theaters, performing in *Pagliacci, Carmen, Aida* and *Fanciulla del West*. In these operas he exhibited a voice that was well-colored, extensive, sturdy and rounded over the *passaggio* notes, though not quite resistent enough to tackle, unscathed, the verist repertory. In fact, in the long run, his original vocal qualities lost their freshness and vigor.

Hipólito Lázaro (Barcelona 1889 – Madrid 1974) had a similar destiny. Having tackled the risky operas of Mascagni, from *Isabeau* to *Parisina* and *Piccolo Marat* (of these two last works he was the first performer in 1913 and 1921 respectively), he was overtaken by the same fate as Fleta and Cortis and retired early from the stage. During his golden years, between 1911 and 1920, this Spanish tenor sang, with style and elegance, but above all with a generous voice (even if affected in the center by an unpleasant *vibrato*) operas such as *Rigoletto, Puritani, Favorita, Elisir d'Amore*, alternately with *Aida, Cavalleria, Trovatore* and the aforesaid Mascagni operas.

It seemed an impossible challenge, but the flexible and brilliant voice of Lázaro overcame every obstacle gloriously. "Remember, you are listening to the greatest tenor in the world!" he would tell the audience, interrupting his performance. Towards the end of the twenties his star began to shine less brightly than in his youthful days, and, little by little, it faded completely. His huge and demanding repertory had robbed him of at least another fifteen years of song.

Pertile, an Isolated Voice

Aureliano Pertile (Montagnana, Padua 1885 – Milan 1952) was one of the most intel-

Aureliano Pertile *as Canio in* I Pagliacci. *(Historic Archives of La Fenice Theater of Venice)*

ligent and sensitive artists of the twentieth century, able to compensate an unattractive vocal color and physical appearance with a style, variety of phrasing and an emotional participation that totally engaged the public. He sang from 1911 until 1946, when he gave a last performance of Boito's *Nerone* at the Rome Opera. He sang mainly in Italy, at La Scala (1918-1937) and all the other major theaters, but also at the Metropolitan Opera from 1921-22, and at Covent Garden from 1927 until 1931.

His favorite operas were *Carmen, Tosca, Cavalleria, Pagliacci, Manon Lescaut, Lucia, Fedora, Ballo in Maschera, Andrea Chénier, Bohème, Rigoletto, Forza del Destino*, and even *Otello* towards the end of his career. In these operas every word, every note had just the right expressive quality, the right accent and the right vibration.

He was Arturo Toscanini's favorite tenor, and the legendary conductor fully understood and exploited the huge potential that could issue from that awkward body. (His critics called him "the Hunchback"). In the higher registers his

voice reached high b′ with ease, though he was often obliged to lower the most difficult arias. Nonetheless, the nuances and inflections with which he flavored each passage he interpreted were such as to overshadow any "theatrical inconveniences".

Caruso's Heir

Giovanni Martinelli (Montagnana, Padua 1885 – New York 1969) was considered Caruso's heir in the United States. The New York Metropolitan adopted him in 1913, the year of his debut in *Butterfly*, until 1945-46, giving him honor and unconditional praise. For about a decade, between the thirties and forties, this tenor used his naturally clear and soaring voice to imitate Caruso, thus enlarging the central notes and darkening the sound. These strainings produced unpleasant slips of intonation and damaged the marvelous quality of his high notes, also robbing him of stylistic flexibility. However, Martinelli managed to escape the Caruso experiment relatively unscathed and after 1935 continued to enjoy world-wide success, his performances ranging from the verist Puccini repertory to *Norma, Forza del Destino, Gioconda, Aida, Carmen* and *Trovatore*. During the last part of his lengthy career he also sang *Otello, L'Ebrea* and *Tristan* together with Kirsten Flagstad.

The Dramatic Tenors of the First Three Decades of the Twentieth Century

Among the dramatic and *spinto* tenors of the first thirty years of the twentieth century are names such as **Giulio Crimi** (Paternò, Catania 1885 – Rome 1939), a great Puccini singer who took part in the first performances of *Il Tabarro* and *Gianni Schicchi* in New York; the Spaniard **Isidoro Fagoaga** (Vera de Bisadea, Navarra 1895 – San Sebastian 1976), who was famous also as a Wagnerian tenor; **Francesco Merli** (Corsico, Milan 1887 – Milan 1976), a Calaf and Otello with golden high notes and a vibrant, robust voice; the Englishman **Alfred Piccaver** (Long Sutton 1884 – Vienna 1958), who is remembered for his impeccable legato and dark timbre, the flexibility of his phrasing and confidence in the high register. He was considered the German Caruso at the Vienna Staatsoper. Also worthy of mention is the Canadian **Edward Johnson** (born Edoardo Di Giovanni; Guelph, Ontario 1878 – Toronto 1959), an acclaimed Chénier between 1912 and 1935. His principal characteristics were the warmth of his timbre and his piercing high notes.

Thill, Roswänge: Ambassadors of Italian Opera in France and Germany

Georges Thill (Paris 1897 – Lorgues 1984) was not really a "dramatic" tenor in the true sense of the word, but rather a *lirico puro* (pure lyric) with exceptional versatility. He was able to sing *Manon*, *Werther*, *Faust* and *Lakmé* while at the same time achieving worthy results in operas such as *Aida*, *Turandot*, *Guglielmo Tell*, *Fanciulla del West*, *Carmen*, and even *Samson and Delilah*.

His career began in Paris in 1918, as Don José, and was concluded, once again in Paris, with a farewell concert in 1955.

Taking into account Thill's undoubted natural talent and his training in De Lucia's school, it can nevertheless be said that the extent of his repertory did little to help his vocal longevity. The first noticeable signs of his decline were already audible in the 1929 performances of *Turandot* at La Scala. However, it is also true that despite his smooth emission and beautiful *mezzavoce*, a certain harshness in his high notes had always been evident, especially when singing in a more demanding repertory. His

Werther, however, remains unsurpassed, equaled only perhaps by that of Schipa.

Helge Roswänge (his real name was Helge Rosenving-Hansen; Copenhagen 1891 – Munich 1972) had an exceptionally long career that began in 1921 (with his debut as Don José at Neustrelitz) and continued until the end of the fifties. He was by then singing exclusively in Berlin and Vienna.

His golden years were, however, from 1926 to 1940. These were years when his voice, with its rich timbre, extension up to high d´´ and capacity for varied dynamic effects, enthralled the public in operas by Mozart, Verdi, Puccini, Leoncavallo, Wagner and Richard Strauss.

Roswänge was actually the first performer of many of Verdi's operas in the German opera theaters during the well-known Verdi revival which began in the nineteen-thirties. Some of his performances which have remained on record are memorable despite the fact that they are sung in a German translation: from "Vesti la giubba" (*Pagliacci*) to "Ah! Sì, ben mio" (*Trovatore*), and how can we forget the perfection of "Giorno di pianto" (*Vespri Siciliani*), where we can admire not only the legato but also the shining high note in the cadenza.

For Roswänge, as for the others, the last part of his career was less fortunate from a vocal point of view. His voice began to wobble, the various registers began to separate, and even his intonation began to slide, as is evident from the recordings made in Vienna during the late forties and fifties. We should not forget his considerable involvement in operetta at the Vienna Volksoper where Roswänge was an acclaimed favorite.

Two other excellent protagonists of the world opera scene who belonged to the same generation as that of Thill and Roswänge were **Richard Tauber** (Linz 1891 – London 1948), who was mentioned earlier in the paragraph on Mozart tenors, and **Galliano Masini** (Leghorn 1896 – 1986), a generous and robust interpreter of so many performances of *Cavalleria*, *Pagliacci*, *Aida* and also *Carmen*, *Andrea Chénier*, *Turandot*, *Adriana Lecouvreur*, and, in 1955, *Otello*.

He was from humble origins but gifted with a formidable theatrical instinct. He used to literally terrify his partners with the force of his performances, throwing fiery glances and even real punches at the poor Carmen or Desdemona of the evening.

The Human Message of Lauri Volpi

Many are unaware that, although the role of the Principe Ignoto was first performed by

Miguel Fleta, it was actually conceived by Puccini for **Giacomo Lauri Volpi** (stage name of Giacomo Volpi; Lanuvio, Rome 1892 – Burjasot, Valencia 1979). He was a vocal phenomenon without equal, at least as far as his voice was concerned, for nowadays his style seems rather old-fashioned.

Between 1919 and 1959 he was the Lone Knight of Belcanto, crusader of the old way of singing, and an ideal lover in operas such as *Puritani, Favorita, Les Huguenots, Rigoletto, Manon, Guglielmo Tell*; but he also sang Puccini (*Bohème, Tosca, Fanciulla del West, Turandot*) and Verdi (*Luisa Miller, Rigoletto, Trovatore, Forza del Destino, Otello*).

His voice had three octaves (ranging from low f to the high f´´ above high c of *Puritani* which he sang in chest voice), of limpid tone-color and clear enunciation, trained to softly caress before passionately exploding. Barilli called it "the happy man's voice".

This exceptional voice was created thanks to the lessons Lauri Volpi took from the great Cotogni, and Maria Ros, his wife, who was herself an excellent soprano, but above all by the determination and intelligence of the artist himself. He was a man of culture and many interests, and also the author of a number of

books: *Cristalli viventi* (Living Crystals), *Voci parallele* (Parallel Voices), the novel *La prode terra* (The Valiant Earth), and the collection entitled *A viso aperto* (With an Open Glance) are the better known examples.

At the summit of his glory and no longer in his youth, the Roman tenor was still easily able to perform the difficult phrase "Talor dal mio forziere" (*Bohème*) in *falsettone*, or the high b´ in the Raul-Valentina duet from *The Huguenots*. When he was sixty he was still singing with an incredible vocal freshness in the roles of Calaf, Arturo, Manrico, Poliuto and Edgardo. Not even the young Corelli managed to perform them all.

A demonstration of the fact that a voice, if well cultivated and trained, never tires and accompanies its owner until death, was given in Lauri Volpi's last concerts: Valencia 1971, Barcelona 1972, Busseto 1976 and Madrid 1977. On this last occasion the "grand old man" (eighty-four years old) once again sang "Nessun dorma" with that final amazing "Vincerò!," which was, to quote Barilli again, the most beautiful "human message" ever launched at the moon.

Many could not accept Lauri Volpi's pompous, out-dated style. Envious colleagues were very hostile towards him, but he always gave as good as he got, replying to his disparagers both orally and in writing. However, as we listen to his recordings today, we cannot help but wonder if some of his vocal habits were really necessary, such as his excessive use of *falsettone* and *portamenti*, his imprecise *solfeggio*, and his occasionally faulty intonation.

Giuseppe Lugo (Sona, Verona 1899 – Milan 1980) was considered by the French to be Thill's successor. He possessed a solid vocal ability at least until the end of the thirties.

He was excellent in parts such as the Duke of Mantua, Rodolfo, Werther, and in the French repertory in general, but not so successful in the Italian repertory, which he undertook after 1936. He found himself in difficulty handling the type of emission used in Italian theaters, and, as a result, his Italian career, although not without its successes, did not last long.

Mario Filippeschi (Pisa 1907 – Florence 1979) is quite a different case. Despite the ease with which this former tram-driver reached the high notes, he had an alternating career which was short-lived due to his lack of style and a sloppy interpretation of certain operas (*Ballo in Maschera, Tosca, Bohème* and *Lucia di Lammermoor*). However, his high c´´s and c´´ sharps, distributed freely in *Trovatore* and *Puritani*, were enough to assure him a noteworthy following during the forties and fifties.

"No, no, principessa altera, ti voglio ardente d'amor!" sings **Lauri Volpi** *and launches his high c´´ to the stars like a luminous comet. This photo depicts the mythical tenor during one of his last performances, in Turandot on June 28, 1958, at the Terme di Caracalla. His partners were Inge Borkh and Onelia Fineschi. (Photo: Oscar Savio. Historic Archives of the Rome Opera)*

On June 28 1953, Caracalla opens with Rossini's Guglielmo Tell, *featuring three ace cards: the baritone* **Tito Gobbi** *in the center, the bass* **Giulio Neri** *and to the right in the estremely difficult role of Arnaldo is* **Mario Filippeschi** *famous for his high C's in chest voice. (Historic Archives of the Rome Opera Theatre)*

The voice and handsome appearance of **Mario Lanza** (the stage name of Alfredo Arnold Cocozza; Philadelphia 1921 – Rome 1959) quickly assured him fame. He was considered the "new Caruso" in the United States, perhaps more because of his many films (the most famous being, not surprisingly, *The Great Caruso*, made in 1951) than because of his voice. Though his voice did, in fact, have a pleasant tone-color, dark and velvety, he frequently produced it in a way that was sloppy and negligent, at times even rough. A sudden heart attack killed him at only thirty-eight years of age, and thus helped to increase the cult-following of this son of Italian emigrants, who had become rich and famous thanks to his Carusian voice color.

Two other famous American tenors were Jan Peerce and Richard Tucker. **Jan Peerce** (born Jacob Pincus Perlemuth; New York 1904 – Fort Rochelle 1984) began his musical career in 1933 as a violinist in a jazz band. He made his debut in 1938 in Philadelphia as the Duca di

Mantova in *Rigoletto*. He became a tenor at Toscanini's urging and made many recordings with this famous conductor, among which *Traviata*, *Ballo in Maschera* and *Bohème*. In his Met career he interpreted a wide variety of Verdi and Puccini roles. And when he was eighty years old, he made a recording which revealed all the old vocal power and high notes!

Richard Tucker (stage name of Rueben Ticker; New York 1913 – Kalamazoo, Michigan 1975) was encouraged to study by Peerce, who became his brother-in-law in 1936. In 1945 he premiered at the Metropolitan singing Enzo in *La Gioconda*, a role so well suited to him that he sang it throughout his entire career. He had excellent vocal gifts, technique (perfect sound placement, brilliant high notes) and timbre. In Italy he sang in *Pagliacci* and *Ballo in Maschera*, in Rome, Florence and the Arena of Verona.

Tucker's career was mainly based in America, from 1945 until 1975; he frequently sang *Pagliacci*, *Carmen*, *Forza del Destino*, *Tosca*, *Rigoletto*,

Richard Tucker *and* **Grace Bumbry**. *It is March 1970 and at Rome there is a new production of* Carmen *in its original edition; and with stage sets by Guttuso that were destined to cause scandal. It was the only appearance the American tenor made in the Italian capital apart from a* Manon Lescaut *in 1968. (Historic Archives of the Rome Opera Theater)*

Thus **Mario Del Monaco** and **Tito Gobbi** close the second act of Otello, put on stage at the Palazzo Ducale of Venice in 1960. Del Monaco was the protagonist of many incredible performances of this, his favorite Verdi opera. Once, at the La Monnaie Theater in Brussels, he sang the difficult phrase "Dopo l'armi lo vinse l'uragano" all in one breath – an "Esultate" that left the public gasping! (Photo: Afi. Historic Archives of La Fenice Theater, Venice)

Elegant and proud, **Mario Del Monaco** *was a vocal phenomenon without precedent; his lung capacity and the brilliance and power of his high notes were exceptional. (Archives of the San Carlo Opera Theater of Naples. Photo: Troncone)*

Lucia, Aida, Ballo in Maschera and Manon Lescaut. During his thirty years of activity at the Metropolitan he sang over six hundred times in approximately thirty different roles. In 1973 he succeeded in attaining one of his dreams by singing Eléazar in Halévy's La Juive at New Orleans.

Mario Del Monaco (Florence 1915 – Mestre 1982) was both the last follower of Caruso and the first of a new school, that of the Del Monaco imitators, of course. It must be said that his vocal qualities cannot be copied; any other vocal or respiratory system would be seriously damaged by imitating his techniques. Already rich and powerful by nature, the voice of this Italian tenor was built on the central tenor notes which were strengthened and thickened, and on the incredible power of his high notes, which were joined to the middle register by an excellent *passaggio*. The result was a declamatory singing, unique in its incisiveness, albeit sometimes exaggerated, which encountered difficulty when utilizing dynamic effects and *mezzavoce*, and sometimes showed little imagination. When guided by a great conductor, such as von Karajan, Del Monaco could adapt to the shadings required by the part; thus he gave the public a superb recording of *Otello* in 1960 (Decca). This Verdi opera was to become his principal role from 1950, when he sang it for the first time at Buenos Aires, until his last performances in the sixties in which his interpretation was based on the power and incisiveness of his high notes.

During the first part of his career from 1941 (he made his debut in *Butterfly*) until 1949, Del Monaco's repertory included *Lucia, Rigoletto, Tosca* and *Bohème*; it seemed that he might continue as a pure lyric. Then came the vocal tidal waves of *Aida, Fanciulla del West, Pagliacci, Otello, Samson and Delilah,* and *Trovatore*. He had made his choice.

Del Monaco did not sing frequently at Covent Garden, appearing for the first time in 1946, on tour with the San Carlo Company from Naples, and once again in 1962 as Otello.

He performed regularly at the Metropolitan from 1951 until 1959.

He retired after a series of performances of *Pagliacci* in Vienna in 1976; but when listening to recordings of songs made shortly before his death, we cannot help but be amazed by the vocal metal and the intact vigor of the many high b´ flats.

The Del Monaco School

A vocal phenomenon of the strength and fame of Del Monaco was sure to be imitated, especially as he dedicated much of his time during the last years of his life to teaching. Moreover, his brother Marcello was also active in this field. Del Monaco's technique, as Kraus confirmed on more than one occasion during his master classes, was nothing more or less than the technique adopted by the great tenors from Caruso on: a voice sustained by a solid breathing technique, maximum opening of the inner throat, the tenor range of two octaves (from low c´´ to high c´´) executed uniformly and with perfect tone-color. I was told by one of Del Monaco's last pupils that after one of his

In I Pagliacci ***Mario Del Monaco*** *used to insert a series of sobs at the end of the famous aria "Vesti la giubba" which were more comical than tragic; and yet one cannot help but be impressed by the drama in his phrase "No, pagliaccio non son." (Historic Archives of the Rome Opera Theater)*

Franco Bonisolli (Rovereto, Trento 1938) and **Teresa Zylis-Gara** in Rossini's Guglielmo Tell *in Nice in 1981. Bonisolli is a rather singular character in the operatic world: he is gifted with excellent high notes (which reach up to high e´´ flat in falsettone). (Archives of the Nice Opera)*

lessons "your voice was completely hoarse, it was a case of natural selection". Quite rightly, if we think about it, opera envisages a certain natural selection, otherwise everyone would be singing. It is also true that mere imitation of Del Monaco could well have resulted in faded, uninteresting photocopies, especially if only his faults had been imitated; it was the quality and impetus of his singing that made him such a unique phenomenon.

Gianfranco Cecchele (Galliera Veneta, Padua 1938), who has been singing now for some thirty-five years, was a pupil of Marcello Del Monaco and one of the Del Monaco school's major exponents. Endowed with a superbly polished, extensive voice, Cecchele is able to tackle a vast repertory ranging from Verdi's early works (*Alzira, Masnadieri, Ernani*) to *Aida, Forza del Destino, Otello*, and including all Puccini's operas and many verismo operas, too. Following a long-standing legal controversy with La Scala, which he won, Cecchele has been unjustifiably ostracized by the Italian opera authorities, singing mainly abroad and at the so-called "traditional theaters", with considerable success.

Other singers of unquestionable talent influenced by Del Monaco's method, though not necessarily pupils of his, include **Gastone Limarilli** (Nervesa della Battaglia, Treviso 1927 – Montebelluna, Treviso 1998), who enjoyed fame and fortune during the first half of his career, but was neglected during the second, in part due to his disorderly life style and a series of financial setbacks; **Flaviano Labò** (Sarmato, Piacenza 1927 – Melegnano, Milan 1991), a specialist in the roles of Radames and Don

Pier Miranda Ferraro *(Altivola, Treviso 1924) was a typical Del Monaco follower who had a noteworthy career, distinguished by his professionalism and the constancy of his vocal performances. (Archives of the Rome Opera Theater)*

Alvaro (who was prematurely killed in a road accident); **Pier Miranda Ferraro** (Altivole, Treviso 1924), who sang in *Otello, Carmen* and even in *Pirata* together with Maria Callas (a somewhat questionable event from a stylistic point of view); **Nunzio Todisco** (Torre del Greco, Naples 1942), endowed with a warm, velvety voice, famous for his Pollione, Don José and Canio; **Mario Malagnini**, a pupil of Pier Miranda Ferraro, who made his name at the Verona Arena in *Aida, Attila, Traviata, Rigoletto* and *Carmen*, thanks to the warm timbre of his voice and captivating stage presence; **Nazzareno Antinori,** one of Mario Del Monaco's last pupils, winner of the Callas competition organized by the RAI in 1981, who has tackled a considerably demanding repertory, but with alternating results.

Though he will be remembered above all for Otello, which he sang on innumerable occasions the world over, **Carlo Cossutta** (Trieste 1932 – Udine 2000), on completion of his studies in Argentina, went on to perform the entire *lirico spinto* and dramatic repertory with success, being acclaimed in London, New York, Buenos Aires and the major Italian theaters. In 1964 he became the first singer to interpret Ginastera's *Don Rodrigo*, while his favorite roles included Turiddu, Radames, Don Carlos, Gabriele Adorno.

Tall and slim, graced with a ringing voice trained at the Melocchi school at Pesaro (who taught both Del Monaco and Corelli), **Giorgio Merighi** (Ferrara 1939) had everything going for him, but for a series of inexplicable vicissitudes his career, though enjoying success, has never quite taken off, and as a singer he has remained on the borders of the mainstream. Nonetheless, Merighi has sung in most major theaters, from the Met to La Scala, performing a vast repertory with preference being given to Verdi and Puccini.

The Four Aces

A special note goes to four singers who have all made their mark in *lirico spinto* and dramatic opera over the last few decades at the world's major theaters: **Franco Bonisolli** (Rovereto 1937), **Nicola Martinucci** (Taranto 1941), **Giuseppe Giacomini** (Veggiano, Padua 1940) and **Lando Bartolini** (Casale di Prato 1937).

Bonisolli has superb vocal gifts and cuts a fine figure on the stage. Tall, handsome, endowed with a voice of extensive range and expressive baritone undertones, he has tackled with incredible versatility operas ranging from Rossini's *Barbiere* to Verdi's *Otello*, alternating virtuosity with

Giuseppe Giacomini in Puccini's Turandot.

the most fervid pages of Verismo. On stage (his favorite theaters are the Vienna Staatsoper and the Verona Arena) he has given full voice to his high E flat in *Lucia* and his radiant c˝ of the "Pira" in *Trovatore*, an opera admirably suited to his natural disposition for the character of the lone knight. Despite the fact that he was favored by Karajan and belonged to none of the record industry's numerous lobbies, he had the audacity to walk out of the dress rehearsal of *Trovatore* staged for worldwide television in 1977. But the Vienna audiences, and all the major American and European theaters where he has appeared, have always been on his side. He abandoned his career in 1993 following serious family problems, but made a remarkable come-back, first as Calaf in a concerted version of *Turandot* organized by the Italian Radio Company in 1998, then in a concert at Vienna and again in Umberto Giordano's *Fedora* (March 1999). In his preparation of an opera, Bonisolli is guided by the recordings of Caruso and Del Monaco, but above all by the tempos and indications suggested by the author. Bonisolli's working methods, both vocal and psychological, are among the most interesting and meticulous to be found today. However, his bad temper and lack of diplomacy have helped neither his fame nor his career in the hypocritical, touchy world of contemporary opera.

Giacomini, too, has an exceptional voice, but he unfortunately suffers terribly from nerves. He is just as likely to give a memorable performance as he is to fall victim to an attack of nervous tension, his voice disappearing after only a few lines never to return. Nonetheless, he has been applauded by audiences at the Met, the Arena of Verona and Vienna for the clarity of his high notes and the timbre of his voice, singularly reminiscent of Corelli's. His winning interpretations include *Aida*, *Andrea Chénier*, *Tosca*, *Pagliacci*, *Forza del Destino* and *Otello*.

Martinucci is more reliable, though he sometimes tires easily during a performance. His voice is rich and voluminous, rising easily to C, but he pronounces the "S" with an irritating lisp. He has become famous in the roles of Radames, Calaf and Don Alvaro, performed many times the world over.

Last but not least is Bartolini, who has settled in America. His is another rich voice, solid and sonorous, well-suited to a wide repertoire, from *Trovatore* to *Otello*, *Andrea Chénier*, *Iris* and *Cavalleria Rusticana*. He is famous especially for his last minute rescue operation during the version of *Turandot* directed by Mehta at the Maggio Fiorentino in 1998 when, wearing his pyjamas and slippers, he was carried bodily into the theater at the beginning of the second act to replace a colleague who had quarreled with the Maestro.

José Cura, the Muscle Man

From the pampas to La Scala can be a shorter step than one might think, and that step has been taken by a new heroic tenor from Argentina, **José Cura** (Rosario 1962). A body builder's physique, an Etruscan profile, and heaps of determination: that's the tenor of the new Millennium, a man concerned not only with his physical condition but also with his musical prowess, which means being able to play the piano, the guitar, compose music and even direct an orchestra. In 2000 he was appointed Musical Director of the Orchestra Symphonia Varsovia, inheriting the commitment from the great Yehudi Menuhin, the first tenor ever to receive such an assignment.

Cura's voice is dark, emitted with impetus and generosity, permitting him to tackle both dramatic roles such as Otello, Samson, Don Alvaro, Radames, and more lyrical parts including Cavaradossi, Don Carlos, Manrico, Corrado in *Corsaro* and even Alfredo in the highly successful television version of *Traviata* filmed in Paris and produced by Andrea Andermann. Thanks to his imposing appearance and that touch of arrogance often seen in handsome young men, Cura has become a

José Cura *together with* **Sylvia Valayre** *in* Aida *(1999). This Arentinian singer is the perfect embodiment of the tenor of the new Millennium, physically fit and highly accomplished musically. (Fondazione Arena di Verona. Photo: Gainfranco Fainello).*

favorite with the ladies, taking the place in the hearts of opera's 'pasionarie' firstly of the legendary Del Monaco and secondly of Domingo. On stage he has created a new way of acting, with movements, gestures and attitudes not normally used by a tenor, emphasis being laid on voice emission and the successful utterance of his B flats. "An actor who sings, rather than a singer who acts", is the motto of this young Argentinian tenor, who seems to pay more attention to his stage presence analyzed with extreme precision, than to a method of singing that could hardly be called orthodox.

1950-1960: Picchi, Poggi, Fernandi – Three Little Men Amongst The Giants

During the period from 1950 until the end of the sixties there was a ferocious competition amongst tenors, especially in the *lirico-spinto* category. Some managed to carve out a small niche for themselves by choosing an unusual repertory or by emigrating overseas. **Mirto Picchi** (S. Mauro a Signa, Florence 1915 – Florence 1980) had begun as a *lirico-spinto* in operas performed by Del Monaco, Corelli and other colleagues who had more vocal weight. He soon decided to employ his particular skills, both vocal and acting, in a rarer repertoire and in new works (*La Figlia di Jorio* by Pizzetti, 1954; *La Sposa Sorteggiata* by Busoni, 1966; *Celestina* by Testi, 1963; *Lorenzaccio* by Bussotti, 1972). In these operas the Tuscan tenor had no rivals.

Gianni Poggi (Piacenza 1921 – 1989) earned himself widespread fame as Alfredo, the Duca di Mantova, Riccardo, Manrico and as a Donizetti singer both in Europe and America. His tone-color was unmistakable and has been aptly described as "full-bodied", that is, rich and dense. His high notes were noteworthy for their brilliance and incisiveness.

Eugenio Fernandi (Pisa 1924 – Millington, USA 1991)) sang frequently in Italy between 1954 and 1960, but emigrated to France where he included the most strenuous dramatic roles in his repertory. His performances were not always successful: his voice often seemed about to crack, probably because of some original intonation problems that were never completely resolved. All the same Fernandi was part of many prestigious casts and worked under the direction of a number of great conductors, one in particular being the Salzburg *Don Carlos* of 1958 with Herbert von Karajan.

A "sherpa" version of **Mirto Picchi** together with the mezzo-soprano **Gianna Pederzini** in I Cavalieri di Ekebu, by Zandonai, during a performance in Rome in January, 1954. Picchi gave highly intelligent and sensitive interpretations of these lesser known parts, investing them with a dignity equal to that of the major roles. (Photo: Oscar Savio. Historic Archives of the Rome Opera)

Corelli: Power and Charm

Like many dramatic tenors, **Franco Corelli** (stage name of Dario Corelli; Ancona 1921) made his debut as Don José at Spoleto in 1951. The first things that were apparent in the young tenor were his exceptional good looks, worthy of a Hollywood film star, and a dark, baritone-like voice of great power and large extension, but affected by a *vibrato stretto* which did not please everyone.

With time and under Lauri Volpi's invaluable guidance, he managed to dam the "gushing river" of his voice, rising to the highest notes of the pentagram and gaining a flexible and smooth emission. Thanks to this technical control he was not only able to sing *Pirata, Trovatore, Turandot, Poliuto* and *Les Huguenots* but also *Werther, Faust*, Gounod's *Roméo et Juliette* and *Don Carlos*, all major roles, during his long permanence at the Metropolitan Opera of New York. He retired in 1976, still in perfect condi-

A suggestive close-up of **Franco Corelli**, who looks more like one of Hollywood's stars than a typical opera singer. Just imagine what that spectator felt like when, after having "booed" Corelli in Trovatore, he turned round to find the tall, handsome tenor in his very box – furious! – This actually happened in Bologna.

What Escamillo could ever compete with such an enchanting Don Jose? This photo depicts **Corelli** and **Giulietta Simionato** in the Carmen performed at Venice, 1956. In the final two acts Corelli used to exihibit a vigor that has never been surpassed. (Historic Archives of La Fenice Theater, Venice. Photo: Giacomelli)

Corelli is hardly recognisable in his costume for Canio in Pagliacci at Caracalla in 1953. His voice was robust and metallic, but also able to express even the most delicate nuances. (Historic Archives of the Rome Opera. Photo: Oscar Savio)

When Pier Miranda Ferraro was suddenly taken ill, the management of the Teatro Regio of Parma immediately called **Franco Corelli** *to fill the part of Pollione in* Norma, *all in less than one day. It was the 1971-72 season, and thanks to the presence of the great Italian tenor, the performance was a triumph. (Historic Archives of Parma's Teatro Regio. Photo: Montacchini)*

tion. He was, however, renowned for his great insecurity and the panic attacks which would grip him before appearing in public. Quite often friends and colleagues would have to literally "launch" him onto the stage.

The Great Vocal Traditions of Emilia: Gianni Raimondi

Gianni Raimondi (Bologna 1923) showed right from the beginning (*Rigoletto*, Budrio 1947) that he possessed a solid vocal ability sustained by a sound vocal technique. His was a voice with a superb consistency and a timbre which, in its clarity and transparency, was similar to that of Di Stefano.

His exceptional high c‴ s and c″ sharps, together with his class and style, made him a belcanto singer in much demand in his time (*Puritani, Favorita, Armida, Mosè, Semiramide, Guglielmo Tell*).

As a pure lyric tenor, Raimondi excelled as Alfredo, Edgardo, Rodolfo and Cavaradossi, and was engaged by theaters all over the world for these parts, including La Scala, where he sang in *Bohème* directed by von Karajan in 1963.

The only criticism that might be leveled at him during his career is that he was sometimes a lazy performer, and had to be pushed to include extra *mezzavoce* and reminded in order to avoid monotonous phrasing; he succeeded if he was guided by a good conductor.

The Authentic Verdi Tenor: Carlo Bergonzi

For the first part of his career, from his initial debut as a baritone at Lecce in 1948 and his

Gianni Raimondi as Arrigo (Vespri Siciliani) in the 1973 performance at Turin under the direction of Di Stefano and Maria Callas. (Historic Archives of the Teatro Regio of Turin. Photo: RG. Naretto)

second debut, this time as a tenor (*Andrea Chénier*, Bari, 1951), until the beginning of the seventies **Carlo Bergonzi** (Vidalenzo, Parma 1924) did not enjoy the same critical acclaim extended to less worthy colleagues. The critics accused him of an unattractive timbre, of having a voice that was too artificial, with no high notes, and of having little stage presence; even his "s" pronounced "sh" in the Emilian way seemed to annoy them. However, few singers in the twentieth century could compete with Bergonzi as far as style, breathing technique and enunciation are concerned.

His perfect legato and vigorous accent made him an ideal Duca di Mantova, Riccardo, Radames, Don Alvaro, Canio and Pinkerton, not to mention his unforgettable Don Carlos. Although he never had sharp high notes because of his insistence in "covering" the notes of the *passaggio*, Bergonzi overcame even the most arduous vocal passages with incredible breath control: great examples are the aria "Quando le sere al placido" from *Luisa Miller* and the prison scene in *I Due Foscari*; he also applied variety and imagination to his phrasing. In this he is to be considered the rightful heir to Aureliano Pertile.

Thanks to his excellent technique Bergonzi gained professional satisfaction even in later years, singing triumphantly in concerts world-wide; especially memorable was the Madison Square Garden event, plus a phenomenal performance of Verdi's *Requiem* at Parma in 1998 and his long-awaited debut in *Otello* at New York's Carnegie Hall in May 2000, thus crowning an artistic career that has few equals.

Domingo the Supertenor

Placido Domingo was born in Madrid. His detractors say that his birth date is in 1934 (who knows why?), but his friends say he was born in 1941. Wisely, we propose both dates and leave the decision to the reader. He studied piano and composition during his youth in Mexico City, which gave him a firm grounding as a musician before he began as a singer. A friend persuaded him to attempt a vocal career, which was not altogether an unknown road to him as both his parents had been successful *Zarzuela* singers.

The steps on Domingo's ladder to success can be summarized as follows: 1959, debut in a small part in Poulenc's *Les dialogues des Carmélites* in Mexico City; 1962, his first lead part; 1963-65, permanent member of the Tel Aviv Opera; 1967, debut at the Metropolitan in *Adriana Lecouvreur*; 1969, Italian debut at Verona and the opening of the La Scala winter season on the traditional December 7 with *Ernani*.

Since then, Domingo's presence in the world's major theaters, arenas, squares, stadiums, film sets, recording and television studios has been constant, almost unbelievable. His repertory has, with time, embraced all the principal tenor roles from Verdi to Donizetti, Puccini, Massenet, Gounod, Wagner; most of these interpretations have been preserved on record.

Until 1975 the Spanish tenor kept the best qualities of his voice intact. Its color was magnificent, warm and sensual, smooth and caressing in quality, a beautiful *falsettone* (of which, unfortunately, he has always made little use), penetrating high notes, and a clear and passionate declamation. If to this we add his intelligence and musical brilliance, not to mention his psychological understanding of his roles, his acting ability, his undoubted charm, and his good looks, it would be easy to proclaim Domingo the greatest tenor of the twentieth century. But alas, his hyperactivity and vast repertory have taken their toll. During the second half of the seventies his voice began to suffer: the high notes (even only a´ and b´ flat) became strained, at times even strangled, as evident in the 1977 Vienna *Trovatore*; the *mezzavoce* became falsetto; he had trouble with his breathing in certain difficult passages; the legato lost its polish.

After the disastrous earthquake which hit Mexico City in 1985, the tenor generously decided to dedicate an entire year of activity to charity performances alone, canceling all his previous engagements with theaters the world over.

With the advent of mega-concerts and notwithstanding the malicious book written by Monica Lewinsky's mother, entitled *The True Story of the Three Tenors*, Domingo's fame has grown. And while continuing to make records, he is constantly adding new roles to his already vast repertoire, showing a level of artistic discipline and love of his profession that are rarely to be found today. He made an excellent attempt at Wagner's *Walküre* and *Parsifal*, was slightly less successful in Mayerbeer's *Profeta* at Vienna (1999), and was nothing less than exceptional in Tchaikovsky's *Queen of Spades*, again at Vienna, considered one of his best ever performances.

The Great Wagnerian Tenors of the Twentieth Century

Giuseppe Borgatti (Cento, Ferrara 1871 – Reno, Lago Maggiore 1950) was the apostle of Wagner's music in Italy. Gabriele D'Annunzio wrote of him: "The Wagnerians have found their Saint Paul." In fact, after his debut in *Faust*, at Castelfranco Veneto, 1892, his repertory was almost exclusively Wagnerian: *Lohengrin* at Milan in 1894, the first Italian *Siegfried* during the La Scala 1899-1900 season and *Tristan* the following season; finally *Tannhäuser* at Buenos Aires in 1901.

Borgatti's vocal abilities were perfectly suited to the difficult *Heldentenor* roles: he had brilliant high notes, smoothness of emission, and an excellent technique. The Italian operas he most frequently performed were *Andrea Chénier, Tosca, Fedora* and *Iris*; however, it appears he had considerable difficulty in sustaining the high notes in these parts from 1905 on. This was probably the reason why he decided, during the last part of his career, to limit his repertoire exclusively to Wagner, in whose operas the tessitura of the tenor voice converge.

From 1904, he triumphed at Bayreuth, the Wagner temple, where he became an essential protagonist of future editions of the festival. In 1914 he sang his last *Parsifal* at La Scala, in concert form, then retired because of ill health.

Placido Domingo *and **Cecilia Gasdia** in* I Pagliacci *(1993). The boom of the megaconcert has considerably increased the popularity of this Spanish tenor, who continues to add new roles to his already vast repertoire. (Fondazione Arena di Verona. Photo: Gianfranco Fainello)*

He suffered from glaucoma which gradually led to complete blindness by 1923.

Despite his advancing years and poor physical condition, his Colombia recordings made in 1928 are amazingly forceful interpretations of the "Ode to Spring" from *Die Walküre* and the finale of *Otello*.

Besides the "Borgatti phenomenon," for whom spreading the Wagnerian *Gesamtkunstwerk* was a true vocation, there were many other great Wagner performers.

The first of this illustrious lineage was **Italo Campanini** (Parma 1845 – 1896), brother of the famous conductor Cleofonte; he was the first *Lohengrin* at Bologna in 1871. He was also active in the French *lyrique* and Italian repertories, especially in London and New York. The tenor from Milan **Ettore Cesa-Bianchi** (1884 – 1952) was a noteworthy *Lohengrin*, and was described by Eugenio Gara as having "a voice of silver, just like the hero's armor". **Fiorello Giraud** (Parma 1870 – 1928) was the first Canio in Milan in 1892 and was Toscanini's favorite *Siegfried*, having been chosen by him for this opera at La Scala in 1907. **Edoardo Ferrari-Fontana** (Rome 1878 – Toronto 1936) was first an operetta tenor but the great Maestro Tullio Serafin persuaded him to take on roles more suited to his abilities, such as *Tristan* or *Tannhäuser*. He triumphed in these roles at the New York Metropolitan.

Amongst the first Germans to champion Wagnerian melodrama in the twentieth century was **Heinrich Knote** (Munich 1870 – Garmisch 1953), famous for his outstanding diction and his super-powerful high notes, which made him very popular as Manrico in Verdi's *Trovatore*. He continued to sing with the same vocal capacity until 1931.

Another *Heldentenor* of rare quality was **Jacques (Jac) Urlus** (Hergenrath, Aachen 1867 – Noordwiik 1935) whose repertory was incredibly wide (apart from the main Wagnerian roles, he could easily perform Tamino in *The Magic Flute*, *Faust* and Raoul in *The Huguenots*). Known for his robust vocal capacity and the smoothness and flexibility of his emission, this Dutch tenor was able to diminish or increase sounds even in the high register.

Karel Burian (Carl Burrian) (Rousinov, Rakovnik 1870 – Senomaty 1924) was very popular in the R. Strauss repertory and especially as Herod in *Salome*. He was the first to interpret this part, in 1905, in Dresden. He also distinguished himself in Wagner, Smetana, and in Lieder works, displaying a technique and style of rare quality.

After having made his debut as a baritone at Wiesbaden in 1891, **Erik Schmedes** (Gjentofte,

The tenor **Giuseppe Borgatti** *in his hairy Siegfried costume. It seems that, to train for this role, he kept a hammer and anvil in his hotel room – much to the disapproval of the other clients!*

Copenhagen 1866 – Vienna 1931) made a second debut as a tenor in 1898 at Vienna, singing the part of Siegfried. He was one of the most acclaimed performers at the Staatsoper during Mahler's management. His biggest successes were *Tristan*, *Lohengrin* and *Parsifal*, apart from his lively portrayals in *Otello*, *Pagliacci*, *Norma* and *Carmen*. He was the first Austrian Cavaradossi in 1910.

Leo Slezak: Humorous and Amiable

Leo Slezak (Schonberg, Moravia 1873 – Rottach Egern, Bavaria 1946) remains the greatest *Heldentenor* of the twentieth century. He made his debut in *Lohengrin*, at Brno, in 1896 and went on to work mainly in Berlin (1898-99), Vienna (1901-09) and New York (1909-13), and then in Vienna and in German opera theaters until 1934.

He was gifted with a voice that was flexible, beautiful in timbre, sturdy, luminous in the high register, warm and sensual in the middle register. His imaginative phrasing allowed him to range from Mozart, Delibes and Charpentier to the most difficult of Wagnerian roles and Verdi's *Otello*. In the latter he triumphed at the Metropolitan in 1911 under Toscanini's baton.

Equally memorable were the musicality and polish with which he sang Lieder songs, showing an artistic talent far superior to that of his Italian contemporaries.

Slezak had an imposing appearance, but also a pronounced sense of humor to which he often gave rein. The management of the Metropolitan Opera had to fine him after a performance of *Aida* for the confusion he had caused among members of the chorus. The remark he made during a performance of *Lohengrin* has remained famous. After singing the "Farewell to the Swan" he casually enquired "When does the next one leave?", making everyone collapse with laughter. His book of memories is appropriately titled *The Clown's Song: Memories of a Starving Tenor*.

François Gauthier, better known as **Paul Franz** (Paris 1876 – 1950), spread Wagner's operas in France; after 1908, when he made his debut his in *Lohengrin* at the Paris Opera, he was clearly one of the most complete dramatic tenors of his generation. He was chosen for many important premieres by composers such as Roussel, d'Indy, Rabaud, and he also participated in Paris performances of Berlioz's *Les Troyens*, Massenet's *Hérodiade* and Halévy's *La Juive*. He

Ivan Ers'ov *was a great interpreter of the Russian and Wagnerian repertory He was exceptional for his total emotional involvement and his stage presence, especially in Lohengrin and Parsifal. (Photo from the Historic Archives of the Kirov Theater of Leningrad, 1910)*

retired from the stage on July 12, 1938, and from then on dedicated his time to teaching.

In Russia, and precisely at the Marynskij Theater, the German repertory was triumphantly upheld by **Ivan Ers'ov** (Novo-

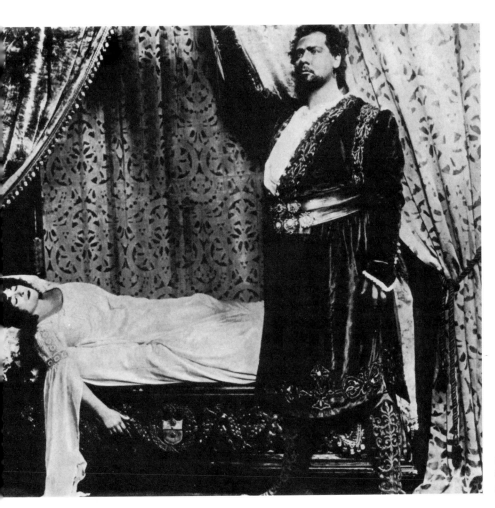

Leo Slezak, *Otello, has just strangled* **Frances Alda**, *Desdemona.*

cerkassk 1867 – Leningrad 1943) from 1895 onwards. Meanwhile, in the Bayreuth sanctuary, shone the bright star of **Alois Burgstaller** (Holzkirchen 1871 – Gmünd 1945). An excellent Sigmund, Siegfried, Erik and Parsifal, he was exiled from the "sacred hill" in 1903 being guilty of having sung *Parsifal* in New York before the exclusive copyright had expired.

Melchior, the Giant with the Golden Voice

Lauritz Melchior (Copenhagen 1890 – Los Angeles 1973) had a truly golden voice. A baritone from 1913 until 1917, he became a tenor in 1918 when he made his debut as Tannhäuser. During the first years of his career

"The Great Dane," **Laurik Melchior**, *in the title role of Wagner's* Tannhäuser. *The greatest* heldentenor *of the twentieth century.*

he dangerously alternated tenor and baritone roles, putting his voice at great risk. He was saved thanks to his incredible physical resistance and a period of hard study between 1921 and 1923 under the guidance of several different teachers.

In 1924, having obtained a valuable engagement at Bayreuth, he began his spectacular rise to fame, and even to cult status in America. He sang at the Metropolitan Opera from 1926 until 1950 when he retired.

When listening to some of the recordings made during the span of his long career, what is most striking is the extraordinary consistency and sonority of that voice with a cutting *Sprechgesang* and spearlike high notes. We can, however, also hear a certain difficulty in molding such vocal bulk in order to respect all the dynamic signs. Sometimes the same difficulty is noticeable in the most treacherous legato passages and in held high notes, as is demonstrated in the live recording of *Tannhäuser* made in 1942 at the Metropolitan.

These were defects due, perhaps, to his original beginnings as a baritone and were never completely resolved or camouflaged. As Lauri Volpi shrewdly noted in his book *Voci Parallele*, "his declamation and sonority were those of a Wagnerian orchestra"; and we might add that his physical stamina was indestructible, in fact he sang Tristan over three hundred times!

A second wave of Wagnerian singers followed the generation of Melchior and Slezak, even though they remained a step below the level of their immediate predecessors.

Julius Patzak (Vienna 1898 – Rottach 1974) was the flag bearer of this new regiment of tenors, singing from 1926 until 1960, particularly at the Vienna Staatsoper. His voice was neither beautiful nor particularly powerful; his art consisted of a rare musicality and sensitivity. Thanks to his uncommon acting ability and his complete adherence to style, he made memorable portrayals of Florestan in *Fidelio*, in Pfitzner's *Palestrina*, as Herod in *Salome*, as Mime in *The Ring*, and in *Lohengrin*, and performed all the most important Mozart roles.

Max Lorenz (Düsseldorf 1901 – Salzburg 1975) started his career in 1927, one year after his colleague, Patzak, in the part of Walther in *The Mastersingers of Nuremberg*. The audiences of Berlin, Vienna, New York, London, Bayreuth, Rome and Milan were able to applaud him until the beginning of the seventies, admiring his passionate declamation and penetrating voice. It is true that his voice had already shown evident signs of tiredness by the fifties, causing problems in certain roles (Tristan, for example), but it is also true that Lorenz emerged victorious from every performance. He is even remembered in opera annals for the much-maligned *Tristan*, superbly performed at La Scala with the mythical conducting of De Sabata in 1948.

Amongst the best Lohengrins and Siegmunds (*Walküre*) between the wars was **Franz Völker** (Neu Ilsenberg 1899 – Darmstadt 1965), who was also famous as Otello and Canio in German theaters. His "Addio alla madre" (Farewell to mother) from *Cavalleria Rusticana* is the most beautiful recording of this piece ever made.

Set Svanholm (Vasteras 1904 – Stockholm 1964) was another singer who began as a baritone, having first appeared in 1930 as Silvio in *Pagliacci*, and then became a tenor in the role of Radames in 1936. This role was well suited to him despite his unexceptional vocal powers and the absence of a "physique du rôle." In the immediate post-war period his dramatically intense interpretations created him the reputation of being virtually irreplaceable in the roles of Tristan and Siegfried.

The German tenor **Marcel Wittrisch** (Antwerp 1901 – Stockholm 1955) distinguished himself in both the Wagnerian repertory and in the operettas of Lehar, succeeding equally well in an incredible stylistic cocktail.

The 1948-49 season: **Ramon Vinay** *sings "Dio, mi potevi scagliar" in the third act of* Otello. *(Historic Archives of the San Carlo Opera Theater of Naples)*

His career lasted for three decades, from 1925 until 1955.

The Wagnerian Meteors

In the nineteen-fifties it was a tenor from Chile who excited the custodians of the Holy Grail of Bayreuth. His timbre was dark, his high notes imposing, his enunciation sculptured, his stage presence magnificent. He seemed a fairy-tale Tristan; his name was **Ramón Vinay** (Chillan 1911 – Puebla 1996). Alas, the dream did not last long. Unresolved technical problems and a heavy repertoire prematurely tired Vinay's voice, which often sounded forced and strained.

In 1962, as a last hope, he returned to his original baritone register, but the parts of Telramondo, Iago, Scarpia, and even Falstaff in no way helped him to find his lost voice.

The same fate awaited the Italian **Gino Penno** (Felizzano, Alessandria 1920 – Milan 1999), who badly abused a naturally rich and generous voice in operas that were too strenuous for him (*Lohengrin, Walküre, Turandot, Aida, Forza del Destino*) and his career was brief. During a *Trovatore* at La Scala in 1954 he had to lower the "Pira" by an entire tone! In 1956, following a few performances of *Boris Godunov* at La Scala, he retired permanently.

Another voice of steel was that of **Hans Beirer** (Wiener Neustadt 1911 – Vienna 1993), who was still performing at the theaters of

Hans Beirer – *Siegfried. A photo from at least fonty years ago. (Historic Archives of the Rome Opera. Photo: W Saeger)*

Vienna and Berlin at over seventy years of age. He was an excellent interpreter of Wagner's operas, with a special predilection for the roles of Tannhäuser, Erik in *The Flying Dutchman* and Siegfried. A master of *Sprechgesang*, with fine, powerful high notes, Beirer also included in his repertoire *Otello, Lohengrin, Parsifal* and a memorable impersonation of Herod in Strauss's *Salome*.

The Twilight Of the Gods

In post war years the number of *Heldentenoren* gradually diminished, revealing a lack of authentic voices and the decline of singing schools.

Wolfgang Windgassen (Annemasse, Geneva 1914 – Stuttgart 1974) was, together with Jon Vickers, the last great Wagnerian singer of the twentieth century. He began his activity in 1941, making his debut at Pforzheim as Don Alvaro in *La Forza del Destino*. After a pause during the war years, he started singing again in the Stuttgart Opera ensemble, and was noticed by Wieland Wagner in 1951. Wagner was favorably impressed by the tenor in Offenbach's operetta *La Belle Hélène* and signed him up for the Bayreuth festival.

Soon Windgassen became irreplaceable in Wagnerian heroic tenor roles, demonstrating a timbre, a technique and an interpretive intelligence of unequalled excellence. During the fifties and sixties he undertook the difficult roles of the German lyric theater, refining his characterizations and always giving the audience new sensations, especially in the revolutionary productions of Wieland Wagner at Bayreuth. He retired from the stage at Stuttgart in 1972, leaving behind him a fine record as singer, director and artistic manager.

Furtwängler's favorite tenor was **Ludwig Suthaus** (Cologne 1906 – Berlin 1971) who had made his debut, as many of his colleagues before him, in the part of Walther in *The Mastersingers of Nuremberg*, in 1928. Because of the volume and the color of his voice, and his penetrating high notes, he was considered Melchior's heir, although he had a relatively early decline. The career of this German artist was formed in all the world's major theaters, up to 1967. He was often part of prestigious companies and sang under the batons of such illustrious conductors as von Karajan, Erich Kleiber and, as mentioned earlier, Furtwängler. On the whole, his renderings of operas such as *Tristan, The Ring*, Strauss' *Elektra, Fidelio* and *Wozzek* were noteworthy, although such a strenuous repertoire was bound to take an early toll on his vocal abilities.

The Canadian tenor **Jon Vickers** (Prince Albert 1926) belongs undoubtedly to the category of Wagnerian tenors, despite the fact that, since 1956, he has also been an excellent Verdi dramatic tenor (*Otello*) and has also sung roles such as Don José in *Carmen*, Samson in Saint-Saëns' opera and Pollione in *Norma*. For all of the sixties and most of the seventies, his voice was robust and vigorous in the center, powerful and secure in the high notes (at least up to b´ flat), able to follow all the dynamic indications in a score and to creatively vary phrasing.

With the passing of years, his voice has been marred by a certain stiffness, a fault which an excellent technique has not been able to remedy, nor has it been helped by his timbre, unexceptional right from the start. However, Vickers has continued to enjoy success, above all in London and America, thanks to his intelligence and artistic sensitivity. Vickers established a long partnership with Covent Garden (beginning in 1957), singing mainly Don José, Aeneas, Don Carlos, Radames, Florestano, Siegmund, and a wonderful Peter Grimes.

The New Generation

Once the stars of **Hans Hopf** (Nuremberg 1916 – Munich 1993), splendid as Walther in *The Mastersingers of Nuremberg*, **Jess Thomas** (Hot Springs, South Dakota 1927 – Tiburon, California 1993), a penetrating Lohengrin and Tannhäusen, **Sàndor Kónya** (Sarkad, Hungary 1923), endowed with a magnificent timbre and phrasing, and of **James King** (Dodge City, Kansas 1925), who, with his strong, piercing voice, made his name singing in both German and Italian operas, had begun to fade, the school of the *Heldentenors* has gradually declined.

Voices such as those of **René Kollo** (Berlin 1937), **Peter Hoffmann** (Marienbad 1944), **Siegfried Jerusalem** (Oberhausen 1940) and **Reiner Goldberg** (Crostan, Saxony 1939), though endowed with good tone-quality and phrasing ability in roles such as Tristan, Lohengrin and so forth, have in the long run been unable to stand up to comparison with the voices of the preceding generation.

Nor have matters improved with the arrival on the scene of singers such as **Richard Versalle**, who was unfortunately killed in an accident on stage at the Met, **Aikki Siukola**, a huge Finn whose tumultuous voice is undermined by a sometimes hesitant intonation, **Ben Heppner**, another heavyweight, well-received in the roles of Tristan and Hüon in *Oberon*, not to mention the many victims sacrificed on the Beyreuth altar.

Other Famous Sopranos

The section dedicated to the most famous tenors of the twentieth century concludes with this chronological table comprising the names of other artists no less worthy of mention. Each name includes the date, place and opera of the singer's debut, plus the principal roles in his repertoire and a brief note on his vocal characteristics and career.

NAME	FIRST PERFORMANCE	BASIC REPERTORY	REMARKS
Ahnsjö, Claes (1942) Light lyric	1969, Stockholm (*Magic Flute*)	Mozart, *Don Pasquale, Barbiere, Falstaff, Mastersingers* (David)	An appreciated concert artist
Albanese, Francesco (1912) Lyric	1942, Venice (*Cenerentola*)	*Traviata, Bohème, Armida*	International career. A soft voice of lovely color
Alcaïde, Tomaz (1901-1967) Light lyric	1925, Milan (*Mignon*)	*Don Pasquale, Traviata, Barbiere, Werther, Faust, Favorita.*	A most polished and refined technique, capable of spinning high and super high notes and soft, persuasive *mezzevoci*
Aldenhoff, Bernd (1908-1959) *Heldentenor*	1938, Darmstadt	Wagner, Strauss	Good, penetrating timbre, of excellent power
Alexander, John (1935-1990) Lyric	1965, Cincinnati	Mozart, *Norma, Anna Bolena, Traviata, Faust*	A noted recitalist and oratorio interpreter
Altmeyer, Theo (1931) Light lyric	1955, Berlin	Bach, Handel, Mozart, Beethoven	Celebrated for his recordings of Bach: Cantatas and Oratorios
Altschewsky, Ivan (1876-1917) Lyric	1901, St. Petersburg	*Roméo et Juliette, Faust, Les Huguenots,* Russian repertory	Foremost exponent of the great Russian tradition of the early twentieth century
Alvarez, Albert (1861-1933) *Lirico spinto*	1886, Geneva (*Faust*)	*Faust, Thaïs, Navarraise, Roméo et Juliette, Pagliacci, Carmen*	Noble declamation, purity of vocal line, efficient actor
Anders, Peter (1908-1954) Lyric	1931 Berlin (*La Belle Hélène* by Offenbach)	*Magic Flute, Ariadne auf Naxos, Fidelio, Der Freischütz, Lohengrin*	First interpreter of *Friedenstag* by R. Strauss at Munich in 1938. Radiant timbre, intense and varied phrasing, magical *mezzevoci*, a formidable Lieder singer
Ansseau, Fernand (1890-1972) Lyric	1913, Dijon (*Hérodiade* by Massenet)	French lyrique repertory. Puccini	Active in Belgium and in the French theaters. Fine timbre, secure technique
Atlantov, Vladimir (1939) *Lirico spinto*	1962, Leningrad	*Carmen, Otello, Queen of Spades, Eugene Onegin, Tosca, Pagliacci, Boris Godunov*	Voice solid and penetrating, phrasing monotonous. From 1977 he has included some baritone roles
Bassi, Amedeo (1874-1949) *Lirico spinto*	1897, Castelfiorentino (*Ruy Blas* by Marchetti)	*Aida, Loreley, Girl of the Golden West, Zazà, Parsifal, Walküre*	A strong voice, luminous in the high register. Acclaimed in the American theater. Among his students in Florence, Ferruccio Tagliavini
Baum, Kurt (1900-1990) *Lirico spinto*	1932, Zürich (*Der Kreidekreis* by Zemlinsky)	*Aida, Guglielmo Tell, Trovatore,* Wagner operas	A burnished timbre color; penetrating voice, slight technical insecurity. Studied with Edoardo Garbin in Milan
Benelli, Ugo (1935) Light lyric	1960, Milan	*Barbiere, Cenerentola, Don Pasquale, Italiana in Algeri, Matrimonio Segreto*	Pleasing timbre, soft emission, some excessive use of falsetto
Berdini, Amedeo (1919-1964) Lyric	1948, Naples (*Lucia*)	*Lucia, Rigoletto, Butterfly, Duca d'Alba*	Died whilst in the full glory of his career. Considered a valid candidate as Gigli's successor

Bergamaschi, Ettore (1884-1975) *Lirico spinto*	1912, Bari (*La Forza del Destino*)	Verdi, Puccini, Mascagni	Became known, thanks to his talent, as the "Caruso of South America"
Breviario, Giovanni (1891-1982) *Lirico spinto*	1924, Pola (*Trovatore*)	*Norma, Cavalleria, Pagliacci, Trovatore*	He never received in Italy the recognition achieved in other countries
Brilioth, Helge (1931) *Heldentenor*	1959, Stockholm (as a baritone); 1965, Stockholm (as a tenor in *Carmen*)	*Otello, Siegfried, Tristan, Parsifal, Ariadne auf Naxos*	A shooting star but of short duration. Dominated Bayreuth from 1969 until 1974
Burrows, Stuart (1933) Light lyric	1963, Cardiff (Ismaele in *Nabucco*)	Mozart, *Fidelio, Traviata*, Lieder and oratorio	Well emitted voice, musical; specialist in *The Damnation of Faust* and Berlioz's *Requiem*
Campora, Giuseppe (1924) Lyric	1949, Bari (*Bohème*)	*Butterfly, Gioconda, Tosca, Simon Boccanegra, Bohème;* operetta	Rich, dark tones, high notes a little forced
Casellato, Renzo (1936) Lyric	1963, Parma (*Elisir d'Amore*)	*Pearl Fishers, Elisir d'Amore, Don Pasquale, Sonnambula, Lucia, Traviata*	Richly grained voice, not very agile but well tuned
Cioni, Renato (1929) Lyric	1956, Spoleto (*Lucia di Lammermoor*)	*Butterfly, Tosca, Traviata, Rigoletto, Lucia*	Lovely color, persuasive phrasing, but expression a little stiff
Conley, Eugene (1908-1981) *Lirico spinto*	Concerts with the N.B.C. Symphony Orchestra in the early forties. From 1948 in the main European theaters	*Puritani, Guglielmo Tell, Faust, Rigoletto*	Exceptionally penetrating high notes, the voice solid and darkened in the center. Excellent musicality
Constantino, Florencio (1869-1919) *Lirico spinto*	1892, Montevideo (*Dolores* by Bretòn)	*Gioconda, Don Carlos, Otello, Trovatore*	Acclaimed in South America for his strong high notes. Famous for his "death rattle" in the death scene of *Otello*
Crooks, Richard (1900-1972) Lyric	1927, Hamburg (*Tosca*)	*Tosca, Rigoletto, Traviata Manon*, concerts and oratorio	Soft, flexible, clean voice, inclined towards a shaded singing without mannerisms or blanching
Dalmorès, Charles (1871-1939) Dramatic	1899, Lyon (Loge in *Das Rheingold*, with his real name, Henri Alphonse Brin)	*The Ring, Lohengrin, Thaïs, Oracolo*, Verdi repertory	Exceptional volume and strength. An idol in American and German theaters in Wagner operas
d'Arkor, André (1901-1971) Lyric	1924, Luttich (Gerald in *Lakmé*)	*Lucia, Rigoletto, Lakmé, Roméo et Juliette, Faust*	Shining, secure high notes; his timbre amongst the most beautiful of the interpreters of the French school

Vladimir Atlantov *with* **Mietta Sighele**, *in* Carmen, 1984.

Richard Crooks.

Davies, Ryland (1943) Light lyric	1964, Welsh Opera (*Barbiere*)	*Falstaff, Idomeneo, Così Fan Tutte, Eugene Onegin*, oratorio	Voice lacking in color, but flexible and pleasantly emitted
de Muro Lomanto, Enzo (1902-1952) Light lyric	1925, Catanzaro (*Traviata*)	*Rigoletto, Lucia, Traviata, Don Pasquale, Barbiere, Don Giovanni*	Refined technique, an inclination for shading in the phrasing. Between 1929 and 1932 he was married to Toti Dal Monte
De Palma, Piero (1916) Light lyric	Towards the end of the thirties with La Scala company	Over two hundred roles as *comprimario* and secondary parts	A regular figure in major opera theaters for almost fifty years. Memorable his recording of Malatestino
Dvorsky, Peter (1951) Lyric	1972, Bratislava (*Eugene Onegin*)	*Lucia, Rigoletto, Bohème, Traviata, Elisir d'Amore, Manon Lescaut*	Radiant timbre, strong high notes, clear diction; but his phrasing lacks variety, and this has harmed his recent experiences in a more *lirico-spinto* repertory
Dyck, Ernest van (1861-1923) *Heldentenor*	1883, Paris (soloist in the cantata *Le Gladiateur* by Vidal)	*Lohengrin, Parsifal, Siegfried, Tannhäuser*	He was the first Werther in 1892, but his recording of "Pourquoi me réveiller" is disappointing
Erb, Karl (1877-1958) Light lyric	1907, Stuttgart	*Mozart, Pfitznert*, Lieder and oratorio	Great musicality and style, flexibility and smoothness
Escalaïs, Léon (1859-1941) *Lirico spinto*	1883, Paris (*Guglielmo Tell*)	*Trovatore, Robert le Diable, Les Huguenots, Faust*	Impressive incisiveness and powerful high notes
Figner, Nikolai (1857-1918) Lyric	1882, Naples (*Philémon et Baucis* by Gounod)	*Queen of Spades, Iolanthe, Ernani, Sonnambula, Rigoletto, Carmen, Les Huguenots*	Exceptionally eclectic. Voice very penetrating and sweet
Filacuridi, Nicola (1922) Lyric	1945, Alexandria (Egypt) (*Cavalleria Rusticana*)	*Manon, Traviata, Adriana Lecouvreur, Werther*	A young, fresh timbre, caressing emission, some forcing in the highest notes
Fisichella, Salvatore (1943) Light lyric	1970, Spoleto (*Werther*)	*Rigoletto, Puritani, Favorita, Faust*	A voice which is not powerful but excellently projected; easy high notes reaching high F
Fusati, Nicola (1876-1956) *Lirico spinto*	1907, Rome	*Ernani, Norma, Aida, Trovatore, Otello*	Exceptional power in the high notes, wide and full central register
Gibin, Joao (1929-1997) *Lirico spinto*	1954, winner, as a baritone, in the "Mario Lanza" competition	*Lucia, Andrea Chénier, Turandot, Don Carlos, Fanciulla*	Nasal sounding emission, and difficulty in singing the *mezzavoce*

Enzo de Muro Lomanto in The King *by Giordano.*

Léon Escalas.

Gilion, Mario (1870-1914) Lyric	1901, Monza (*L'Africana*)	*Huguenots, Guglielmo Tell, Robert le Diable, Faust*	Easy and penetrating high notes, even if his recordings do not justify his fame
Giorgini, Aristodemo (1879-1937) Light lyric	1903, Naples	*Bohème, Sonnambula, Don Pasquale, Mefistofele*	Voice marked by a vibration and mannerism typical of "Liberty-style" singers
Giraudeau, Jean (1916-1995) Light lyric	1947 Paris (*Pearl Fishers*)	*Barbiere, Thaïs, Les Troyens, Faust.*	Pleasant vocal color, smooth and caressing singing, fine sound in the *falsettone*
Grassi, Rinaldo (1885-1946) *Lirico spinto*	1904, Novara (*Bohème*)	*Mefistofele, Tosca, Butterfly, Cavalleria Rusticana, The Girl of the Golden West, Faust*	A notable dramatic temperament and passionate acting
Häfliger, Ernst (1919) Light lyric	1942, in concert	*Don Giovanni, Fidelio, Magic Flute, Oedipus Rex*	Excellent method, perfect diction, grace and style
Hislop, Joseph (1884-1977) Lyric	1914, Stockholm (*Faust*)	*Lucia, Rigoletto, Bohème, Traviata.*	One of the best Anglo-Saxon tenors for correct technical positioning and fluid singing
Hollweg, Werner (1936) Light lyric	1962, Vienna Chamber-opera	All Mozart; Lieder and oratorio	Rich middle register, but some problems in the high register
Ilosfalvy, Robert (1927) Lyric	1953, Budapest (*Hunyadi Laszlo* by Erkel)	*Butterfly, Manon Lescaut, Traviata, Rigoletto*	Splendid natural vocal ability governed by an excellent technique. Inexplicable is his lack of fame and the absence of this great singer in Italy
Imbart de la Tour, Georges (1865-1911) *Lirico spinto*	1890, Geneva (*Les Huguenots*)	*Aida, Carmen, Faust, Tannhäuser*	Major exponent of the French school of singing at the end of the nineteenth century
Jagel, Frederick (1897-1982) Lyric	1924, Leghorn (*Bohème*, with the name of Federico Jeghelli)	*Traviata, Bohème, Aida, Peter Grimes*	Very equal voice over all the range, solid in the center and easy high notes
Jörn, Karl (1873-1947) *Heldentenor*	1896, Fribourg (*Martha*)	*Faust, Carmen, Parsifal, Tristan and Isolde*	Stable member of the Metropolitan Opera until 1914; noted as an exceptional Wagner singer
Kiepura, Jan (1902-1966) Lyric	1924, Lwow (*Faust*)	*Bohème, Traviata, Rigoletto*; operetta	Handsome appearance, pleasant voice. Famous for the films made together with his wife, the soprano Martha Eggerth
Knote, Heinrich (1870-1953) *Heldentenor*	1892, Munich, Bavaria (Georg in *Waffenschmied* by Lortzing)	*Tristan and Isolde, Rienzi, Trovatore, Lohengrin, Queen of Sheba*	Rivalry with Caruso at the Met at the beginning of the twentieth century
Koslowski, Ivan (1900-1993) Lyric	1920, Poltawa	*Sadko, Werther, Orfeo, Lohengrin, Roméo et Juliette, Eugene Onegin*	A sweet timbre and smooth emission. At seventy years of age he was still amazing the Soviet public
Kozma, Lajos (1938) Light lyric	1962, Budapest	Lieder and oratorio, *Lucia, Così Fan Tutte*, contemporary repertory	Lovely timbre, warm, not particularly extensive but flexible
Kozub, Ernst (1925-1971) *Heldentenor*	1950, Berlin (*Zar und Zimmermann* by Lortzing)	*Siegfried, Aida, Mastersingers, Die Frau ohne Schatten, Flying Dutchman* (Erik), *Carmen*	Some slight technical problems in the *passaggio* hindered a varied phrasing. His natural vocal abilities, however, were of excellent quality
Krenn, Werner (1943) Light lyric	1966, Berlin (*The Fairy Queen* by Purcell)	*Don Giovanni, La Clemenza di Tito, Lucio Silla, Il Re Pastore*, Lieder and oratorio	First bassoon player of the Vienna Symphony for three years. Noteworthy Mozart interpreter in innumerable productions
Kullmann, Charles (1903-1983) Lyric	1929, American Opera Company (*Madama Butterfly*)	*Così Fan Tutte, Die Entführung aus dem Serail, Don Giovanni, Oberon, Faust*	Fine timbre, perfect technique. He was a star at the Met between 1935 and 1962

Lavirgen, Pedro (1930) *Lirico spinto*	1964, Mexico City (*Aida*)	*Carmen, Trovatore, Turandot, Aida, Tosca*	Splendid natural voice ruined by technical problems and a tendency to "push" the high notes
Lemeshew, Sergei (1902-1977) Lyric	1920, Moscow (*Eugene Onegin*)	*Werther, Rigoletto, Roméo et Juliette, Traviata*	Excellent singing method. *Mezzevoci* and *smorzature* of high quality; good high notes
Lewis, Richard (1914-1990) Light lyric	1939, Carl Rosa Opera Company (*Barbiere*)	*Don Giovanni, Peter Grimes, Così Fan Tutte, The Rake's Progress*, Lieder and oratorio	Interpreter of many first-ever performances in England, gifted with exceptional musicality
Luccioni, José (1903-1978) *Lirico spinto*	1931, Rouen (*Tosca*)	*Carmen, Otello, Aida, Samson and Delilah, Esclarmonde*	Incisive, fiery, penetrating and passionate voice which was never exaggerated. Chiseled enunciation and formidable stage presence
Malipiero, Giovanni (1906-1970) Lyric	At the end of the twenties in small provincial theaters	*Lucia, Mefistofele, Bohème, Favorita, Roméo et Juliette* (Zandonai)	An authentic specialist in the role of Faust, be it that of Boito or Gounod. He knew how to sing with taste and feeling
Mazaroff, Todor (1907-1975) Dramatic	1935, Sofia (*Prince Igor*)	*Aida, Forza del Destino, Guglielmo Tell*	An idol of the Vienna State Opera from 1937 until 1953. Noted for the power and beauty of his voice
Melandri, Antonio (1888-1970) *Lirico spinto*	1924, Novara	*Isabeau, Fedora, Turandot, Cavalleria, Ernani*	His voice resembled that of Aureliano Pertile. A singer very much appreciated at the Colòn in Buenos Aires
Minghetti, Angelo (1887-1957) Lyric	1911	*Bohème, La Fiamma*	First performer of *La Fiamma* in 1934 at Rome. Because of technical errors he was already having problems as early as the thirties
Nash, Heddle (1894-1961) Light lyric	1924, Milan (*Barbiere*)	*Don Giovanni, Mastersingers* (David), *Cosi fan Tutte*, oratorio and recitals	Studied with Borgatti at Milan and was a singer of impeccable and gracious style
Nessi, Giuseppe (1887-1961) Light lyric	1910, Saluzzo (*Traviata*)	All the most important *comprimario* and support roles of the popular repertory	A major protagonist at La Scala Opera Theatre from 1921 until his death. He took part in the first-ever performances of *Turandot* and *Nerone*
Ochman, Wieslaw (1937) Lyric	1959, Bytom	*Eugene Onegin, Tosca, Vespri Siciliani, Boris Godunov, Lucia, Idomeneo, Anna Bolena, Salome*	An exceptionally wide repertoire, ranging from the Baroque to contemporary opera. Made many recordings

Kark Jörn
in Faust.

Heinrich Knote
in Otello.

Oncina, Juan (1925) Light lyric	1946, Barcelona (*Manon* by Massenet)	*Cenerentola, Matrimonio Segreto, Comte Ory, Don Pasquale, Barbiere*	A dark and caressing voice
O'Sullivan, John (1878-1948) *Lirico spinto*	1909	*Les Huguenots, Guglielmo Tell, Trovatore, Otello*	He certainly did not deserve the phrase "Tenor of only two notes" coined by Carelli to describe him. His middle voice was rich and with a lovely color, but his acting was a little stiff
Paoli, Antonio (1870-1946) *Lirico spinto*	1899, Paris (*Guglielmo Tell*)	*Trovatore, Otello, Samson and Delilah, L'Africana, Pagliacci*	Radiant high notes, great stage temperament
Pattiera, Tino (1890-1966) *Lirico spinto*	1915, Dresden (a sentinel in *The Magic Flute*)	*Andrea Chénier, Tannhäuser, Queen of Spades, Ariadne auf Naxos, Forza del Destino*	Very active in the "Verdi Renaissance" in Germany in the twenties-thirties
Pauli, Piero (1898-1967) Lyric	1929, Trieste (*Faust*)	*Bohème, Mefistofele, Gianni Schicchi, Traviata, Falstaff, Carmen, Tosca*	An interpreter of great possibility, secure and homogeneous over the entire scale
Pears, Peter (1910-1986) Light lyric	1942, London (*Tales of Hoffmann*)	*Peter Grimes, The Rape of Lucretia, Billy Budd, Death in Venice, Acis and Galathea*	The favorite singer of Benjamin Britten and the first interpreter of all his most important compositions. Voice inclined towards falsetto, but passionate
Piccaluga, Nino (1890-1973) *Lirico spinto*	1918, Novara	*Tabarro, Francesca da Rimini, Roméo et Juliette*	Highly esteemed by Zandonai who wanted him as principal singer in many of his operas. He had to interrupt his career in 1935 because of illness
Poncet, Tony (1921-1979) *Lirico spinto*	1955, Luttich	*La Juive, Pagliacci, Guglielmo Tell, Carmen, Aida, L'Africana, Trovatore, Faust*	Easy, tone-colored high notes, full middle register, but little inclination for expressive shadings
Prandelli, Giacinto (1914) Lyric	1942, Bergamo (*Bohème*)	*Bohème, Traviata, Lucia, Rigoletto, Peter Grimes, Adriana Lecouvreur, Francesca da Rimini, Mefistofele*	A pleasant, homogeneous voice, very clear in enunciation. He has a repertoire of over fifty roles
Prevedi, Bruno (1928-1988) *Lirico spinto*	1958, Milan (as a baritone, Tonio in *Pagliacci*); as a tenor in 1960	*Don Carlos, Norma, Macbeth, Aida, Carmen, Ernani, Trovatore*	Some problems in the *passaggio*, never completely resolved, but a beautiful color and an intense participation in his roles
Riegel, Kenneth (1938) Light lyric	1965, Santa Fe (*König Hirch* by Henze)	*Don Giovanni, Così Fan Tutte, Die Entführung aus dem Serail, Elisir d'Amore, Traviata, Lulu*	A vast repertory with alternating results; good in contemporary operas but not nearly as successful in the major operas, in which he cannot compete with better quality, better prepared voices
Rogatschewsky, Joseph (1891-1985) Lyric	1922, Toulouse	*Manon, Rigoletto, Traviata, Eugene Onegin, Werther*	Elegance, expressive variety, a liking for vocal nuances, secure technique
Salvarezza, Antonio (1901-1985) *Lirico spinto*	1935	*Guglielmo Tell, Turandot, Tosca, Rigoletto, Puritani*	An idol in America and South America, but his star shone for a brief time only
Scaramberg, Emile (1863-1938) *Lirico spinto*	1893, Paris (*Richard Coeur de Lion* by Grétry)	*Lohengrin, Werther, Roméo et Juliette*	Active above all in the principal French theaters until the end of the first decade of the twentieth century, when his voice began suddenly to deteriorate
Schmidt, Joseph (1904-1942) Lyric	1928, Berlin (*Idomeneo*, a concert performance for the radio)	Concerts all over Europe, North America, Mexico and Cuba. Many recordings, and films with celebrated arias	Crystalline timbre and outstanding high notes, with a capacity for effortless phrasing at high level, but he was too short ever to appear on stage. He died in a concentration camp
Schock, Rudolf (1915) Lyric	1937, Braunschweig	*Magic Flute, The Mastersingers, Carmen, Fidelio, Lohengrin, Tiefland, Tosca, Fra Diavolo*; also operettas by J.Strauss and Lehár	Connected to the great German tradition; very eclectic; excellent phrasing. Protagonist of many famous films

Schreier, Peter (1935) Light lyric	1957, Desden (*Matrimonio Segreto*)	*Magic Flute, Don Giovanni, Così Fan Tutte, Mastersingers* (David), *Das Rheingold* (Loge), *Capriccio*	A noteworthy musician, with a voice that was not particularly impressive but based on a good technique. Excellent phrasing, a superb concert singer of Bach oratorios. A good Lieder singer. Also an orchestra conductor
Sénéchal, Michel (1930) Light lyric	1952, winner of the Geneva Competition	*Platée, Comte Ory, Dame Blanche, Thaïs*	A full flexible voice, gracious *falsettone*, controlled emission. Excellent in many character roles
Shirley, George (1932) Light lyric	1960, Spoleto (Herod in *Salome*)	*Così Fan Tutte, Idomeneo, Barbiere, Traviata, Bohème*, Lieder and oratorio	Much appreciated at the Met, London and Glyndebourne during the sixties-seventies
Simoneau, Léopold (1918) Light lyric	1943, Montreal (*Mignon*)	*Magic Flute, Così Fan Tutte, Don Giovanni, Idomeneo, Ifigenia in Tauride, Orfeo, Traviata*	A Mozart interpreter with a smooth, *sfumato* voice of caressing timbre; an excellent recitalist
Smirnoff, Dimitri (1881-1944) Lyric	1903, St. Petersburg (*Camorra* by Esposito)	*The Demon, Rigoletto, Tabarro, Lakmé, Fedora, Traviata, Sadko, Butterfly*	Rival of the great Sobinov, he fared best in more lyrical roles
Spiess, Ludovico (1938) *Lirico spinto*	1962, Galati (*Rigoletto*)	*Tosca, Carmen, Aida, Dalibor, Turandot, Fidelio, Boris Godunov*	Although gifted with an interesting voice, his career was brief
Stolze, Gerhard (1926-1979) Light lyric	1949, Dresden (Augustin Moser in *The Mastersinger*)	*Mastersingers* (David), *Magic Flute* (Monostatos), *Elektra* (Aegysth), *Salome* (Herod), contemporary repertory	An unequal singer-actor in Wagner and Strauss operas
Taccani, Giuseppe (1882-1959) *Lirico spinto*	1905, Bologna (*Andrea Chenier*)	*Trovatore, Aida, Forza del Destino, Nerone, Fedora*	Dazzling high notes, burnished middle register, great temperament
Tappy, Eric (1931) Light liric	1964, Paris (*Zoroastre* by Rameau)	*Magic Flute, Pelléas et Mélisande, Oedipus Rex, Orfeo*	Great elegance and taste, very smooth emission
Treptow, Günther (1907-1987) *Heldentenor*	1936, Berlin (*Der Rosenkavalier*)	*Siegfried, Tristan, Fidelio, Otello, Tannhauser, Mastersingers*	A less gifted artist than his more famous colleagues, but a good professional and an intense interpreter
Uhl, Fritz (1928) *Lirico spinto*	1950, Graz	*Das Rheingold* (Loge), *Flying Dutchman* (Erik), *Salome* (Herod), *Elektra* (Aegysth), *Tristan, Antigonae*	Excellent in the minor roles of the Wagner and Strauss repertory
Unger, Gerhard (1916) Light lyric	1947, Weimar	*Mastersingers* (David), *Die Entführung aus dem Serail* (Pedrillo), *Butterfly* (Goro), *La Finta Giardiniera, The Barber of Baghdad*	An exceptional *Spieltenor* and singer of Masses, concerts and oratorio (Bach, in particular)
Uzunow, Dimiter (1922) *Lirico spinto*	1946, Sofia	*Otello, Forza del Destino, Pagliacci, Aida, Boris Gudonov*	Stylistically unconvincing, but gifted with dazzling high notes
Valero, Fernando (1854-1914) Lyric	1878, Madrid (*Fra Diavolo*)	*Faust, Pearl Fishers, Cavalleria Rusticana, Rigoletto, Favorita*	He studied with the famous Tamberlick and was one of the last singers of the legendary school of the eighteen hundreds. His recordings are therefore useful in helping us decipher that style
Vesselovsky, Alexander (1895-1964) Lyric	1917, Moscow	*Manon Lescaut, Kovantchina, Traviata, Rigoletto, Fedora, Lohengrin*	Called by Toscanini to La Scala in 1925 to interpret *Kovantchina*. He was one of the best Russian singers of the twentieth century and one of the best of his generation
Vezzani, César (1886-1951) Lyric	1911, Paris (*Richard Coeur de Lion* by Grétry)	*Faust, Carmen, Pagliacci, La Juive, Trovatore, Guglielmo Tell, Werther, L'Africana*	An extraordinary voice and temperament, solid as steel. He died during a rehearsal at Toulon, his voice still intact

Heddle Nash.

Alessandro Ziliani in Madama Butterfly.

Léopold Simoneau.

Francisco Vignas in Aida.

Vignas, Francisco (1863-1933) *Lirico spinto*	1888, Barcelona (*Loehgrin*)	*Cavalleria Rusticana, Carmen, Lucia, Tristan, Tannhäuser*	Considered the successor of the great Gayarre, he had unforgettable triumphs at the Met, Covent Garden and La Scala
Villabella, Miguel (1892-1954) Lyric	1918, Poiters (*Tosca*)	*Lakmé, Bohème, Manon, Barbiere, Tosca, Traviata, Rigoletto, Don Giovanni*	World Champion Rollerskater. He was a student of Lucien Fugère and endowed with a clear, crystalline voice
Winbergh, Gösta (1943-2002) Light lyric	1971, Göteborg (*Bohème*)	*Don Giovanni, Don Pasquale, Così Fan Tutte, Barbiere, Traviata*; Lieder and oratorio	Engaged by important record companies and esteemed by illustrious conductors, he nonetheless has some evident unresolved technical problems, especially in the high register
Zanelli, Renato (1892-1935) Dramatic	1916, Opera of Chile (Valentino in *Faust*, as a baritone); 1924, Naples (Raoul in *Les Huguenots*, as a tenor)	*Otello, Lohengrin*	One of the most beautiful "natural" voices there has ever been. His brother, Carlo Morelli, had considerable success as a baritone
Ziliani, Alessandro (1906-1977) Lyric	1928, Milan (*Butterfly*)	*Gioconda, Traviata, Tosca*; operetta	Very popular in America and Germany. He was the first interpreter of many operas of Peragallo, Pannain, Pedrollo, Respighi and Wolf-Ferrari

The French coloratura soprano **Lily Pons**, in the title role of Lucia di Lammermoor. She was Met star from 1931 until well into the 1950s.

The Sopranos

The Soprano Voice: Extension and Emission

The soprano voice is the highest of the female voices. Its ideal tessitura goes from g´ to g´´, and the full extension usually reaches from c´ up to c´´´ or d´´´.

The dramatic soprano can reach down to an a´ or an a´ flat while a coloratura soprano easily surpasses high f´´´. The mythical Lucrezia Agujari, called "la Bastardella," ranged from g´ up to c´´´´, according to Mozart's testimony; whilst in more recent times Mado Robin could exhibit high a´´´ and b´´´ flats, without any apparent effort (and could reach high d´´´´ flat when vocalizing!).

The Different Soprano Categories

During the twentieth century the soprano voice was divided into various categories: *coloratura soprano*, or *soprano leggero* (a union of the nineteenth century soprano *à roulades* with the soprano *sfogato* voice), a voice suited for virtuoso roles such as *Barbiere*, *I Puritani*, *Rigoletto*, *Lucia*, *Sonnambula*, *Traviata*, *Ariadne auf Naxos* and *Le Rossignol*. The pure lyric soprano (who stands exactly between the late-Verdi *soprano di forza* and the virtuoso soprano) has a voice which is not greatly extended but constantly engaged on the first high notes with a passionate and vehement phrasing; ideal for the operas of Massenet, Puccini (*Butterfly*, *Suor Angelica* and Liù in *Turandot*) and those of the Verist composers in general (Mascagni's *Iris*, Cilea's *Adriana Lecouvreur* and Leoncavallo's *Zazà*). The *lirico spinto* soprano is suited to the heavier Verdi operas (*Forza del Destino*, *Don Carlos*, *Aida*), Puccini (*Turandot*, *Tosca*) and the early Wagner and Strauss roles. The dramatic soprano (*dramatischer-Sopran*) has a solid, powerful voice that can dominate the complex orchestras of the operas of Wagner (Brünnhilde in *The Ring*, Kundry in *Parsifal*, Isolde in *Tristan und Isolde*) and Strauss (*Salome*, *Elektra*, *Die Frau ohne Schatten*). Finally, there is the *soprano soubrette* for the parts of the cunning little maidservants in the eighteenth-century comic operas (Despina in *Così Fan Tutte*, Susanna in *Nozze di Figaro*).

THE COLORATURA SOPRANO IN THE TWENTIETH CENTURY: THE EMPEROR'S NIGHTINGALES

At the beginning of the twentieth century there was an extraordinary flourishing of coloratura sopranos, coming mainly from Spain. The song of these phenomenal nightingales, however, was not immune to the vices and licenses of the Liberty style then in vogue. Alongside high notes of crystalline purity they alternated exaggerated *cadenze* and decorations which were, at times, decidedly annoying. Moreover, their limited volume in the middle and lower registers and their mechanical stage presence seriously discredited roles originally written for the *soprano drammatico d'agilità* (*Lucia*, *Sonnambula*, *Puritani*).

Amongst the historical singers of the first half of the twentieth century we should remember **Maria Barrientos** (Barcelona 1883 – St. Jean de Luz, Low Pyrenees 1946), who made her debut at only fifteen years of age and was singing in all the world's major theaters until

Amelita Galli-Curci in Traviata. *In order to better demonstrate her vocal extension she often sang the arias a tone higher. She was forced to retire because of a throat illness. After an operation in 1935 she tried to return to the stage with La Bohème at Chicago; but the results convinced her to give up her career.*

1890, when she made her debut in Florence in Meyerbeer's *L'Africana*, until her last American concerts in 1932.

She made use of an almost transcendental virtuosity built on pyrotechnical trills, *picchiettati*, breath-taking melismic passages and giddy *cadenze*. But often she exaggerated, exceeding the expressive limits of certain roles. For example, her recording of Oscar's aria from *Il Ballo in Maschera* where, in the finale, she inserts a long *cadenza*, which was frankly out of place.

Antonietta Meneghel, stage name **Toti Dal Monte** (Mogliano Veneto, Treviso 1893 – Pieve di Soligo, Treviso 1975) was by far the most important coloratura soprano before the revolutionary advent of Maria Callas.

Having completed her studies with Barbara Marchisio and Antonio Pini-Corsi, she made her debut at La Scala in 1916 as Biancofiore in *Francesca da Rimini*. During her entire career (she retired in 1943), she successfully alternated the lyric repertory (*Butterfly*, *La Rondine*, *Bohème*, *Lodoletta*) with true coloratura roles (*Lucia*, *Barbiere*, *Rigoletto*, *Mignon*), succeeding in gaining the approval of a world-wide public and of one of the "gods of music," Arturo Toscanini.

Toti's best quality was the color of her voice: light, almost infantile in certain inflexions, ethereal even. It had a timbre which, united with the luminescence of her high notes, bewitched her listeners, so that they literally held their breath. We have only to listen to her

Mercedes Capsir Tanzi (Barcelona 1895 - Suzara Mantova 1969). Here photographed as Butteffly, she had a notable interpretative temperament as well as an excellent voice. In contrast to colleagues more adventurous and powerful in the higher octave she offered an impressive elegance of phrasing and softness of tone. (Historic Archives of the Rome Opera Theater)

about 1920. With her great flexibility, soaring high notes and crystalline timbre, she formed a mythical duo with Hipólito Lázaro, and was widely acclaimed as Elvira in *Puritani*, Lakmé and Amina in *La Sonnambula*.

Amelita Galli-Curci was Italian (Milan 1882 – La Jolla, California 1963). She made her debut as Gilda in *Rigoletto* (1907) and remained faithful to this role until the mid-twenties when she was singing mainly in North American theaters. Thanks to the brilliance of her high notes and the precision of her *roulades* she was able to compete with her Spanish rivals, Pareto, De Hidalgo, Barrientos, Galvany and Capsir, and shared the favor of the Italian public with Tetrazzini.

Luisa Tetrazzini (Florence 1871 – Milan 1940) had a very long career, spanning from

A beautiful photograph of **Toti Dal Monte** in the costume of Gilda, a role which remained associated with her name for many years. The La Scala performances in 1922 with Toscanini on the podium were unforgettable. It was Toscanini who chose her for "his" Rigoletto, after she had sung with him in Beethoven's Ninth Symphony at Turin. With the end of her singing career, and after a period on stage as a dramatic actress, "Totina" dedicated her life to teaching.

Mad Scene from *Lucia* or Gilda's "Caro Nome" from *Rigoletto* to appreciate this. They are still unequalled. However, the Venetian soprano can be accused of a lack of psychological depth in decisive roles such as Violetta, Mimì or Butterfly; she tended to overcome such difficulties merely with the beauty of her voice.

The beautiful and gifted Alice Joséphine Pons, stage name **Lily Pons** (Draguignan, 1898 – Dallas 1976) also belongs to legend. She made her debut in *Lakmé* in 1927 (she had already made a concert debut in 1917) and continued her activity at the Metropolitan for over thirty years (from 1931 until 1961) as well as performing in many other important theaters.

Apart from a particularly attractive appearance, nature had also given her an agile voice which extended above high f‴, ideal for the acrobatic passages contained in *Lakmé, Dinorah, Lucia, Tales of Hoffman* and *Barbiere*.

Pons' timbre was neither beautiful nor powerful; but she knew how to govern her breath, completely controlling the vocal stream at will. Thus she obtained dynamic effects without effort, interminable *filature*, resonant high notes and all the true virtues of belcanto.

Her first vocal successes were in France (Cannes, Deauville, Montpellier). But once discovered by Zenatello and recommended to Casazza, Director of the Met, she was brought to New York and began her Met career in 1931 in Donizetti's *Lucia*. She continued with the Met until 1959. Married to the conductor André Kostelanetz, she made many recordings and was much in demand for movies, thanks not only to her fine voice but also to her beauty.

Among the coloratura sopranos active in the Russian, French, German and Italian repertory there were also **Lidia Lipkovska** (Babino, Bessarabia 1880 – Beirut 1955); **Antonia Nejdanova** (Kryvoje Balka, Odessa 1875 – Moscow 1950); **Eidé Norena** (Norten, Oslo 1884 – Lausanne 1968); **Graciela Pareto** (Barcelona 1888 – Rome 1973); **Olimpia Boronat** (Genoa 1867 – Warsaw 1934); **Fritzi Jokl** (Vienna 1895 – New York 1974); **Frances Alda** (Frances Davies; Christchurch, New Zealand 1883 – Venice 1952), who was able to sing both Gilda and Leonora from *Trovatore* but with a dubious technique as her high notes were whistling and unsustained, and her timbre light and colorless; **Regina Pacini** (Lisbon 1871 – Buenos Aires 1965); **Irene Abendroth** (Lemberg 1872 – Weidlind, Vienna 1932); **Ada Sari** (Wadowice,

Krakow 1886 – Kriowoshnek 1968); **Miliza Korjus** (Warsaw 1907 – Culver City, California 1980), **Emma Luart** (Brussels 1892-1968); the amazing **Mado Robin** (Yseures-sur-Creuse, Tours 1918 – Paris 1960); **Wilma Lipp** (Vienna 1925); **Anneliese Rothenberger** (Mannheim 1924); **Erika Köth** (Darmstadt 1927-1989); **Selma Kurz** and **Frieda Hempel** (whom we will discuss in the chapter dedicated to the lyric sopranos); and, finally, **Maria Ivogün** (Ilse von Gunther, Budapest 1891 – Beatenberg, Switzerland 1987), the first Zerbinetta in the newer version of Strauss' *Ariadne auf Naxos*, which was performed in Vienna in 1916. She was active in the lyric and coloratura repertories of Italian, French and German opera between 1913 and 1933. Elizabeth Schwarzkopf was one of her students.

Between 1927 and 1956 the star of **Lina Pagliughi** (New York 1907 – Savignano sul Rubicone, Forlì 1980) shone brightly on an international scale. Hers was one of the purest and best-placed voices ever heard in the roles of Gilda, Lucia or Amina. Hampered by her physique, Pagliughi could not compete on stage with her more attractive colleagues, but she outclassed them in musicality and vocal emission. In *Traviata* she revealed a rare temperament and passion, as witnessed by her recordings, both the official and the "pirate" ones.

Sharing the favors of the public in the vocal pirouettes of Lucia, Amina, Gilda and Violetta in the sixties were **Roberta Peters** (New York 1930) and **Anna Moffo** (Wayne, Pennsylvania 1935), the latter being also attracted to a more lyric repertoire.

Peters amazed her audiences with her remarkable agility and her extension beyond high f''', while Moffo enchanted the public with her fascinating and elegant appearance as well as her voice (which was, however, always considered small and more suited to the recording studio than the opera theater). With her model looks and gifts as an actress, she often starred in movies.

In 1965 **Cristina (Engel) Deutekom** (Amsterdam 1932) appeared for the first time as the Queen of the Night – the part which would consign her to musical history. At last, the terrifying role of the Mozart queen was liberated from the peaky chirpings of the small voiced sopranos and returned triumphantly to a true *soprano drammatico d'agilità*. Alas, with the passing of time and with the difficult repertory chosen (*Puritani, Norma, Armida, Lucia*), Deutekom's voice became worn and uneven in all the registers. Her vocal agility is in the Tryol yodel style, hers being a unique compromise between legato and aspiration of the notes.

The Contemporary Coloratura Soprano: Serra, Gruberova, Devia

Two singers have taken the place of Toti Dal Monte and Lily Pons. They are **Luciana Serra** (Genoa 1946) and **Editha Gruberova** (Bratislava 1946).

Serra sang for years in Teheran, where she performed as the "Shah's nightingale" and can truly be defined as Dal Monte's heir. She has many similarities with the famous Venetian singer: a clear, child-like voice, a perfect legato, a silvery high register, a rare perfection in high passages and an all-over agility. Her intonation is not always perfect, but when she is at her best she can evoke with surprising emotion all the ghosts of *Lucia*, the legends of *Lakmé*, the clockwork acrobatics of Olympia in the *Tales of Hoffmann*, and Amina's painful love in *Sonnambula*. During the last ten years Serra has gradually cut down her engagements in the coloratura field, to tackle a more lyrical repertoire (*Anna Bolena, Traviata*) with alternating, but on the whole satisfactory, results.

Editha Gruberova was born in Bratislava, but studied in Vienna. She has been a stable member of the Vienna State Opera ensemble for years, where she regularly triumphs in operas such as *Lucia, Traviata, Die Entführung aus dem Serail, The Magic Flute, Rigoletto* (she was the first to perform the critical edition conducted by Riccardo Muti), and especially *Ariadne auf Naxos*: the elegance and confidence with which she performs Strauss' terrifying melismas while amiably twirling Zerbinetta's parasol cannot be

A photo showing the suffering of Lucia, here interpreted by **Luciana Serra**. *(Historic Archives of the Teatro Regio of Parma)*

equaled. Her voice is sweet and flexible, richer in harmonics than that of Serra; she easily performs *smorzature* and *rinforzandi* and reaches up to high f´´. During more recent years Gruberova has directed her repertory towards the so-called Donizetti "queens": *Maria Stuarda, Anna Bolena* and *Roberto Devereux* (Elisabetta), though she has not entirely abandoned her pet roles. It is above all in the many performances of *Puritani* that Gruberova gives full rein to her talent, from the superb *messe di voce* (the swell and diminish of tones) in the madness scene to the crystalline notes in *pianissimo* of the big *concertato*.

We must not forget these other important protagonists of the belcanto coloratura repertory: the Welsh soprano **Norma Burrowes** (Bangor 1944), who has been a regular member of the English National Opera since 1971 and a renowned Blondchen, Despina, Zerlina, Fiorilla in *Turco in Italia* and Nannetta in *Falstaff*; **Ruth Welting** (Memphis, Tennessee 1949 – Ashville, North Carolina 1999), who made her debut in the part of Blondchen in New York in 1970, and went on to perform in all the major international theaters in the roles of Zerbinetta, Gilda, Lucia, the Queen of the Night and Adele in *Die Fledermaus* (she also sang in a vast repertory of Lieder and oratorio); the Italians **Alida Ferrarini** (Villafranca, Verona 1947) and **Patrizia Pace** (Turin 1964), who specializes in an extraordinary characterization of Oscar the page; and, above all, **Mariella Devia** (Chiusavecchia, Imperia 1948). Devia is one of the most important singers of today, whose style, virtuosity and pleasing voice is well suited to Bellini's lunar heroines (Amina, Giulietta, Elvira) and also to some of the lesser known Rossini and Donizetti operas and oratorio. With patience, precision and an obstinate refusal of the diva role, she has consolidated her fame and improved her stage presence, succeeding in offering her audiences a convincing characterization of Violetta in *Traviata*. She made a memorable *Lucia* at the Maggio Fiorentino directed by Zubin Mehta and was perfect as Fiorilla in *Turco in Italia*.

Janet Perry (Minneapolis 1947), a polished, all-round singer, is one of those classical examples of an artist whose talent has not been fully recognized. After her debut at little more than twenty years of age, her career got off to a brilliant start in Germany and Austria, with splendid performances (and recordings) together with Karajan, Harnoncourt and Kleiber, in a vast repertoire in which Adele in *Die Fledermaus*, Sophie in *Der Rosenkavalier*, Zerbinetta in *Ariadne auf Naxos*, Blondchen and Kostanze in *Die Entführung aus dem Serail* soon proved to

Anna Moffo *as Marie in Donizetti's* La Fille du Régiment.

be her forte. Her perfect emission, the beautiful, smooth timber of her voice and her musicality have enabled her to sing the Italian repertoire, too (Norina, Adina, Nannetta, Gilda, Lucia), but these are roles Perry has performed in the main outside Italy. A fact which surely is a loss more for Italy than for the artist herself.

However talented, I would hesitate to include **Cinthia Lawrence** and **Kathleen Cassello** (Wilmington 1958) among the rightful heirs of Roberta Peters or Anna Moffo, but I would name among the stars of the latest generation **Valeria Esposito** (Naples 1961), **Stefania Bonfadelli** (Bussolengo, Verona 1967), both endowed with a pleasant tone-color and fluid vocalization, and the French coloratura soprano **Natalie Dessay** (1965), much in demand by theaters and world-wide recording companies. Dessay possesses a smooth, extremely extensive voice which, though not particularly voluminous, is of a rarely to be found intonation. I would add that the precision of her entries and the purity of her emission over the entire range

Mariella Devia *at the end of the "Mad Scene" from* Lucia di Lammermoor, *presented in Bologna in 1986.*

are her true forte. What is so especially amazing about this young French artist, apart from her spectacular virtuosity, is her almost surreal ability to sing equally well in a variety of positions: lying down, head down, back to the audience, running or jumping like a grasshopper, as can be seen from the video *Orphée aux enfers*, published in the late nineties. But Dessay is also an excellent interpreter of Mozart, Handel, Delibes' *Lakmé*, Thomas' *Hamlet* and Bellini's *Sonnambula*, performed triumphantly at La Scala.

Following in the footsteps of her better-known colleagues, Devia and Dessay, is **Eva Mei** (Fabriano, Marche 1967), endowed with a confident voice and considerable extension, rising to high f in Mozart's terrifying concert arias, plus an unquestionably convincing stage presence. She has given excellent performances in *Don Pasquale*, *Elisir d'Amore*, *Tancredi*, not to mention *Figlia del reggimento*, *Die Fledermaus*, Donna Anna in *Don Giovanni* and *Capuleti e Montecchi*.

The Lyric Sopranos of the Twentieth century

The long list of the greatest lyric sopranos of the twentieth century starts with **Emma Carelli** (Naples 1877 – Montefiascone, Viterbo 1928),

one of the most intense and fiery singing actresses to have trod the opera stage.

Her interpretations of *Zazà*, *Wally*, *Bohème*, *Siberia*, *Adriana Lecouvreur* and *Arlesiana* deeply moved the audience, even to tears, and not infrequently it was the soprano herself who was the most moved of all, crying on stage and thus beginning the tradition of the sobbing Verist *prime donne*.

Right from her debut in *La Vestale* at Altamura in 1895, her voice was shown to be neither particularly beautiful nor widely extended; so Carelli had to make her way using her passionate temperament and "the sweetness of her heart", as Eleonora Duse, one of her great admirers, chose to put it. It was Carelli who

Emma Carelli *in the role which made her famous – Floria Tosca. Her farewell to the stage was in Rome in 1924, with a memorable Iris. She was a shrewd business-woman and theatrical agent, having gained experience with her husband, Walter Mocchi, who ran the Rome Opera and the Colon of Buenos Aires. (Historic Archives of the Rome Opera Theater)*

The beautiful **Carmen Melis**, who was able to prepare her Minnie with the help of Puccini himself. "Vibrant, exquisite, very beautiful" raved Puccini, captivated by the excellence and beauty of this exceptional singer-actresss.

Zazà by Leoncavallo: sitting together are the baritone **Mario Sammarco** and the soprano **Rosina Storchio**, a famous Butterfly, Violetta, Mignon, Mimì. She retired in 1923 in Barcelona after a last Butterfly. (Historic Archives of La Fenice Theater, Venice)

invented the solemn rites that conclude the second act of *Tosca*, immediately after Scarpia's death. Those well-studied movements send a shiver up your spine and have been copied by every other soprano. From 1912 until 1926 she and her husband managed the Costanzi Theater of Rome, earning esteem as theatrical agents who discovered many new singers.

One of the most important Massenet and Puccini performers was **Rosina Storchio** (Venice 1872 – Milan 1945). She made her first appearance in Milan in *Carmen* as Micaëla in 1892. Her voice was essentially small, but it was very penetrating and animated by an exceptional artistic spirit. She gave the right expressive value to each note, to every accent, every movement, even those that were apparently insignificant. Storchio created extremely dramatic portrayals. Her Butterfly (she was the first-ever performer), her unequalled Violetta, Iris, Zazà, Manon and Mimì will never be forgotten. She retired after a final *Butterfly* in Barcelona in 1923. Puccini wrote that hers was "the sweet little voice that comes from the soul".

Another historic performer in the French repertory, from Massenet to Debussy (of whom she was a great friend) was **Mary Garden** (Aberdeen 1874 or 1877-1967), the first to perform *Pelléas et Mélisande*, in 1902. She was beautiful, ethereal and misty like Debussy's harmonies; careful, like few others, to analyze the phrasing and detail of the spoken word even more than the sung note. The Scottish soprano created the title role of Louise in Charpentier's opera in 1900, and was a wonderful interpreter of Massenet (*Chérubin*, *Thaïs*, *Manon*), Leroux (first to perform *La Reine Flammette* in 1903) and Erlanger (*Aphrodite*). She continued to sing at the Chicago Opera until 1913, and retired after a final performance of *Carmen* in an open-air theater in Cincinnati.

A mention is due to **Fanny Heldy** (Liège 1888 – Paris 1973) who was chosen by Toscanini to sing Louise and Mélisande at La Scala. She was gifted with a lovely timbre and a notable virtuosity which made it possible for her to successfully sing, during the years from 1913 to 1939, both in the French *lyrique* and Italian *lirica* repertoires in operas such as *Barbiere* and *Traviata*.

Geraldine Farrar (Melrose, Massachusetts 1882 – Ridgefield 1967) possessed a magnifi-

Gilda Dalla Rizza *in Act IV of* Traviata. *Puccini composed* La Rondine *for her. Giulia Dalla Rizza was also the first performer in Italiy of Suor Angelica and Lauretta.*

cently forceful voice. Agile, despite some problems in the high register, she was one of the most acclaimed interpreters of *Butterfly, Zazà* and *Manon*, especially in the theaters of North America. Her popularity was enormous, even among the younger generation, to the extent that every one of her performances was attended by flocks of so-called *Gerry-Flappers*. Farrar had first sung at ten years of age in a Christmas pageant where she played the part of Jenny Lind. She made her second debut at the Hofoper of Berlin in 1901 as Marguerite in *Faust*. In 1906, after a perfection course with Lilli Lehmann, she joined the Metropolitan Opera and stayed there until 1922, singing five hundred performances of twenty-nine different operas. She was the first to perform Mascagni's *Amica* (1905), *Madame Sans-Gêne* (1915), and *Suor Angelica* (1918). Geraldine also wrote a delightful autobiography, *Such a Sweet Compulsion* (1938), and made at least a dozen successful films.

Carmen Melis (Cagliari 1885 – Longone al Segrino, Como 1967) boasted a rich voice, docile in modulation, together with an attractive physical appearance and an uncommon acting ability. From 1905 until the year of her withdrawal from the stage in 1935 she was an exceptional Manon (both in Massanet's opera and Puccini's), a fantastic Salome, Minnie (*La Fanciulla del West*), Nedda (*Pagliacci*) and Thaïs. Renata Tebaldi was one of her pupils.

Favored by Puccini who wanted her as the first performer of Magda in *La Rondine* (1917), Suor Angelica and Lauretta in *Il Trittico* (1919),

Gilda Dalla Rizza (Isola della Scala, Verona 1892 – Milan 1975) was a magnificent *Traviata* under Toscanini's baton. She was guided by a stage instinct which has few comparisons. She made her debut at Bologna in 1910 as Charlotte in *Werther* and retired with a final *Suor Angelica* at Vincenza at the 1942 Puccini celebrations.

Salomea Krusceniski (Tarnopol 1872 – Leopoli 1952) had a superb figure, a passionate temperament and a perfect singing technique. She was the magnificent *Butterfly* who brought the opera to success at Brescia in 1904 after its original failure at La Scala. The flexibility and expressive possibilities of her voice made her so suited to both the lyric and dramatic repertory that it is impossible to give a precise definition of this Polish soprano.

In his book *Voci Parallele* Lauri Volpi defined Krusceniski as an extraordinary singer: "Amazing for the beauty of her voice, her perfect technique and style".

In the Italian and above all the German repertory, the most applauded lyric sopranos were Frieda Hempel and Selma Kurz. **Frieda Hempel** (Leipzig 1885 – Berlin 1955) could pass with ease from singing the Marschallin in *Der Rosenkavalier* to the Queen of the Night; from Rosina and Eva in *The Mastersingers* to Oscar in *Un Ballo in Maschera* and Euryanthe. **Selma Kurz** (Biala, Galicia 1874 – Vienna 1933) became a superstar by virtue of her trills and incredible versatility – between 1895 and 1927 she sang Wagner, Donizetti, Verdi and even Puccini. Her favorite aria was "Lockruf" from *The Queen of Sheba* by Goldmark in which she could give full voice to her mythical, inimitable trill.

We should not forget these other important pure lyric sopranos of the early part of the twentieth century: **Angelica Pandolfini** (Spoleto 1871 – Lenno, Como 1959); **Emma Eames** (Shanghai 1865 – New York 1952); **Lina Cavalieri** (Rome 1874 – Florence 1944), who was applauded in many Verist operas, more perhaps for her beauty than for her vocal gifts; **Bessie Abbott** (Bessie Pickens; New York 1878-1919), famous as Juliette and Mimì at the Met; **Maria Kuznetsoya** (Odessa 1880 – Paris 1966), one of the most authoritative Russian singers specialized in the roles of Tatyana, Juliette, Mimì, Marguerite in *Faust*, Elsa and Carmen; **Miura Tanaki** (1884 – 1946), the most important Japanese soprano, who gave successful performances in the roles of Mimì, Manon, Iris and Santuzza; **Germaine Lubin** (Paris 1890 – 1979); **Maria Zamboni** (Ponti sul Mincio, Mantova 1891 – Peschiera, Verona 1976); **Rosetta Pampanini** (Milan 1896 – Corbola 1973); **Alma Gluck** (Bucharest 1884 – New York 1924);

Joan Cross (London 1900 –1993); **Ninon Vallin** (Mantalieu-Vercien 1886 – Lyon 1961); **Cesira Ferrani** (Turin 1863 – Pollone, Biella 1943), who was the first *Manon Lescaut* and Mimì at the Regio Theater of Turin; **Adelaide Saraceni** (Rosario, Argentina 1895 – 1995); **Josefina Huguet** (Barcelona 1871 – 1951); **Margaret Sheridan** (County Mayo, Ireland 1889 – Dublin 1958), a respected Puccini singer and a specialist in the part of Mimì; **Lotte Schone** (Vienna 1891 – Paris 1977); **Maggie Teyte** (Wolverhampton 1888 – London 1976), whose voice was flexible and delicate.

Before the revolutionary advent of Maria Callas, towards the end of the forties, many lyric sopranos with beautiful voices appeared on the scene. They were all equally gifted, but still tied to the old-fashioned way of singing, a style of singing which would soon be swept away by the philological rigor of the great Maria, and by the belcanto revival. Voices like those of **Licia Albanese** (Bari 1909), a legendary Violetta and Butterfly at the Metropolitan (until 1966); **Mafalda Favero** (Portomaggiore, Ferrara 1903 – Calolziocorte, Lecco 1981), a refined Mimì and Manon; and **Iris Adami-Corradetti** (Milan 1904 – Padua 1998), famous interpreter of *Francesca da Rimini* and of almost all the roles created by Wolf-Ferrari. They were rich voices, guided by noteworthy artistic talent, but all too

Mafalda Favero *here photographed as Cho-Cho-San, first sang, as Liù, in Parma in 1927. During a long career she was much appreciated as Mimì; Manon, Adriana Lecouvreur, Thaïs. (Historic Archives of La Fenice Theater of Venice. Photo: Camuzi)*

It is difficult to resist so seductive a Salome: **Salomea Krusceniski***, perhaps inspired by her name, knew how to captivate her audience with her vibrant voice and sinuous movements.*

Intelligent and versatile, **Iris Adami-Corradetti** *had a repertory of about eighty operas and a particular fondness for the works of Wolf-Ferrari. Among her students,* **Katia Ricciarelli***. (Historic Archives of La Fenice Theater of Venice. Photo: Giacomelli)*

*An elegant **Tito Gobbi** (Sharpless), with **Magda Olivero** (Cho-Cho-San) and the tenor **Gianni Poggi** (Pinkerton) – the main characters of a Rome staging of* Madama Butterfly. *(Historic Archives of the Rome Opera Theater)*

*The 1959-60 season at the San Carlo Opera (Naples) opened with Adriana Lecouvreur. **Giulietta Simionato** (Princess of Bouillon) hugs **Magda Olivero** (Adriana) who, at the last moment, splendidly replaced Renata Tebaldi who had been taken ill. (Historic Archives of the San Carlo Theater, Naples)*

often tempted by verist excesses that went beyond the limits of good taste.

It is a different story for the Brazilian **Bidù Sayao** (Baldwina de Oliveira; Niteroi 1902 – Lincolnsville, Maine 1999), who studied with the legendary Jan De Reszké. Between 1926 and 1958 she distinguished herself as a measured and sensitive performer of Manon, Mimì, Juliette (Gounod), Mélisande, Zerlina, Gilda, Violetta and Susanna. All her performances were characterized by artistic taste and elegance.

We should also mention **Margherita Carosio** (Genoa 1908); **Jarmila Novotná** (Prague 1907 – New York 1994), active at the Metropolitan from 1939 till 1954 as an unforgettable Donna Elvira and Manon; **Dame Joan Hammond** (Christchurch, New Zealand 1912), who studied with Dino Borgioli and possessed a smooth and caressing voice ideal for Puccini's operas; **Dorothy Kirsten** (Montclair, New York 1917 – 1992), who sang at the Met from 1945 until 1975 and specialized in the roles of Louise (which she studied with Charpentier), Manon Lescaut, Minnie and Cho-Cho-San; **Janine Micheau** (Toulouse 1914 – Paris 1976); **Grace Moore** (Jellicoe, Tennessee 1901 – Copenaghen 1947), who had a sensitive personality and a delightful voice capable of singing a double repertoire, the lyric and light lyric; **Onelia Fineschi** (Florence 1921), who enjoyed a brief but exciting career; and **Ilva Ligabue** (Bagnolo in Piano, Reggio Emilia 1928 – Palermo 1998), who sang a vast and varied repertory.

Art Is Ageless: Magda Olivero

Madga Olivero (Saluzzo 1910) was a remarkable person for her time, and she prepared the ground for Maria Callas. Even without possessing exceptional vocal means, especially as far as timbre and volume were concerned, she outclassed all of her colleagues in style and vocal longevity. As well as having an incredible technique (right up to the end of her career she was able to perform *filati* and *diminuendi* with ease) she proved herself to be an artist of great sensitivity and intelligence, always fully immersed in her roles, acting passionately but never "hamming." She made her debut in 1933 at Turin, as Lauretta in *Gianni Schicchi*, and in her early career she sang the light-lyric repertory with success (Gilda, Zerlina, Violetta). In *Traviata* she easily reached a high e''' flat, and exhibited an acrobatic series of *vocalizzi* that were nothing short of amazing.

In 1941 she abandoned the stage, having married, only to return in 1951 with a verist repertory. Her intense renderings of *Adriana*

Lecouvreur, *Tosca*, *Manon Lescaut*, *Francesca da Rimini* and *Butterfly* are unforgettable. In a crescendo of emotion she would alternate from cutting, burning phrases to estatic or melancholic moments of incomparable intensity. She was able to do this thanks to her incredible breath control.

By virtue of her technique, Olivero continued her career into the eighties (*La Voix Humaine* by Poulenc at Verona in 1981, and a concert at Voghera during that same year where she performed a perfect "Pace, pace, mio Dio" from *La Forza del Destino*). In 1990, at Cosenza, she sang the aria "Adieu, notre petite table" (*Manon*) and the finale of *Butterfly*, closing with a b'' flat that would make a thirty-year-old green with envy. In recent years she has recorded Cilea's entire *Adriana* (published by Bongiovanni Editore) and in the summer of 1999, at Palermo, a selection from Puccini's *Bohème*.

An Angel's Voice

Renata Tebaldi (Pesaro 1922) is still defined by every opera lover as a *voce d'angelo*, that is, "the voice of an angel." It is difficult to find even one among her colleagues, past or present, who can equal the smooth, velvety quality of her voice: a precious vocal instrument formed by the great school of Carmen Melis and Ettore Campogalliani.

Tebaldi made her debut in 1944 at Rovigo as Elena in *Mefistofele* and from then on, but especially following 1946 (after Toscanini had asked her to participate in the concert that re-opened La Scala after the war), became a legend in the greatest theaters and in a wide repertoire which reached its highest peaks with the roles of Desdemona, Mimì, Tosca and Maddalena di Coigny. She was especially loved in Italy and in America. She sang at Chicago from 1955 until 1969 and at the Metropolitan from 1954 until 1973, leaving behind her indelible memories.

During the years in which Callas represented a blazing return to a protoromantic style of singing, Tebaldi, virtuoso and radiant (but always profoundly expressive), incarnated the typical post-verist soprano: a large, beautiful voice that unfolded sumptuously over a Puccini or Verdi melody, a luminous timbre, and a warm, forceful phrasing.

This was the context in which it is possible to talk of rivalry between Callas and Tebaldi. Not because there existed any actual disagreement between the two divas, but because they conceived vocal interpretation from two completely opposing viewpoints. On the one hand

Renata Tebaldi in La Forza del Destino, *an opera particularly adapted to her vocal characteristics. (Historic Archives of La Fenice, Venice)*

But just look how the applause of the audience has made **Giangiacomo Guelfi**'s *Scarpia as poised as a court dandy and* **Tebaldi**'s *Tosca as coy as Musetta. (Historic Archives of the Rome Opera Theater)*

Tebaldi in full swing in the first act of Tosca *under the gaze of* **Mario Del Monaco**. *(Historic Archives of the Rome Opera Theater. Photo: Savio)*

there was dramatic agility and analytic phrasing (Callas), and on the other the pure luxury of sound, the ecstatic abandonment to melody, the dulcet sound of a Stradivarius without equal (Tebaldi).

It is not easy to make a judgment about Victoria Lopez, stage name **Victoria De Los Angeles** (Barcelona 1923) which will satisfy everyone. She is a singer who has been either idolized (especially in Anglo-Saxon countries) or harshly criticized. Her debut took place in her native city as the Countess in *The Marriage of Figaro* in 1945; but her repertory, during her lengthy career, numbered a huge variety of roles, ranging from Elsa *(Lohengrin)* to Rosina, Cenerentola, Carmen, Violetta, Manon, Mimì and Marguerite *(Faust)*, as well as including an almost obsessive Lieder activity. All these numerous opera roles were characterized by a refined interpretation, aided by a noteworthy stage presence and great musicality; but they were hampered by precise technical limits. For example, her usual rise to the high register was not correctly breath sustained thus rendering the sound hard and strained and any modulation impossible.

Northern Charm

Three sopranos from three different generations, each with a vast repertory, deserve a special mention: **Hilde Güden** (Vienna 1917 – Munich 1988), **Elizabeth Söderström** (Stockholm 1927 – 1998) and **Anja Silja** (Berlin 1940).

Güden was a light-lyric soprano of enormous possibilities. She swept easily from Mozart to Lehar, from Strauss' "King of the Waltzes" to Richard Strauss (her Sophie in *Rosenkavalier* was wonderful), and even included Verdi and some modern operas.

Söderström did not have a pure and crystalline voice like that of Hilde Güden, but she was an intelligent and versatile artist. She was noted for her elegant singing of Mozart and Strauss (superb her Countess in *Capriccio*), and she kept close ties with contemporary composers (Berg, Britten, Henze).

Beautiful, alluring Anja Silja was launched in public while still an adolescent. Her years of glory went from 1956 (the year of Rosina at Berlin) until the second half of the seventies when she sang, without respite, *Lulu, Turandot, Die Entführung aus dem Serail, The Flying Dutchman, Fidelio, The Ring, Elektra, Salome*, and many contemporary works. Then began her vocal decline, and the spell was broken; the wobbling and harshness of her high register could not be compensated even by her exceptional stage presence.

Leontyne Price, *a gorgeous Donna Anna in Mozart's* Don Giovanni – *a role she approached with exemplary precision.*

La Scala, on tour in Japan, performed La Bohème with **Peter Dvorsky** and the best Mimì of recent years **Mirella Freni**. (Photo: Bunka Kaitan, Tokyo. September, 1981)

Leontyne Price: A noble Aida of the purest vocal qualities. (Historic Archives of the Rome Opera Theater. Photo: Mélançon)

Another photo of the La Scala version of Bohème in Japan with **Mirella Freni**. Here, we are in the third act. (Bunka Kaitan, Tokyo. September, 1981)

A singing lesson for **Mirella Freni**, a pleasing Maria in La Fille du Régiment. (Historic Archives of the Teatro Comunale of Bologna)

Price and Freni: Two of von Karajan's Pupils

Leontyne Price (Laurel, Mississippi 1927) had a clarity and brilliance in her high register, but also a purity that few other sopranos have ever been able to boast. To a certain extent this compensated for the fact that she was never able to overcome a certain opacity in the middle register, which was often irritating. The beautiful American took her diploma at the Juiliard School of Music in 1952, and then began her prestigious career as a typical lyric and *lirico-spinto* soprano.

Although she is principally identified with *Aida*, Price was also great as Elvira in *Ernani*, in *Butterfly*, as Leonora in *Trovatore*, and in *Forza del Destino*, showing a style and a brilliance which was rare even in the greatest sopranos of the century. She retired from the stage after one final *Aida* at the Metropolitan in the late eighties, but she continues to make concert appearances, singing many of her *pièces de résistance*. She is particulalry fond of the city of Rome, where as a young girl she perfected her singing technique at Maestro Ricci's school.

It seems impossible to believe, but over forty

Another photo from the La Scala tour of Japan. Simon Boccanegra, directed by Strehler and conducted by Abbado, thrilled the Japanese. **Mirella Freni** *is a wonderful Amelia and here she is receiving an ovation after the aria "Come in quest'ora bruna" during the first act. (Bunka Kaikan, Tokyo. September, 1981)*

In 1980, invited and expressly encouraged by von Karajan, **Freni** *attempted the perilous role of Aida and emerged victorious. Supported by von Karajan's authoritive conducting of the orchestra, the soprano overcame every difficulty and gave the role of the Ethiopian slave a lyrical flow and sweetness which very few dramatic sopranos have been able to achieve. (Archives of the Salzburg Festival)*

years have passed since **Mirella Freni** (Modena 1935) made her debut as Micaela in a *Carmen* staged at Modena in 1956. Freni has a solid technique and an uncommon intelligence. With a scrupulous respect for the score and its expressive signs, she first emerged as Susanna in *The Marriage of Figaro*, Zerlina in *Don Giovanni* and Marie in *La Fille du Régiment*; then she introduced parts into her repertory that were more suited to her voice, such as Mimì, Liù, Marguerite in Gounod's *Faust*, Adina in *Elisir d'Amore*, *Puritani* (Rome, 1971) and even an unjustly criticized *Traviata* at La Scala in the 1964-65 season.

Under the guidance of exceptional *Maestri* such as von Karajan, Carlos Kleiber and Abbado, Freni has provided perfect characterizations of roles such as Amelia in *Simon Boccanegra*, which opened La Scala in 1971-72 (directed by Strehler, conducted by Abbado), Elisabetta in *Don Carlos*, Desdemona and Aida at Salzburg with von Karajan as mentor – thus managing to succeed in a repertory that seemed beyond her means. Freni has also been able to include the roles of Manon Lescaut, Adriana Lecouvreur, Tatyana in *Eugene Onegin* and Lisa in *The Queen of Spades* in her vast repertory, with surprising results, thanks to her intelligent evolution as a singer. She seems to have developed a special feeling for *Fedora*, *Eugene Onegin* and Giordano's *Madame Sans-Gêne*, operas in which she has literally identified herself over the last few years. Her perfect breathing and a calm, moderate life-style have guaranteed her a unique vocal longevity and vocal characteristics, in particular the fine timbre and *pianissimi* and the elegance of her legato, that have been virtually untouched by time. A point of curiosity: throughout her long career Freni has persistently refused to sing in open-air theaters.

Raina Kabaivanska (Burgas, Black Sea 1934) is another fine example of vocal longevity. Her official debut was in 1959 when she sang in *Tabarro* staged at Vercelli. Despite being employed by major theaters and applauded by public and critics, the soprano from Bulgaria did not initially manage to make the "big-time." However, from the seventies on, Raina has won herself a place in the heart of the opera public. Her repertory is wide, ranging from Verdi to Puccini's masterpieces (especially *Tosca*, *Butterfly* and *Manon Lescaut*), from Bellini's *Pirata* and *Beatrice di Tenda* (Agnese and Beatrice) to Donizetti's *Fausta* and *Roberto Devereux*, up to the Verists (*Francesca da Rimini*, *Adriana Lecouvreur*) and Strauss (*Capriccio*); she also made an excursion into the comic field and operetta (*Merry Widow* in 1989, in Naples, Venice and Rome). Because of her talent as an actress and certain obvious timbrical and technical similarities (*filature*, *rinforzandi*, and a liking for expressive nuances), Kabaivanska can be considered a worthy heir of Magda Olivero. In recent years she has added new roles to her repertoire, wisely chosen on the basis of her vocal and stage abilities: *The Makropoulos Affair*, *The Turn of the Screw*, *La voix humaine*, *Jenufa*.

There were other important names on the opera billboards of the fifties and sixties. **Clara Petrella** (Milan 1914 –1987), for example, was not called the "Duse of the singers" for nothing. She was a sensitive and intelligent interpreter of a vast repertory. **Herva Nelli** (Florence 1909 – Sharon, Connecticut 1994) was chosen by Toscanini for the now famous recordings of *Aida*, *Ballo in Maschera*, *Otello*, *Falstaff* and *Requiem*; she sang mainly in important American theaters. **Virginia Zeani** (Solovastru, Romania 1925) studied with Lipkovska in her homeland and with Pertile in Italy. She was versatile to the point of being able to perform Rossini's *Zelmira* and *Otello* while singing equally well in *Manon Lescaut*, *Bohème* and *Lohengrin*, and she managed a fantastic portrayal of the three heroines in *The Tales of Hoffmann*, which she sang with her husband, the bass Nicola Rossi Lemeni. **Rosanna Carteri** (Verona

A ride in a gondola between one performance and another for the beautiful **Marcella Pobbe**. From humble origins, she managed to succeed thanks to indomitable will power. She made her debut at Spoleto in 1948 as Margherita in Gounod's Faust. Her repertory was vast. (Historic Archives of La Fenice Theater, Venice)

Rosanna Carteri started her career in 1949, after having won a competition on the Italian national radio. She was very musical and versatile and was often the protagonist of first-ever performances: Ifigenia by Pizetti, Flavia in Prosperina e Lo Straniero by Castro, Natasha in the European premiere of War and Peace by Prokofiev. (Historic Archives of La Scala, Milan. Photo: Piccagliani)

1930) was an attractive and precise specialist of the roles of Liù, Adina, Mimì and Violetta. **Antonietta Stella** (Perugia 1929) was considered Tebaldi's heir because of the natural beauty of her voice, but she retired early, a victim of a bad choice of repertory. **Marcella Pobbe** (Montegaldo, Vincenza 1921) performed in many operas of the lyric and *lirico-spinto* repertory, the best of which were *Faust*, *Otello* and *Adriana Lecouvreur*.

In the following generation we find **Margherita Rinaldi** (Turin 1933), one of the best and most refined of the Italian singers, endowed with a warm and homogeneous voice ranging over two octaves. She was active in the classic light-lyric repertory, with a few interesting escapades into the lyric repertory and an intensive oratorial and concert activity (*Le Prophète* by Meyerbeer at the RAI in 1970 is among her best achievements). We must not forget the Puccini singer **Mietta Sighele** (Rovereto 1936), one of the most applauded Liùs, Butterflys and Mimìs of recent decades. She is a singer who is technically and musically well-prepared, capable of giving an intimate portrayal of each character.

Of the latest generation, two names stand out among the many, **Angela Gheorghiu** (1965) and **Fiorenza Cedolins** (Gorizia 1966).

Gheorghiu, who was born in Romania, rapidly climbed the ladder of international success thanks both to the auspices of Placido Domingo but especially to a solid grounding, an attractive stage presence and considerable determination. Her fiery temperament was behind the epic clash she had with Muti during a rehearsal of *Pagliacci* at Ravenna. "I am not taking any lessons!" she announced, leaving Muti dumbfounded. Her voice is not particularly full, but this is more than compensated for by her phrasing and expressiveness, especially as Adina (*Elisir d'Amore*) and in *Traviata*, her forte. She has made many recordings together with her husband Roberto Alagna (especially interesting are their recordings of Puccini's *La Rondine*, *Manon* and *La Bohème*).

Cedolins comes from Friuli but was trained outside Italy. She sprang to fame with a vast repertoire including *Cavalleria Rusticana*, *Trovatore*, *Norma*, *Aida*, *Tosca*, *Butterfly* and *Adriana Lecouvreur* which she has already performed in many Italian theaters. Her vocal characteristics are more those of a lyric soprano; her voice is clear, easily executing the *pianissimi*, with elegant phrasing and sweet timbre. She also has an attractive stage presence and administers her vocal qualities well and without exaggeration.

Beautiful Katia

A favorite of the greatest conductors and directors, **Katia Ricciarelli** (Rovigo 1946) has been singing now for more than thirty years, having made her debut at Mantua in 1969. Her repertory reaches from Rossini to Puccini, even if her pure timbre and delicate emission are unsuited to verist exaggerations, whereas the abstract, ecstatic abandon of Bellini's and Donizetti's melodies are perfectly suited to her vocal characteristics. Let one example stand for all: that of her triumphant *Anna Bolena* at the Regio Theater of Parma during the 1976-77 season. The final aria "Al dolce guidami castel natio" was performed by the Venetian soprano with surprising *pianissimo* effects and an impeccable legato, proof of the greatness of the school of Iris Adami-Corradetti.

Thanks to her ease in fast vocalizing passages, her fluid emission of trills and *roulades* (especially if sung at *mezzavoce*), Katia Ricciarelli has been able to alternate performances of *Tosca*, *Ballo in Maschera*, *Trovatore* and *Aida* with Rossini's lesser known and now finally rediscovered operas: *Donna del Lago*, *Tancredi*, *Armida*, *Assedio di Corinto*, *Bianca e Falliero*, *Semiramide* and *Gazza Ladra*. The critics have accused the singer of overlooking the authentic Rossini virtuosity *di forza* in favor of an emission almost exclusively performed at *mezzavoce*, and have perceived signs of fatigue in the soprano's voice. However, for all opera lovers Katia remains the sweetest and most beautiful Desdemona to have appeared on stage. This is fully confirmed by Zeffirelli's film, which is masterfully brought to life by Ricciarelli and Placido Domingo.

After her marriage to TV showman Pippo Baudo, Ricciarelli's fame has spread to audiences other than opera lovers, thanks to her frequent appearance in a variety of TV programs. We have seen her dance, argue, answer quiz questions, introduce shows and, of course, sing, though not necessarily Handel or Puccini, but theme songs of TV programs, too. She has made many debuts: in *Barbiere di Siviglia*, *Cenerentola*, *Andrea Chénier*, *Werther*, *Fedora*, *Adriana Lecouvreur*, Handel's *Agrippina* and Lehar's *Eva*.

The Myths of Jessye Norman and Margaret Price

In the Mozart repertory, the Lieder repertory, and in a few of Verdi's operas (especially in *Aida*) Jessye Norman and Margaret Price have made their mark.

Jessye Norman (Augusta, Georgia 1945),

with her extended and expressive voice, is one of the greatest concert artists of all time. She studied at Harvard University in Baltimore and at the University of Michigan, making her debut in Berlin in 1969 as Elizabeth in *Tannhäuser*. In 1973 she made her debut in Paris at the Salle Pleyel in *Aida*.

Her performances have aroused great enthusiasm among opera audiences. She was particularly applauded in Rameau's *Hippolyte et Aricie* in 1983 and Strauss' *Ariadne auf Naxos* in 1985 at Aix-en-Provence, and at the Metropolitan in Berlioz's *Les Troyens* (1983) and Wagner's *Parsifal* (1991). She also shines in oratorio and Lieder concerts, of which there are numerous recordings. She has also made a number of records, together with many of the most famous singers of the last fifty years. She is renowned for the tone-color of her voice, dark and full on the low notes, keen and clear on the high and especially agile in the use of *pianissimi*. She made a memorable recording, together with Karajan, of the finale of *Tristan* and was extraordinarily accomplished, especially in her phrasing, as Kundry in *Parsifal* directed by Levine in New York.

Margaret Price (Blackwood, Wales 1941), an exceptional Pamina, Fiordiligi, Donna

A refined stylist, in possession of a rich voice, ranging from warm deep notes to the most luminous filature, **Jessye Norman** *amazed the Roman audience in a splendid performance of* Dido and Aeneas *by Henry Purcell. The perfection of her phrasing, the moving intensity of her expression, make her one of today's great artists. (Photographic Archives of Philips. Photo: Z. Dominic)*

Anna and Countess in *Marriage of Figaro*, sings also in German theaters performing in Italian operas such as *Norma, Otello* and *Aida*. She made her debut in 1964 as Cherubino at Covent Garden.

One of the rare operatic appearances of **Jessye Norman** *– an outstanding Phèdre in Rameau's* Hippolyte et Aricie *at Aix-en-Provence. It was during her studies at Michigan University with Pierre Bernac, a legendary French chansonnier, that Norman became interested in German Lieder and especially in the beautiful songs of Poulenc, Faure, and Satie. (Mariano Delle Rose Collection)*

Price is famous for the purity of her entries, her use of *mezzavoce* and the delicacy of her timbre, all qualities well suited to the repertoire she chose in the early years of her career. Unfortunately, whether by choice or persuaded by the dictates of the industry, Price gradually abandoned her original repertoire to embark on a disastrous and suicidal attempt at the more complex dramatic genre, such as *Gioconda*, *Norma*, *Adriana Lecouvreur*. Though singing with some success the more lyrical passages, her voice, obviously in difficulty in these unsuitable roles, lost both polish and clarity on the high notes.

Stars and Meteors on the Threshold of the Third Millennium

After her debut in belcanto, **Daniela Dessì** (Genoa 1957), gifted with a particularly sonorous voice and a passionate temperament, was bound sooner or later to tackle operas such as *Aida*, *Tosca*, *Ariadne*, performed tirelessly and without respite. She has heaps of natural talent backed by a solid technique. Her voice is typically Italian, rounded, rich, extended with fine mezzavoci. And yet, not everything has gone right for her. Her approach at the Verdi repertoire (above all *Vespri Siciliani*, *Don Carlos* and *Trovatore*) was unconvincing, as was her *Butterfly*, even though she sang well, while her rendering of *Tosca* at Bologna in 1999 was judged to be too tormented. Dessì tends to be inconsistent, perhaps trying to cover too much ground in too short a time, adding debut to debut without the necessary concentration. Nonetheless, hers is the most attractive voice of her generation, and has enabled her to achieve excellent results in *Otello*, *Aida*, *Iris*, *Traviata*, and particularly in Giordano's *La cena delle beffe*.

In less than ten years, the young singer who had begun her career as a resplendent star, full of promise, became instead a transient meteor. **Fiamma Izzo d'Amico** (Rome 1964), after having savored the grandeur of Saltzburg with Karajan (she sang *Don Carlos*, *Carmen* and *Tosca* under his guidance), inexplicably faded from the scene towards the end of the eighties. Hers was a characteristic voice, neither powerful, nor particularly homogeneous over all the registers, but sustained by an exceptional ability in phrasing and an amazing capacity for expressing emotion, to the extent that she may rightfully take her place alongside another famous singer of similar character, Clara Petrella.

Two illustrious victims of the "ghost of Callas" are **Lucia Aliberti** (Messina 1956) and **Tiziana Fabbricini** (Asti 1958)), the former more talented than the latter but both intent on imitating Callas, and sadly her weak rather than her strong points. Aliberti, at the beginning of her career (she won the Spoleto Festival in 1978), expressed limpid high notes and a fluid agility in her song, but gradually she began to make use of enclosed notes, which eventually compromised both timbre and phrasing. The voice of Fabbricini, who was launched by an exaggerated publicity campaign, which did more harm than good, after her successful *Traviata* at La Scala in 1989, soon began to show signs of a precocious decline, losing uniformity in the registers and manifesting poor intonation.

The fascinating **Anna Caterina Antonacci** (Ferrara 1961), one of the world's best actresses, has become identified with a role that might not be among the best known in opera, but one that only she has been able to render so perfectly: Rossini's *Ermione*. Poised between the characteristics of the mezzo-soprano and the belcanto of the *soprano di agilità*, Antonacci has revived the myth of Isabella Colbran, the famous nineteenth-century virtuosa known not so much for her voice (which was often criticized for its lack of uniformity in the registers), but rather for her ability to excite the audience. A shy and conscientious artist, Antonacci has triumphed at La Scala in Gluck's *Armide* and at her American debut in *Cenerentola*, roles admirably suited to the limited extension of her voice.

The Callas myth, which has created and destroyed over the years so many "new Callases", has been revived yet again by **Maria Dragoni** (Procida, Naples 1957), gifted with a magnificently full, extended voice, capable of rising to high f (last rondò of *Sonnambula*) and reaching down to low d (Persiani's *Ines de Castro*), with excellent *agilità appoggiata*, accents and *mezzevoci*. Dragoni, an intelligent and sensitive singer, has not had an easy time, however, and has often had to face the hostility of a frequently inimical environment. Her best performances include *Norma*, *Turandot*, *Aida*, *Don Carlos* and a splendid Verdi *Requiem* conducted by Giulini.

From the other side of the ocean, hails **Kallen Esperian** (1961), a highly appreciated singer of Verdi's operas, with a special predilection for the role of Desdemona and Luisa Miller. Esperian, who is half Armenian, half American, is graced with a superb physique and considerable dramatic force, together with a gentle, ductile, well-trained voice. Other young talents include the lovely **Svetla Vassileva**, highly applauded as Violetta Valéry conducted by

Mehta at the Maggio Fiorentino in 2000 and equally so as Nedda in *Pagliacci*; the Greek singer **Dimitra Theodossiou** who, in a rapid climb to fame, has achieved a number of successes in the early Verdi repertoire, for instance in *Stiffelio* at Trieste, *Traviata* in Rome, *Masnadieri* at Palermo in 2001; the Albanian singer **Inva Mula,** sensitive interpreter in the roles of Gilda, Violetta and Lucia di Lammermoor, much in demand in Vienna and the Arena di Verona; the Chilean singer **Cristina Gallardo-Domas** (Santiago 1967), applauded in major European theaters again singing Verdi (particularly interesting was her recording of *Aida* conducted by Harnoncourt).

A word apart in due to **Barbara Frittoli** (Mercallo, Varese 1966), who, moving gradually from Mozart to Verdi's *Otello, Falstaff, Trovatore, Luisa Miller*, with the support of a number of famous Maestros, not least among whom Muti and Abbado, has established a prominent place for herself in the opera world and has even earned the admiration of the great Mirella Freni. This famous soprano has on more than one occasion named Frittoli as her heir. Frittoli

is unquestionably endowed with vocal qualities and technique that make her an outstanding artist: exceptional musicality, controlled emission, easily executed *pianissimi* and purity of expression, plus heaps of confidence and an impressive stage presence. Nonetheless, Verdi is perhaps not the most suitable repertoire for her. Frittoli is another purely lyric soprano projected, somewhat by force, into the dramatic repertoire which, in the long run, might fail to produce the expected results. It could be added at this point that Verdi sopranos need a more powerful voice of sturdier timbre, in order to sustain not only the tessitura but also the resonance demanded, today more than ever before, by the Verdi orchestras.

Blond, attractive, **Renee Fleming** (1959) has tried her hand at many different repertoires but has yet to make a conclusive decision as to her precise role. She has unquestionable talent as a belcanto singer which enables her to perform Donizetti's more difficult operas (from *Emilia di Liverpool* to *Lucrezia Borgia*) or Rossini's *Armida*, but her interpretations of Massenet's *Thais* or Strauss's *Arabella* are equally intense. Her voice

Daniela Dessì in Aida (2001). This singer from Genoa is backed by a solid technique but has perhaps tackled too much in too short a time. Nonetheless, hers is one of the most attractive voices of her generation. (Fondazione Arena di Verona. Photo: Gianfranco Fainello)

has a pleasant color, and though not strong is very extended (in *Lucrezia Borgia* at La Scala she even produced a high f), while her alluring stage presence is hard to forget (her rendering of *Armida* at the Rossini Festival at Pesaro was immensely forceful).

What can we say about the singer who was once rashly described "la voix absolue"? **Cheryl Studer** (Midland, Michigan 1955) is an illustrious example of how a career can be constructed in theory, only to be inevitably sacrificed on stage. In actual fact, Studer, one of Hans Hotter's pupils, has always alternated great performances (*Lohengrin* in Vienna under the baton of Maestro Abbado) with incredible fiascos (*Vespri Siciliani* at La Scala conducted by Muti, *Trovatore* in Vienna with Mehta, *Viaggio a Roma* at Ferrara with Abbado), proving herself to be the victim of nerves rather than of vocal failings. Without doubt, she is more at home making records. Her voice on stage is sometimes unrecognizable as the voice that sings on record, for Deutsche Grammophon, roles ranging from Lucia to Gilda, from Regina della Notte to Ariadne, from *Tannhäuser* to *Semiramide*, a variety of roles so diverse as to make life extremely difficult for poor Cheryl, perhaps a trifle confused amidst all these different characters.

Mozart Lyric Sopranos

Three important names open the section on the most famous and acclaimed Mozart sopranos of the twentieth century: **Maria Cebotari** (Chisinau, Bessarabia 1910 – Vienna 1949), **Elisabeth Grümmer** (Diedenhofen, Alsace-Lorraine 1911 – Berlin 1986) and **Rita Streich** (Barnaul 1920 – Vienna 1987).

The beautiful and ill-fated Cebotari was prevented from continuing her promising career as Susanna, the Countess, Donna Anna, Salome and Sophie (*Der Rosenkavalier*) when she died of a tragic illness at only thirty-nine years of age. She sang from 1931 until 1949, and was the first to perform the parts of Aminta in R. Strauss' *Die Schweigsame Frau* (1935) and Lucilla in *The Death of Danton* by Einem (1947). She also participated in several important first performances of works by German composers.

Elisabeth Grümmer had a refined and highly musical voice, with a beautiful timbre. Her only handicap was that of having the same repertory as the great Elizabeth Schwarzkopf, thus being faced with a fearful rival in operas such as *Così Fan Tutte* and *Don Giovanni*, not to mention Wagner (*Lohengrin, The Mastersingers*). She did, however, find a space of her own, remaining

*And here is Susanna par excellence: **Irmgard Seefried**, darling of all the great conductors of recent decades. In her final years, before her death, the Viennese artist became interested in dramatic art.*

an unsurpassed Agathe in *Der Freischütz*. From 1941 until the sixties she sang in Berlin, Vienna, London, Bayreuth and Hamburg; she was often conducted by Furtwängler, who was particularly appreciative of her vocal and scenic talents.

As for Rita Streich, we need only say that she was taught, in Berlin, by Maria Ivogün, Erna Berger and Willy Domgraf-Fassbänder: groundwork that made her an acclaimed singer of Mozart (Queen of the Night, Konstanze) and Strauss (Zerbinetta, Sophie) over a long period of time and in many famous theaters.

The beautiful **Lisa Della Casa** (Burgdorf, Bern 1919) was a famous Strauss and Mozart singer. Her artistic beginnings were very precocious. She was part of a theatrical company when seven years old, performing Shakespeare and Shaw; in the meantime her vocal studies were directed by Margaret Haeser. After her debut as Butterfly in 1941 at Solothurn-Biel, Lisa commenced a brilliant career which included her memorable *Arabella, Nozze di*

The beautiful Swiss soprano **Lisa Della Casa**, as the Countess Rosina in Mozart's Le Nozze di Figaro.

Figaro, Don Giovanni (Donna Elvira and Donna Anna), Der Rosenkavalier (in the roles of Sophie, Octavian and the Marschallin), Così Fan Tutte (Fiordiligi) and Ariadne auf Naxos, performing in the world's major theaters: the Staatsoper of Vienna (State Opera), the Metropolitan, Covent Garden, La Scala, Salzburg, and the Colón in Buenos Aires. The best vocal characteristics of the Swiss soprano were her superb legato, her uniformity in all registers, and her soft, sweet timbre, while her elegant appearance accentuated her charm.

A number of other important Mozart sopranos of the twentieth century are worthy of mention: **Minnie Nast** (Karlsruhe 1874 – Füssen im Allgau 1956); the great **Elisabeth Schumann** (Merseburg 1888 – New York 1952), who was also an excellent Lieder singer; **Maria Stader** (Budapest 1911 – Zurich 1999); **Suzanne Danco** (Brussels 1911 – Fiesole, Florence 2000); **Jo Vincent** (Amsterdam 1898); **Audrey Mildmay** (Murstmonceaux, Vancouver 1900 – Glyndebourne 1953); and **Aulikki Rautawaara** (Vassa, Finland 1906). And we must not forget the great **Edda Moser** (Berlin 1931), who enjoyed a brief, but magical moment as an unequalled Queen of the Night and Donna Anna.

Eleanor Steber (Wheeling, W. Virginia 1914 – Langhorne, Pennsylvania 1990) deserves a paragraph apart, by virtue of her luminous and intense voice. In her vast and eclectic repertory, some brilliant highlights came in her Mozart roles of The Countess, Fiordiligi and Donna Anna. She made her debut at the Met in 1940 as Sophie in *Rosenkavelier*, and she remained a bright and active star there until 1970. Thanks to an enormous vocal talent, reinforced by a solid technique and an extraordinary expressive capacity, she was able to sing Puccini, Wagner, contemporary operas (she was the first interpreter of Samuel Barber's *Vanessa* in 1958) and Strauss (the first American Arabella).

Four Queens of Song:
Seefried, Schwarzkopf, Stich-Randall and Jurinac

Irmgard Seefried (Köngetried, Baviera 1919 – Vienna 1988) was a sensitive and extremely refined performer especially in the Mozart repertory, where she shone as one of the best Susannas of the post-war period. She began in the small part of the priestess in *Aida* conducted

Eleanor Steber, a Met star from 1940 on, she created the title role in Barber's Vanessa.

by von Karajan at Aquisgrana in 1938. Until the second half of the sixties she performed in all the principal theaters of the world, with, however, a decided preference for the Vienna State Opera and Salzburg, where she continued to sing in acclaimed *Liederabende*.

Amongst her characteristics were her spicy, good-humored stage presence, her innate musicality, and her excellent vocal technique, the result of continuous study.

The uncontested queen of Lieder and German opera is **Elizabeth Schwarzkopf** (Jarocin, Poznan 1915). After her beginnings as a light-lyric soprano (Flower maiden in *Parsifal*, Berlin 1938), she immediately emerged as a lyric soprano of great talent: in Mozart and in Strauss (her Marschallin in *Der Rosenkavalier* is unforgettable); in Verdi (*Falstaff, Requiem*) and Puccini; she also performed many contemporary composers (she was, for example, the first Trulove in Stravinsky's *The Rake's Progress*, Venice, 1951).

After 1947 Schwarzkopf's star began to shine in all the most important European and international theaters. From 1947 until 1951 she sang regularly at Covent Garden, where she returned in 1959 for a triumphant *Rosenkavalier*. She was acclaimed at La Scala between 1948 and 1963, at San Francisco in 1955, in Chicago in 1959, at the Metropolitan between 1964 and 1966. She made her farewell to the stage after a last, moving performance of the Marschallin in Brussels in 1972.

An intelligent and cultured artist, Schwarzkopf never overlooked one note or one phrase in a performance, giving each its true expressive value. This was also made possible by a sound technique which permitted her to give coloring and shadings and to easily overcome all the difficulties of perilous tessituras.

The vast selection of records made by Schwarzkopf is today a legacy of immense historical value, and includes all the soprano's most famous roles. Especially memorable are the performances entrusted to the batons of Furtwaengler, Karajan and Böhm, which include *Mastersingers* at Beyreuth, *Rosenkavalier, Così fan tutti* with Kraus and Strauss's *Vier Letzte Lieder*.

Another refined Mozart interpreter was **Teresa Stich-Randall** (West Hartford, Connecticut 1927). She made her debut as Aida at the age of fifteen. In 1952 she was engaged at the Vienna Staatsoper, where she was immediately given the title part in *Traviata*. From then on her activity extended to all the major operatic theaters, mainly in America, England and Italy.

Among her favorite operas were *Rosenkavalier* (Sophie), *Così Fan Tutte* (Fiordiligi), *Don Giovanni* (Donna Anna), *Magic Flute* (Pamina) and

Elizabeth Schwarzkopf *refined her talent with the help of her husband, Walter Legge, general manager of a big international recording company. Every new recording was prepared with meticulous care; every nuance, every note, each single inflexion which added to the psychological insight of the character was studied and refined and nothing left to chance. The Marschallin of* Der Rosenkavalier *(photo) was one of the most successful results of this exacting work, both on stage and in recordings. (San Francisco Opera: Giandonato Crico Collection)*

Teresa Stich-Randall *in Ariadne auf Naxos by Richard Strauss; a photo taken in 1963. (Giandonato Crico Collection)*

Ariadne auf Naxos which she performed with a crystalline voice of incredible purity.

We must not forget **Sena Jurinac** (whose real name is Srebrenka, born at Travnik, Jugoslavia 1921), an exceptional Cherubino, Fiordiligi, Ilia (*Idomeneo*), Donna Elvira, Donna Anna, Pamina and the Countess of Almaviva. Her voice was pure and she had a beautiful legato. Thanks to her noteworthy extension she was an excellent Octavian in *Der Rosenkavalier* and Marschallin in the same opera, second only to that of Schwarzkopf, and she was equally successful as the Composer in *Ariadne auf Naxos*, as Desdemona, Butterfly, Elisabetta in *Don Carlos*, Mimì and Suor Angelica.

Two singers who had a long career and distinguished themselves for their versatility, style and flexible voices were the Spanish soprano **Pilar Lorengar** (Saragozza 1921 – Berlin 1996) and the German singer **Gundula Janowitz** (Berlin 1937). The former made her debut in Barcelona in 1949 and spread her repertory over Verdi, Puccini and various contemporary composers, but she obtained her best results with Mozart. Janowitz performed most frequently in Mozart (Countess, Fiordiligi, Donna Anna), often adding Wagner (Elsa, Eva, Senta, Sieglinde) and Strauss (Marschallin, Ariadne, Arabella) and has often sung at Salzburg under

Kiri Te Kanawa *can be considered the heir of Lisa Della Casa as regards repertoire and vocal characteristics; she has a sweet and soft timbre, perfect legato, and good extension. She began her studies as a mezzo-soprano, but on the advice of the celebrated conductor, Richard Bonynge, she changed to a soprano. Her first important success came in December, 1971, when she sang the role of the Countess in a new production of* The Marriage of Figaro, *conducted by Colin Davis, at Covent Garden. (Giandonato Crico Collection)*

the baton of von Karajan. At times her notes were a little fixed, but her timbre was sweet and penetrating. Today she is an opera-director.

Our list of great Mozart interpreters must also include **Graziella Sciutti** (Turin 1927 – Geneva 2001), an unforgettable protagonist of innumerable Neapolitan comic operas as well as an unparalleled Mozart *soubrette* (Despina, Zerbina, Susanna). She made her debut in Rome in 1948 in Mozart's *Oca del Cairo*, demonstrating an innate musical talent, even though her voice was neither particularly extended nor very strong. From 1958-1962 she sang regularly at Covent Garden, from 1958-1966 at Salzburg, and at the Glyndebourne Festival from 1954-1959, having become an indispensable part of the great comic repertory. From the mid-seventies on she turned to music teaching and opera directing as her main interests, being particularly involved with Neapolitan opera, Mozart and Poulenc (she had been an unequalled performer of *La voix humaine*).

Dame Kiri Te Kanawa (Gisborne, New Zealand 1944), a magnificent Donna Elvira in *Don Giovanni* and Countess in *The Marriage of Figaro*, is much loved in Great Britain, France and the United States. She made her debut at Camden in 1969 as Elena in Rossini's *Donna del Lago*. Since 1970 she has ties with Covent Garden, where she is acclaimed and loved in her wide repertory.

Dame Te Kanawa began her music studies as a mezzo-soprano, with Vera Rosza at the London Opera Centre. Richard Bonynge first suggested her move to the soprano range and a Mozart specialization. With a fascinating *portamento*, a light and delicate timbre, Te Kanawa has been applauded worldwide. Hers is a truly vast repertory which includes the roles of Mimì, Desdemona, Arabella, the Marschallin in *Rosenkavelier*, Manon Lescaut and even Violetta Valéry. However, she achieves greater success in Mozart and Strauss than in Verdi or Puccini, since her voice is a trifle limited for the latter repertory. In Lieder concerts Kiri receives enthusiastic acclaim, both live and on records.

Ileana Cotrubas (Galati, Romania 1939) was a sensitive interpreter of so many Susannas, Paminas and Mélisandes (Debussy). She was applauded both for her exquisite vocal technique and her expressive and emotional acting. She made her debut in Bucharest as Yniold in *Pelléas* in 1964 and was a major performer until 1990 when she retired after a series of performances of *Werther* in Lisbon and Vienna. Without doubt she preferred Mozart roles (Susanna, Pamina, Konstanze), but she was also able to create a sensitive, exciting Mimì at La Scala in

1979 with Kleiber conducting. Kleiber insisted on having her as Violetta Valéry in the Deutsche Grammonphon recording. Cotrubas has also earned due fame as a concert and oratorio performer.

Elly Ameling (1938) is an exceptional Lieder singer but is rarely seen on the operatic stage except for a few, infrequent, but nonetheless valuable, Mozart performances. Finally, **Lucia Popp** (Bratislava 1939 – München 1993), gracious and refined as Pamina, Sophie in *Der Rosenkavalier*, Zerlina, Zerbinetta, Marcellina (*Fidelio*), Rosalinde in *Die Fledermaus* and wonderful in a wide Italian light-lyric repertory (Norina, Gilda, Musetta) and, naturally, in Lieder, ranging from Mozart to Mahler. In later years, prior to her premature death, she followed a natural evolution towards heavier roles, including in her repertoire characters such as that of the Marschallin, the Countess in *Figaro*, Eva in *The Mastersingers of Nuremberg* and Elsa in *Lohengrin*.

Emmy Loose (Ustìnad Labem, Bohemia 1914 – Vienna 1987) belonged to the "bright and breezy" category of *soubrette* sopranos. She was a regular member of the Vienna State Opera from 1943 onwards. She was applauded there as Zerlina, Despina, Musetta, Norina, Gilda and, above all, as Adele in *Die Fledermaus*. **Erna Berger** (Cossebande, Dresden 1900 – Essen 1990) gave performances in the Austrian and German theaters that remain unforgettable. She was one of Furtwängler's favorites. Her voice was small but well positioned and sweetly colored, enabling her to interpret Gilda, Rosina, and Zerlina with grace and elegance. **Reri Grist** (New York 1932) was a spirited Despina, Susanna and Zerlina, but also famous as Zerbinetta, Sophie and Rosina in *Barbiere*.

An example of perfect stylistic and musical adherence to the dictates of Mozart's music is to be found in **Edith Mathis** (Lucerne 1938), the impeccable and refined artist of innumerable performances and an equally consistent number of recordings, made under the guidance of many famous conductors. She is remembered especially in the roles of Cherubino, Pamina, Marcellina, Despina, but also as Sophie in *Rosenkavalier* and Melisande. Yet she has never entirely abandoned chamber music and oratorio, and is a widely applauded interpreter of Bach cantatas, Brahms' *Deutsche Requiem* and in Leider concerts.

Judith Blegen (Missoula, Missouri 1943) made a name for herself as Blondchen in *Die Entführung aus dem Serail*, but also as Susanna and Despina. Similarly, **Helen Donath** (Corpus Christi, Texas 1940), who sings mainly in Ger-

Barbara Hendricks, *an American soprano especially popular in France. Her Lieder concerts are widely acclaimed.*

man theaters, especially in Munich, specializing in C.M. von Weber's *Freischütz*.

Christiane Eda-Pierre (Port de France, Martinique 1940) has been applauded in theaters world-wide as Kostanze, but she is also famous as Zerbinetta, Queen of the Night and Rosina. A special word goes to the highly popular **Barbara Hendricks** (Stephens, Arkansas 1948), who has become a veritable star of the French operatic stage. A pupil of Tourel at the Juiliard school, she made her debut in 1974 in Cavalli's *Ormindo*. Her voice was deemed to be small and lacking in special qualities, though well sustained by excellent phrasing and a strong sense of musicality. She rose to fame thanks to her records, nearly all of which dedicated to a Leider repertoire, and to many concert and TV appearances, where her charm and geniality soon made her a favorite. In recent years, after having starred in Comencini's film-opera *La Bohème* (1987), she has become an active defender of children's rights cooperating with UNICEF, and has devoted herself almost exclusively to concert performances.

Kathleen Battle (Portsmouth, Ohio 1948), capricious as an eighteenth-century primadonna, is an attractive, extremely well-prepared singer, whose voice is, however, lacking in certain areas, having for instance a rather sharp timbre and limited volume. Consequently, Battle has emerged thanks mainly to a vigorous publicity and recording campaign, and for having taken part in large-scale productions such as *Don Giovanni* with Karajan at Saltzburg, *Ariadne auf Naxos* with Levine at the Metropolitan, failing nonetheless to reach maximum levels.

The eighties saw the arrival on the scene of other excellent singers such as the Hungarian **Andrea Rost** (1958), launched at La Scala in a much-publicized version of *Rigoletto* conducted by Muti and as Pamina (far more successful) in *The Magic Flute*; the Italo-Norwegian singer **Elisabeth Norberg-Schulz** (Oslo 1959), perfect heir to Graziella Sciutti, having the same lively stage presence and similar vocal qualities, although she has gradually shifted to a more lyrical repertoire; **Karita Mattila** (Somero 1960) from Finland, who has participated in numerous record releases and many important Mozart productions.

Ambassadors of the Russian Repertory

Galina Vichnevskaya (Leningrad 1926) gave magnificent La Scala performances of Tchaikovsky's *Eugene Onegin* and Prokofiev's *Semyon Kotko* on tour with the Bolshoi in 1973. She had splendid vocal qualities, incisive in the

dramatic phrases, soft and caressing in the *mezzavoce*.

These gifts made her insuperable in the Russian repertory, and also in chamber music, so much so that Shostakovich (and he was not the only one) dedicated his seven *Romanze op. 127* to her voice.

Tamara Milashkina (Astrakhan 1934) was a regular member of the Moscow Bolshoi during the sixties and seventies, interpreting the great Russian repertory (Tchaikovsky, Rimsky-Korsakov and Borodin) as well as performing some Italian operatic melodramas and being an excellent Lieder singer.

The nineties saw the rapid rise and unexpectedly sudden decline of the talented **Nina Rautio** (Bryansk 1957), the latter unfortunate circumstance due perhaps to too much work, badly organized by the singer's agents. **Galina Gorchakova** (1962), gifted with an agile voice and masterly stage presence, has proved a splendid.interpreter of *Sadko* and *Eugene Onegin*, and also of many Italian operas, such as *Forza del Destino* performed at St. Petersburg (conducted by Gergev and recorded by Philips). Similarly talented is the statuesque **Maria Guleghina** (Odessa 1959). **Ljuba Kazarnovskaja** (Moscow 1956), better known in her own country than on the international scene, is a specialist in the Puccini repertoire. As with many singers of the Russian school, she has a powerful, extended voice and a strong temperament, well-suited to characters such as Manon Lescaut, Leonora in *Trovatore* and, of course, the heroines of the Russian repertory.

THE *LIRICO-SPINTO* SOPRANOS OF THE TWENTIETH CENTURY

Emmy Destinn (Ema Kittlovà; Prague 1878 – Ceské Budejovice 1930) dominated the stage during the great Verist era, not only because of her vocal power, but also because of her stylistic gifts, her moderation, and the expressive intensity with which she played the roles of Tosca, Salome, Butterfly, Santuzza and especially Minnie in *The Girl of the Golden West* (of which she was the first interpreter at the Metropolitan in 1910, with Toscanini).

She began her singing career at Dresden in 1897 in *Cavalleria Rusticana*, and retired in 1921, her voice showing marked signs of tiredness; her cutting high c‴ and her impeccable polish were severely compromised. Only the art and the intelligence of the great singer remained.

"La divina" **Claudia Muzio** (Pavia 1889 – Rome 1936) was a singer-actress of unequalled

Claudia Muzio *crowned with laurel. (Historic Archives of the Rome Opera Theater)*

Rosa Ponselle *as Elvira in Verdi's Ernani, one of the many notable revivals organised especially for her. She starred at the Met from 1981 to 1936.*

bravura in the parts of Violetta, Tosca, Desdemona, Manon Lescaut and Leonora in *Trovatore*, all characters veined with a subtle melancholy, pushed by fate to their tragic end, involved in impossible loves. In these roles Muzio demostrated an artistic temperament without comparison in the twentieth century, with the exception of Maria Callas.

Despite the fact that she possessed a voice that was limited in extension, agility and volume, she was able to resolve every moment of her performances with the variety of her coloring and shading, an intense and imaginative phrasing, and her passionate acting and attractive stage presence.

She sang from 1910 until 1934, when she died of heart disease (although rumors spoke also of tuberculosis and suicide). Her most sublime creation was that of Refice's *Cecilia*, at the Rome Opera.

Rosa Ponselle (R. Ponzillo; Meriden, Connecticut 1897 – Baltimore 1981) was a lucky discovery made by Enrico Caruso. In 1918 the famous tenor heard her by chance and suggested that she should study opera. Only six months of lessons with her teachers Thormez and Romani were required, and then the young Rosa made her debut by Caruso's side, at the Metropolitan, in *La Forza del Destino*.

She sang until 1937, emitting one of the softest, most velvety voices in the history of opera. Although her voice was flexible, equal in all registers and resonant in the first high notes, she had precise limits in her extension, being unable to reach high c‴ with ease. Her stylistic quality, the noble composure of her singing, and her physical beauty compensated for these shortcomings and helped create the legendary interpretations of *Ernani*, *Trovatore*, *Aida*, *Gioconda* and *Norma* during the nineteen-twenties and thirties.

Giannina Arangi Lombardi (Marigliano, Naples 1891 – Milan 1951), a genuine belcanto singer in a period little inclined towards variations and vocal decorations; she was the first true *soprano drammatico d'agilità* of the twentieth century, paving the way for Callas.

After her debut as a mezzo-soprano in 1920 in Rome she went on to sing Aida at La Scala in 1925 and from then on was the star of many splendid performances of *Gioconda*, *Trovatore*, *Lucrezia Borgia*, *La Vestale*, and even Rossini's *Mosè* (Florence 1935) and Bellini's rediscovered *Beatrice di Tenda* (Catania 1935).

It was not by chance that she withdrew from the stage with *Vespri Siciliani* at Palermo in 1937, for the role of Elena has all the characteristics of the *soprano drammatico d'agilità*.

Arangi Lombardi was also an excellent singing teacher at the Conservatorium of Milan. From 1947 on she taught at Ankara, Leyla Gencer being one of her prized students there.

The heir of Arangi Lombardi, as regards beauty and fullness of voice, was **Maria Caniglia** (Naples 1905 – Rome 1979), one of the most applauded performers in *Tosca*, *Andrea Chénier*, *Traviata*, *Adriana Lecouvreur*, *Trovatore*, *Forza del Destino*, *Ballo in Maschera* and *Aida* during the two decades from 1930 to 1950. Caniglia's best characteristic was the natural capacity of her voice to expand in the central register and in the first high notes like a river of sonority ("Io son l'umile ancella" in *Adriana* and "Amami Alfredo" in *Traviata*). The only thing which occasionally ruined her singing style was her fiery temperament, for it often led her into excesses in the exciting moments of the Verist operas. She was unforgettable when singing with Beniamino Gigli, especially in *Tosca*, *Traviata* and *Fedora*.

Gabriella Gatti (Rome 1908) was an impeccable stylist and a refined singer in an era which was still tied to the powerful and exuberant verist voices. She began distinguishing herself in 1934 (the year of her debut in Monteverdi's *Orfeo*), becoming an irreplaceable interpreter of new and rare operas. She sang in first-ever performances by composers such as Robbiani, Malipiero, Frazzi, Casella, Alfano, Gnecchi, and also in Busoni's *Turandot*, *Wozzek*, *Enfant Prodigue*, *Rinaldo*, *Der Freischutz* (Agata), *Oberon* (Rezia), *William Tell* (Matilde), while also singing the more normal repertoire of the *lirico-spinto* soprano: *Tosca*, *Traviata*, *Forza del Destino*, *Norma*, *Tannhäuser*.

Let us move on to some other great *lirico-spinto* sopranos. **Margherita Grandi** (Hobart, Tasmania 1894 – Milan 1971), a famous Lady Macbeth and Tosca; **Margarete Teschemacher** (Cologne 1903 – Bad Wiesse 1959); **Celestina Boninsegna** (Reggio Emilia 1877 – Milan 1947), much acclaimed in *Trovatore* and *Aida*; **Dusolina Giannini** (Philadelphia 1902 – Zurich 1986); **Ester Mazzoleni** (Sebenico, Dalmazia 1883 – Palermo 1982), a great Medea and Giulia in *La Vestale*; **Rosa Raisa** (Bialystok 1893 – Los Angeles 1963), first to perform *Turandot* and *Francesca da Rimini*; **Giannina Russ** (Lodi 1873 – Milan 1951); **Yvonne Gall** (Paris 1885 – 1972); **Maria Nemeth** (Kormend, Hungary 1897 – Vienna 1967), a wonderful Tosca and Amelia in *Ballo in Maschera*, but also able to sing the Queen of the Night; **Ina Souez** (Windsor, Colorado 1903 – S. Monica, California 1992), famous in the Mozart repertory; **Rose Bampton** (Cleveland 1908), from 1932 until 1950 a diva at the Metropolitan Opera in a wide repertoire, she went from mezzo-soprano roles to the parts of Donna Anna, Kundry, and Sieglinde; **Lucrezia Bori** (Gandia, Valencia 1887 – New York 1960), primadonna at the Met from 1912 until 1936; **Lina Bruna Rasa** (Padua 1905 – Cernusco sul Naviglio, Milan 1984); **Maria Farneti** (Forlì 1877 – 1955); **Eugenia Burzio** (Poirino, Turin 1882 – Milan 1922); **Bianca Scacciati** (Florence 1894 – Brescia 1948), a powerful Turandot and Tosca; **Eileen Farrell** (Willimantic, Connecticut 1920 – New York 2002), one of the most sought after singers for the roles of *Medea* and *Gioconda* during the years when Maria Callas was already dominating the scene.

Brief but dazzling was the parabola of **Caterina Mancini** (Genzano, Rome 1924), who, from

1950 for some ten years, amazed audiences with the power and beauty of her voice, singing without respite in a very difficult repertoire (*Nabucco, Aida* and early Verdi operas in general).

Gabriella Tucci (Rome 1929) made her debut in *Traviata* in 1951 at Lucca and the year after sang Leonora in *Forza del Destino* (after having won the Spoleto Festival). Her ductile, confident voice made her highly suited to roles such as Aida, Maddalena of Coigny, Nedda and Desdemona. **Gigliola Frazzoni** (Bologna 1927), with her fiery temperament (Tosca, Minnie, Santuzza), was part of the cast of the first ever performance of Poulenc's *Dialogues des Carmélites* at La Scala in 1957. **Rita Orlandi Malaspina** (Bologna 1937) and **Luisa Maragliano** (Genoa 1931), both with high-reaching, confident voices, are especially suited to Verdi and Puccini repertoires.

The splendid **Dame Eva Turner** (Oldham 1892 – London 1990) was one of England's most extraordinary voices. After having heard her sing, Toscanini brought her to La Scala where she made her debut in 1924 as Freia in *Rheingold*. From that time on her career was crowned with one success after another, especially when she sang *Turandot, Aida* or Amelia in *Ballo in Maschera*, roles which she regularly performed from 1928-1948 at Covent Garden, in Chicago, Buenos Aires and Lisbon, to name but a few of the world's most famous opera theaters where she shone. Her voice had excellent emission, a beautiful color, and a famous capacity to achieve uniformity over a range of more than two octaves.

Martina Arroyo (New York 1935), though gifted with magnificent vocal qualities, never completely solved the rise to the high notes. She was excellent in *Aida, Ballo in Maschera, Tosca, Macbeth,* and *Forza del Destino*. **Anna Tomowa-Sintow** (Stara Zagora, Bulgaria 1941) was one of von Karajan's favorites, and an excellent Elsa (*Lohengrin*), Leonora in *Forza del Destino* and *Aida*.

Angeles Gulin (Ribadavia Orense, Spain 1937), another extraordinarily powerful and penetrating voice, made her debut as Queen of the Night but became famous also as Abigaille, Norma, Gioconda and in dramatic roles in general. **Maria Chiara** (Oderzo, Treviso 1939) became virtually identified with the role of *Aida,* which she performed numerous times at the Arena di Verona and at La Scala, although she was particularly suited to Puccini characters (Liù, Mimì, Suor Angelica, Tosca, Manon Lescaut).

During the eighties and nineties three excellent Verdi voices appeared on the scene: the English singer **Rosalynd Plowright** (Worksop 1949), an extremely attractive figure on stage but with problems in the high register; the American **Leona Mitchell** (Enid, Oklahoma 1949), gifted with magnificent vocal qualities but hindered by poor enunciation (a specialist in *Aida, Forza del Destino, Ernani*); the exuberant **Aprile Millo** (New York 1958), capable of an incredible parabola.

Millo, a highly unconventional character, made her debut in *Aida* at Salt Lake City in 1980, and her remarkable vocal qualities were instantly clear: extension, splendid color, easily executed *pianissimi*. Unfortunately, influenced by her character and temperament, she soon began to assume primadonna attitudes reminiscent of the past, overacting on stage with tears and speeches, tantrums, scenes and other hysterical manifestations. A pity, because operas such as *Aida, Ballo in Maschera, Don Carlos, Otello, Trovatore,* not to mention *Andrea Chénier* and *Turandot* (some of which recorded with Sony), seem to be written specially for her.

The American school fosters a constant league of *lirico-spinto* sopranos, many of whom are also endowed with impressive physiques; thus the theaters of the new millennium have hosted some authentic amazons such as **Sharon Sweet** (1951), **Deborah Voigt** (1960) and **Alessandra Marc**, whose voices would appear to go hand in hand with their dimensions. It seems strange that in an era in which anorexic top models triumph in the fashion world, on the opera scene the exact opposite is the case. These three singers are engaged by the world's major opera companies, in repertoires that include Verdi, Puccini and also Rossini and Wagner, with intermittent results. The charming voice of **Kathleen McCalla** (Mount Ayr, Iowa 1954) has won her acclaim as *Turandot* and Abigaille, while **Ines Salazar**, who hails from Venezuela, played *Tosca* at the Rome Opera company's centenary. The Italian **Silvia Ranalli** (Torrice, Frosinone 1960), who was a pupil of Antonietta Stella, has specialized in the roles of *Tosca* and *Adriana Lecouvreur*, while the Italo-American **Francesca Patané** (Milan 1959), daughter of Giuseppe, the famous orchestra conductor, gifted with one of the most charming silhouettes to ever tread the opera stage, is much in demand in *Turandot* and *Macbeth*, where she can make the most of her best vocal qualities: the trill of her high notes and the power of her accents.

A word apart is reserved for **Maria Guleghina**, who is today the most important *soprano drammatico d'agilità* of her generation. Her greatest international successes are tied to the key characters of Lady Macbeth and Abigaille. Thanks to the sensational results achieved worldwide in the mid-nineties, especially at La Scala, the Metropolitan and the Arena di Verona, literally taken by storm, Maria has been able to enlarge her repertoire to include *Tosca, Aida, Manon Lescaut, Norma, Ernani, Trovatore, Forza del Destino, Ballo in Maschera*, each time showing exceptional vocal ability. Above all she may be admired for the beauty of her tone-color, the ease with which she reaches the high register (up to e flat in the duet with Nabucco), her vocal agility (such as to enable her to execute variations in the *da capo* of the *cabaletta* of Abigaille and of Odabella in *Attila*, the first singer of her century to attempt such an exploit), not to mention her intense stage presence and fine acting. Following a stormy performance of *Ballo in Maschera* at La Scala in 2001, and the clash with the gallery, Guleghina has decided not to appear again at the Milanese opera house.

The *Lirico-Spinto* sopranos of the German repertory

Lotte Lehmann (Perleberg, Brandenburg 1885 – Santa Barbara, California 1976) was a great interpreter of Wagner and Strauss. Her solid preparation and sensitive acting allowed her a long career which stretched from her appearance at Hamburg in *The Magic Flute* (Third Boy) in 1909 until her last concerts in America in 1951 (she withdrew from the stage in 1946 in Los Angeles, performing the Marschallin in *Der Rosenkavalier*). Her recitative was impetuous and dramatic, her voice sweet and delicate in the elegiac passages, elegant and sensual in the love scenes. Lotte Lehmann was the best performer of *Rosenkavalier, Fidelio, Lohengrin* and *The Mastersingers of Nuremberg* between the years 1920-1940, as well as being the first to interpret many of Richard Strauss's operas (the Composer in *Ariadne auf Naxos* in 1916, the wife of Barak in *Die Frau ohne Schatten* in 1919, Christina in *Intermezzo* in 1924). She was also much acclaimed in *Manon Lescaut, Tosca* and *Suor Angelica*.

Maria Jeritza (Mimi Jedlitzka; Brno, Moravia 1887 – New York 1982) had an extremely attractive voice and stage presence and was the perfect incarnation of Salome and Thaïs, both women of bewitching charm, bursting with sensuality. Her interpretation of the Dance of the Seven Veils and the Final Scene in *Salome* have become legendary. Strauss himself wanted Jeritza as the first performer of *Ariadne auf Naxos* in Stuttgart in 1912, and of *Die Frau ohne Schatten* (as the Empress) in Vienna in 1919.

Hers was a voice with a good timbre and resonance, sustained by a noteworthy technique. She was able to perform in many operas by Wagner and Puccini, gaining great success in *Tosca, Butterfly* and *Turandot*. Her scenic follies in *Cavalleria Rusticana* and *Carmen* have remained proverbial (the Americans went crazy over them): in Bizet's opera Jeritza used to chew on an apple in a deliberately vulgar way during Don Jose's imploring aria, while as Santuzza she would launch the curse "A te la Mala Pasqua" after having rolled down all the stairs of the church.

Elisabeth Rethberg (Lisabeth Sättler; Schwarzenberg, Saxony 1894 – Yorktown Heights, New York 1976) sang from 1915 (when she made her debut in Johann Strauss' *Gypsy Baron* at Dresden) until 1944, stunning the American and Central European audiences with her rich, well-modulated voice, capable of tackling over one hundred roles. Due to the uniformity of her song and her stylistic fidelity she was a divine Aida, Desdemona, Brünnhilde, Mimì, Elisabeth in *Tannhäuser*, Leonora in *La Forza del Destino*, Amelia in *Un Ballo in Maschera*, and also the first to sing in Richard Strauss' *Ägyptische Helena* at Dresden in 1938.

But her performances were sometimes cold, she seemed incapable of transmitting deep emotions to the audience, perhaps because of her majestic stature which made her little inclined to dynamic acting. However, this weakness was amply compensated by her style and the purity of her timbre, characterized by her typical German "r."

The beautiful **Giuseppina Cobelli** (Manerbio, Brescia 1898 – Salò, Brescia 1948) spread the Wagnerian message throughout Italy in the twenties and thirties. She was a wonderful Isolde and Sieglinde but also a superb Fedora, Minnie, Adriana Lecouvreur and the first to perform Respighi's *La Fiamma*.

Régine Crespin (Marseille 1927) studied with Germaine Lubin and performed in a very wide repertoire from Mozart to Wagner. She made her debut in *Lohengrin* (1950) and specialized immediately in roles requiring dramatic vocal qualities (Leonora in *Fidelio*, Kundry, Brünnhilde, Tosca, Fedora, Pizzetti's Fedra, the Marschallin) until, towards the end of her career, she demonstrated a fantastic comic verve (*La Périchole, La Belle Hélène, La Grande-Duchesse de Gerolstein*) and an incredible dramatic intensity which she brought to her noteworthy characterization of the old Mother Superior in Poulenc's *Dialogues of the Carmelites*. During the golden years of her career she presented a brilliant voice and intelligent, psychologically detailed acting.

Elisabeth Rethberg, *German soprano, as Sieglinde in Wagner's* Die Walküre.

Let us look at a list of possibly secondary, but nonetheless important, sopranos active in the German *lirico-spinto* repertory: **Meta Seinemeyer** (Berlin 1895 – Dresden 1929), the unforgettable protagonist of the Verdi revival in Germany who died of leukaemia; **Florence Austral** (Richmond, Australia 1894 – Newcastle, Sydney 1968); **Sophie Sedlmair** (Hannover 1857 – 1939); **Lucie Weidt** (Troppau, Bohemia 1879 – Vienna 1940); **Margarethe Siems** (Breslau 1879 – Dresden 1952), excellent in the R. Strauss repertory; **Florence Easton** (Middlebrough 1884 – New York 1955), who was able to undertake a wide repertory (from Carmen to Brünnhilde) singing a total of eighty-eight different roles; **Rose Pauly** (Rose Pollak; Eperjes 1894 – Tel Aviv 1975), a famous Elektra much loved by Strauss; **Giulia Tess** (Giulia Tessaroli; Verona 1889 – Milan 1976), acclaimed as Salome and Elektra and in the works of Wolf-Ferrari; **Martha Fuchs** (Stuttgart 1898 – 1974); **Nanny Larsén-Todsen** (Hagby, Sweden 1884 – Stockholm 1982); **Elisabeth Ohms** (Arnheim, Holland 1888 – Marquardstein, Bavaria 1974); **Hilde Konetzni** (Vienna 1905 –1980) and her sister **Anny Konetzni** (Ungarisch-Weisskirchen 1902 – Vienna 1968); **Suzanne Juyol** (Paris 1920-1994), famous Isolde and Kundry in France; **Johanna Gadski** (Anklam, Pomerania

1872 – Berlin 1932); the above-mentioned **Germaine Lubin**; **Viorica Ursuleac** (Czernowitz, Romania 1894 – Ehrwald, the Tryol 1985), favored by Strauss, who conducted her many times; **Helen Traubel** (St. Louis 1898 – Santa Monica, California 1972), star of the American theaters and famous also in operetta; **Maria Reining** (Vienna 1903 – London 1991); **Tiana Lemnitz** (Metz 1897 – Berlin 1994), who had a vast repertory thanks to her perfect technique; **Sylvia Fisher** (Melbourne 1910), who was active at Covent Garden from 1949 until 1958, especially in her favorite roles of the Marschallin, Leonora in *Fidelio*, and Sieglinde. Closer to our times there are **Ingrid Bjöner** (Kraakstad, Norway 1928); **Gré Brouwenstijn** (Den Helder, Holland 1915 – Amsterdam 1999); **Catarina Ligendza** (Stockholm 1937); **Helga Dernesch** (Vienna 1939); **Hildegard Behrens** (Varel, Oldenburg 1946); **Jeanine Altmeyer** (Pasadena, California 1948); and **Marita Napier** (Johannesburg, South Africa 1939);

Giuseppina Cobelli *made her debut in 1924, at Piacenza, in* La Gioconda; *but her career really took off the next year when she sang Sieglinde at La Scala. Wagner and other modern composers were the strong point in her repertoire. She was the first to sing* La Fiamma, *by Respighi, and* La Notte di Zoraima, *by Montemezzi.*
(Historic Archives of the Pome Opera Theater)

Dame Josephine Barstow (Sheffield 1940), who has sung regularly at Covent Garden since 1969, and also performs in the contemporary English repertoire; **Elizabeth Connell** (Johannesburg 1946), who is known especially for her performances of Lady Macbeth, and Ortrude (*Lohengrin*); **Rita Hunter** (Wallasey 1933), who studied with Eva Turner and was memorable for the extraordinary power and incisiveness of her voice. During the nineties, Wagner operas, or at least the most important productions, have brought into the public eye both **Deborah Polaski** (1949), especially good in the roles of Kundry and Isolde, although she has proved a far better actress than singer, and especially **Waltraut Meyer** (Braunschweig 1954), splendid Sieglinde and Leonore in *Fidelio*.

The Dramatic Sopranos of the Twentieth Century

Top of the list of famous twentieth-century dramatic sopranos is **Olive Fremstad** (Olivia Rundquist; Stockholm 1868 – Irvington, New York 1951). She made her debut as a contralto in 1895 (Azucena at Cologne), and became a soprano in 1903 after her Sieglinde in *Die Walküre* at the Metropolitan. She was one of the most applauded performers of Isolde, due to the metallic brilliance of her high notes and her dramatic impetus. At the end of her farewell

Régine Crespin, one of the most important French opera singers of the twentieth century.

performance (*Lohengrin* at the Met in 1914) she received nineteen curtain calls and over twenty minutes of applause.

Another wonderful Isolde, Kundry, Brünnhilde and Sieglinde was **Melanie Kurt** (Vienna 1880 – New York 1941), who made her debut as a singer in 1902 after having begun her artistic career as a pianist.

Anna Mildenburg-Bahr (Vienna 1872-1947) and **Gertrude Kappel** (Halle 1884 – Munich 1971) both had piercing high notes, robust central and lower registers, great temperaments and stage presence, in other words two veritable Wagner virtuosi. The latter was also an exceptional Elektra and Marschallin during the two decades from 1910 to 1930.

"A veritable vocal hurricane" is the only way to describe **Félia Litvinne** (St. Petersburg 1866 – Paris 1936), the famous Wagnerian soprano of French theaters, in which she was the first to perform Isolde and Brünnhilde in the *Ring*. Her recordings, alas, do not give the right idea of what one of the most powerful and incisive voices of the time must really have been like. They do, however, bring to light some of her blatant stylistic shortcomings (her "Ho-jo-to-ho" is proof). Showing equally prestigious vocal qualities, but far better style was **Maria Müller** (Theresienstadt, Bohemia 1898 – Bayreuth 1958), who had smooth extension, equal in each note, with lightning-like high notes, and a magnificent consistency. From 1930 until 1944 she was a cornerstone of the Bayreuth "Temple".

Frieda Leider (Berlin 1888-1975) had very few rivals in parts such as Brünnhilde or Isolde during the period stretching between the two wars. Her full, warm and luminescent voice was also flexible enough to allow her to sing operas such as *Don Giovanni*, *Trovatore*, *Aida* and *Tosca*, all parallel with her Wagnerian repertoire.

The artistic story of **Kirsten Flagstad** (Hamar, Oslo 1895 – Oslo 1962) was exceptionally long and triumphant. Her debut was in 1913 in Albert's *Tiefland*, while her farewell was given in December 1953, in Oslo. In 1955, her vocal characteristics still intact, Flagstad went on a long concert tour and recorded Gluck's *Alceste* for the B.B.C. It would be difficult to find any other female singer in the history of opera who had such a powerful and incisive voice, but one which was always contained within the limits of an absolutely secure technique. The most stunning thing about this operatic "Berta Krupp" (as she was defined by Riemens) was her fluidity of style and the uniformity of her registers, which persisted through the years despite the fact that she constantly ran the risks involved in tackling too grueling a repertory.

Isolde, Brünnhilde, Leonora in *Fidelio*, Kundry, Elsa and Elisabeth are roles which are all associated with Flagstad, who often performed together with Melchior and Svanholm.

Gina Cigna (Angers 1900 – Milan 2001) was on stage from 1927 until 1947, but still amazing for her style and vocal condition in some chamber arias recorded towards the end of the seventies. She was *Gioconda*, *Norma* and *Turandot* par excellence, imposing powerful and silvery sounds on a merciless tessitura.

Due to her technical and stylistic virtues she could include in her repertoire Bellini's *La Straniera*, Donizetti's *Lucrezia Borgia*, Gluck's *Alceste* and Monteverdi's *Incoronazione di Poppea*, even if this last role may very well have made a philologist's hair curl.

Great fame as a *lirico-spinto* soprano was gained by **Zinka Milanov** (Zagreb 1906 – New York 1989), exceptional in the operas of Verdi

An imposing stance taken by **Olive Fremstad**, a powerful and spirited Brünnhilde.

Helen Traubel, as Brünnhilde in Wagner's Götterdämmerung. After Flagstad left the Met in 1941, she was regarded as its leading Wagner soprano. In 1953 she stopped singing there because the director, Rudolf Bing, objected to her performing also in night clubs.

(*Trovatore*, *Forza del Destino*, *Ballo in Maschera*, *Aida*) and in *Gioconda*, *Tosca*, *Fanciulla del West*, and even in Wagner (Sieglinde) and Richard Strauss (the Marschallin). After her debut at Lubiana in 1927, she sang at Zagreb from 1928 until 1935, when she moved to Prague and then the New York Metropolitan, where she became uncontested diva over the following twenty years. Her voice was extraordinarily robust and penetrating, technically solid enough to resolve Verdi's many dynamic indications (legato singing, *pianissimi*, *smorzandi*, *rinforzandi*). However, during the fifties her voice became somewhat strained, with an inevitable loss of flexibility.

Marjorie Lawrence (Dean's March, Melbourne 1909 – Little Rock, Arkansas 1979) was a divine Wagner singer, intense and shining as Brünnhilde, Elisabeth in *Tannhaüser*, *Tosca* and *Thaïs*. Struck by poliomyelitis in 1941, she had to abandon the stage, but continued to sing oratorio. However, she did perform a much-acclaimed *Elektra* in Chicago in 1947 in concert form.

The heir of Flagstad towards the end of the sixties was **Astrid Varnay** (Stockholm 1918), gifted with a magnificent voice but not sustained by a sufficiently solid technique. From 1941, the year of her debut at the Metropolitan as Sieglinde, until half way through the sixties, she relentlessly sang all the most difficult Wag-

Frieda Leider began at Halle in 1915, singing Venus in Tannhäuser. She continued to sing until the forties, having a repertoire ranging from Wagner, Strauss and Verdi to 18th century works such as Armida and Don Giovanni. (Historic Archives of the Rome Opera Theater. Photo: Pieperhoff)

nerian roles, especially Brünnhilde. Then her voice began to deteriorate: her high notes wobbled, the various registers split apart and her beautiful vocal polish tarnished completely.

After twenty years of superb Strauss characterizations (Clytemnestra, Herodias and the Nurse in *Die Frau ohne Schatten*) Varnay sang tiny parts such as Mamma Lucia in *Cavalleria* in German theaters, but of those high notes which had seemed like golden comets there remained only the slightest, most pitiful shadow.

Birgit Nilsson (West Karup, Sweden 1918) had, in contrast to Varnay, great control over her voice, managing to hurl her vocal bolts of lightning up until 1979-80 in some memorable performances of *Elektra* and *Die Frau ohne Schatten* at the Vienna State Opera. Because of her immense vocal possibilities, Nilsson was able to include all the most complex Wagner and Strauss roles in her repertoire as well as *Tosca, Aida, Don Giovanni, Macbeth, Fidelio, Oberon, Fanciulla del West* and, above all, her legendary *Turandot*.

In the part of the Ice Princess the Swedish artist launched her incredible vocal spears in theaters all over the world, often singing together with Franco Corelli.

Birgit made her debut in Stockholm as Agathe in C.M. von Weber's *Freischutz*. Her

career continued in Swedish theaters where she sang her favorite operas: *Macbeth, Tannhaüser, The Flying Dutchman* and *Don Giovanni*. It was her Elsa in a 1953 *Lohengrin* at Bayreuth that launched her to international fame. Audiences and critics alike were stunned by her powerful voice and penetrating high notes, and further amazed to note the ease with which this voice adapted to even the most delicate *mezzevoci*. Nilsson sang frequently at Covent Garden from 1957 onwards, but her strongest ties were with the Metropolitan (1959-1975) and the Vienna Staatsoper, where she performed until 1982.

Martha Mödl (Nuremberg 1912 – Stuttgart 2001), after making a late debut as Cherubino in *The Marriage of Figaro* in 1942 at Remscheid, alternated mezzo-soprano and dramatic soprano parts throughout her career. She possessed a fine voice which was particularly extended and of ambiguous color, somewhat steely, and suited especially to fiendish characters (Lady Macbeth, Clytemnestra in *Elektra*, and Kundry). She sang in all the most important theaters world-wide, gaining great acclaim as Isolde for her subtle, poignant rendering, as Brünnhilde, for the variety of her vocal and stage performance and as Leonora in *Fidelio*. But she was showing signs of vocal strain and harshness as early as 1955.

Even though she lost confidence in the high register, Mödl gained even greater acting skill as time went by, continuing to grace the stage in Germany and to gather widespread applause.

Even fifty years after her debut, she made frequent appearances in the part of the Mother in Fortner's *Bluthochzeit* and in some contemporary works, preferably in her hometown theater in Nuremberg. In 1989 she performed the role of the Countess in the *Queen of Spades,* much to everyone's amazement.

One of the most beautiful and sensual Salome's of the twentieth century was **Ljuba Welitsch,** whose real name was Ljuba Velickova (Borissova 1913 – Vienna 1996). During her golden years, between 1936 and 1950, she boasted a pure but penetrating voice, with brilliant high notes, like bolts of lightning, and an acting skill worthy of a true professional: a lioness of the stage.

She sang Donna Anna, Butterfly, Tosca, Aida, Amelia; but her favorite, and the public's favorite too, was the perilous role of Salome. She studied it with Richard Strauss himself in 1944. The final scene, as demonstrated by her recordings of the role (especially the live one conducted by Fritz Reiner), took on a truly apocalyptic aspect when performed by the Austrian redhead. Her high "Ich habe deinen Mund gekusst" (I have kissed your mouth) would triumph radiantly over the storming orchestra. It expressed both the frenzy of victory and the realization of her own evildoing.

Welitsch continued to sing small parts at the Vienna Staatsoper until the beginning of the eighties.

We must include in our list of the greatest Wagnerian sopranos the powerful and resonant voices of **Gertrud Grob Prandl** (Vienna 1917-1995), who sang during the forties and fifties and was a wonderful Isolde, Leonora and Turandot; **Amy Shuard** (London 1924 – 1975), one of the most impressive voices heard at Covent Garden between 1954 and 1974, who was famous as Turandot, Aida, Amelia, Santuzza, Brünnhilde, Elektra, and Jenufa; **Leonie Rysanek** (Vienna 1926 – 1998), who made her debut at Innsbruck in 1949 and was still singing in Vienna and American opera theaters after forty-five years, thanks to the force and purity of her high notes, which easily dominated the Wagner and Strauss orchestras. Rysanek also achieved great success in character roles, performed with expressive intensity: Clytemnestra, Herodias, Kostelnicka (*Jenufa*), Kabanikha (*Katya Kabanova*), the Countess (*The Queen of*

The riddle scene of Turandot. The Princess is **Birgit Nilsson**. At her side an unusual Calaf, **Carlo Bergonzi**. This photo was taken during a performance in Naples in 1976. (Historic Archives of the Teatro San Carlo of Naples. Photo: Troncone)

Marjorie Lawrence, Australian soprano. She was notably athletic, riding her horse into the scenic flames when performing Brünnhilde in Götterdämmerung.

The mighty **Astrid Varnay** captured in a dramatic moment. She sings here the part of Herodias in Richard Strauss's Salome at Nuremberg in 1973. (Historic Archives of the Opera Theater of Nuremberg. Photo: Bischof and Broel OHG)

A dramatic expression by **Martha Mödl** *as Maria in Berg's* Wozzek *(Dusseldoff, 1947). She was an excellent actress as well as a singer of sound vocal ability.*

The splendid Salome of **Gwyneth Jones,** *engrossed in the dance of the seven veils. (Giandonato Crico Collection)*

Ljuba Welitsch *here as Butterfly, a role in which she enchanted the public with her penetrating high register, but even more so with her physical beauty – blue eyes, fiery red hair, and sensuous movements.*

Spades). The German **Inge Borkh** (Mannheim 1917) was a torrential voice for all the most difficult roles in the German repertory. She had a soft spot for *Elektra* and *Salome*, which she tackled with fiery vocal temperament. **Dame Gwyneth Jones** (Pontypool, Wales 1936) began as a contralto but became a dramatic soprano in 1964 and specialized in the parts of Brünnhilde, Senta, Kundry, Turandot, and, above all, Salome, where her perfect interpretation was helped by her superb figure. Her Elektra was imposing. **Eva Marton** (Budapest 1943) has been the rival of Ghena Dimitrova for many years in the roles of Turandot, Tosca, Aida; but she is also active in the Strauss repertory.

The dramatic soprano category has been suffering a serious crisis, only partially compensated by the imposing vocal presence of **Ghena Dimitrova** (Pleven, Bulgaria 1941). Her training took place in her homeland and she began her climb to fame in the Central European theaters during the sixties, improving year by year. Initially her voice seemed like a huge machine for producing high notes, with a few problems in the *passaggio* and in more whispered singing. But a strict self discipline and much study made her voice more homogeneous and pliable, capable of bending to all the subtleties required by scores such as *Turandot, Nabucco, Tosca, Ballo in Maschera, Macbeth* and *Don Carlos*.

In this last Verdi opera, Dimitrova has given a particularly eloquent rendition of the character of Elizabeth, noble and melancholy, with optimum use of her vocal qualities and subtle undertones of chiaroscuro.

CALLAS AND THE BELCANTO DIVAS

What can be described as "the Callas era" began in the summer of 1947 when, at the Verona Arena, there was a new production of *Gioconda*, featuring a young soprano making her debut in Italy: **Maria Callas** (Mary Anne Kalogeropoulos; New York 1923 – Paris 1977).

Right from that very first evening her unusual vocal structure and exceptional performing gifts were obvious. Callas' voice was divided into three well-defined registers, ranging from the corpulent low notes of the mezzo-soprano (she reached low a´) up to the high notes of a coloratura soprano (in Proch's *Variazioni* she reached f´´´), all of which was held together by a refined technical knowledge and by the varied, imaginative and authentic phrasing of a virtuoso.

With her numerous "voices" Callas had a virtually unlimited repertoire, recalling the famous divas of the eighteenth and nineteenth centuries. She could resurrect Rossini's *Armida* (Florence 1952) with its pyrotechnical virtuosity, or create grand classical figures such as Medea, Norma, Giulia (*Vestale*), divining the true tragic accent. Or yet again she could overcome all the difficulties of parts once entrusted to the *soprano drammatico di agilità*, such as Lady Macbeth, Elena (*Vespri Siciliani*), Amina, Violetta, Imogene (*Pirata*) and Lucia.

Combined with her vocal gifts, which not everyone understood and appreciated, Callas offered an unequalled acting and scenic skill: her gestures, her visual expression, every tiny movement contributed to her portrayal of the character, from the evil Lady Macbeth to the neurotic Violetta, from Norma's noble grandeur (her "Teneri figli" is unforgettable) to Abigaille's wild arrogance, and then to her wonderful Tosca, so real and feminine.

Callas was also famous for the unexpected "gifts" with which she would surprise the audience: at the end of the second act of *Aida* in Mexico City in 1951 she launched a fantastic high e´´´ flat that was not part of the score.

January 8, 1953. *Maria Callas* before the diet: a gorgeous doll wrapped in metres and metres of spotted taffeta, with the tenor **Francesco Albanese**, in the second act of Traviata. The sublime artist had a unique way of expressing phrases such as "Dite alla giovane," "Alfredo, Alfredo, di questo core," "Teneste la promessa…" (Historic Archives of La Fenice Theater, Venice)

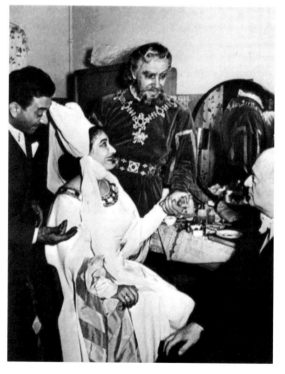

The 1951 staging of Vespri Siciliani in Florence, with conducting by Erich Kleiber (at right in the photo), and with **Maria Callas**, the baritone **Mascherini** (standing), and the tenor **Kokolios**. It was a performance of considerable importance, despite the numerous cuts in the score. (Historic Archives of the Teatro Comunale of Florence)

*The legendary Armida created in Florence in 1952 by **Maria Callas**. The Rossini opera proposed by Francesco Siciliani, artistic director of the Florence May Festival, and by Maestro Serafin, was greeted with general scepticism. Thanks to the extraordinary presence of the Greek artist, in striking vocal form, the choice fired the public's enthusiasm. With scenes and costumes by Alberto Savinio, conducted by Serafin, the performance featured tenors such as Filippeschi, Raimondi and Albanese. All contributed to the triumphal and historical success of that evening. (Historic Archives of the Teatro Comunale of Florence)*

Her perfect voice placement in the facial mask allowed her full control of the high register and super-high register as well as an extremely precise and beautiful legato.

Much has been said about the precocious deterioration of Maria Callas' voice; in reality, the Greek artist had twenty years of fabulous success, having made her debut in *Cavalleria Rusticana* in Athens in 1938, and she possessed all her best vocal prerogatives until 1958, the year in which her real decline began. Her voice not only suffered from her much-famed diet, it was also strained by the arduous repertoire she had tackled for two decades. She lost the homogeneous quality of her voice which became relentlessly more wobbly in the high register. Nonetheless, her myth was not at all damaged. Her last *Norma* at the Paris Opera in May 1965 and her triumphal concerts with Giuseppe Di Stefano in 1973-75 were acclaimed by delirious ovations, which shows that the public (more than some critics) had understood the unequalled greatness of this last diva.

The advent of Callas determined the reproposal of many belcanto operas which had been forgotten in the bottom drawer during the *verismo* boom, and a return to a more correct approach to interpretation.

Joan Sutherland: the Australian Nightingale

The foremost amongst Callas's successors was **Dame Joan Sutherland** (Point Piper, Sydney 1926). She was at the center of the rediscovery and renaissance of the great Baroque operatic repertory (with Handel in the lead) and was also a divine belcanto singer of early romantic operas (Bellini, Donizetti).

Her debut was in Henry Purcell's *Dido and Aeneas* in 1947, but she was really launched in 1957 with a triumphant performance of Handel's *Alcina* at the London Opera Society. Sutherland's voice was not particularly attractive in timbre (if you exclude her radiant high register), but she was armed with an awe-inspiring technique: long breaths, tight trills of exceptional consistency, high notes (up to e‴) of rare brilliance, a taste for variations and expressive modulations. These were characteristics that made her ideal for roles such as Lucia, Amina, Gilda, Elvira in *Puritani*, Norma, Alcina, Lucrezia Borgia and Semiramide, at last liberated from the chirpings of the coloratura sopranos and reclaimed by the *soprano drammatico di agilità*.

Thanks to the power of her voice and her technique, Sutherland was able to perform Desdemona (Verdi's *Otello*), Eva in *The Mastersingers of Nuremberg*, and even Adriana

Maria Callas sings "Teneri figli" from Norma. *The famous diet has already had its effect, giving the singer an enviable silhouette. We are in the second half of the fifties and Callas is already a living legend. During a procession for Carnival in Switzerland there were dozens and dozens of people masquerading as Maria Callas. (Historic Archives of the Rome Opera Theater Photo: Reale)*

Medea, June 22, 1955. An expression typical of **Callas***, a singer capable of revealing all the depth of a character with a look or a slight inflexion of the voice. (Historic Archives of the Rome Opera Theater Photo: Oscar Savio)*

January 15, 1953. **Maria Callas** *and* **Francesco Albanese** *together for Traviata. Few know that during a concert in Greece, in the forties, Maria Callas sang a passage from Verdi's Otello, and immediately after (prophetically anticipating the Rossini revival) she sang a scene from Rossini's. The strange thing was that the young singer did not perform in Rossini's opera as Desdemona but as Otello. For the "Willow Song" by Verdi she wore a white dress, whilst for the part "en travesti" she wrapped herself in a large red cloak. (Historic Archives of the Rome Opera Theater Photo: Oscar Savio)*

Lecouvreur. On record she has created a bel-canto-style version of *Trovatore*, an astral *Turandot* and a *Suor Angelica* that is perhaps a little too cold and measured.

Forty years after her debut, Sutherland still possessed an enviable voice, to the point of being able to keep almost all of her favorite roles in her repertoire (from Norma to Semiramide), often performing together with Marilyn Horne. Rome audiences will never forget her memorable performance in *Lucrezia Borgia* in May 1980, highlighted by a high e''' flat as dazzling as a comet.

In 1990, after a final series of performances of *Les Huguenots* in Sydney, Sutherland retired from the stage. She sometimes attends singing competitions and also accompanies her conductor husband on tour. She was involved in a controversy over Pavarotti ("Luciano should retire"), after the "tenorissimo's" appearance in *Elisir d'Amore* at San Carlo in December 1998.

Queen Leyla

Leyla Gencer (Istanbul 1927) was another belcanto specialist, interpreting many impor-

The young **Sutherland** in the costume of the sorceress, Alcina. Handel's opera was performed in Venice during the 1959-60 season. Due to her particular singing technique, the Australian artist succeeded in obtaining mysterious echo effects in the difficult aria "Tornami a vagheggiar," (Historic Archives of La Fenice Theater, Venice)

Joan Sutherland.

tant Donizetti operas (*Roberto Devereux, Caterina Cornaro, Maria Stuarda, Belisario,* and *Les Martyrs*). She had a wide repertoire, including Gilda, Lucia, Violetta, Elvira, Lucrezia in *I Due Foscari*, Aida, Leonora (*Trovatore* and *Forza del Destino*), Elisabetta (by Rossini), Liù, Suor Angelica, Odabella, Donna Anna, and many, many others, including her satanic Lady Macbeth.

Her best years were from 1950 to 1970, years in which she could reach high e''' flat, alternate different shadings, hold golden *filatura*, overcome with ease *bravura* variations, execute a phrasing that followed the text perfectly and had great dramatic expression. An exceptional example is her furious "Figlia impura di Bolena" in *Maria Stuarda*. These characteristics belonged to a voice which was neither powerful nor beautiful in the classical sense, but rendered flexible by constant study. More recently Gencer has dedicated herself mainly to concert activity, very successfully. Regrettably, by virtue

The duet, Norma-Adalgisa, in the second act of Bellini's opera. Singing are the soprano **Joan Sutherland** and the mezzo-soprano **Margareta Elkins**. In the role of the Druid priestess Sutherland has restored a belcanto of absolute purity, typical of nineteenth century prima donnas. (Archives of the Australian Opera. Photo: W. Mosely)

We are in her dressing room at the Metropolitan Opera in 1964 and **Joan Sutherland** is preparing for Lucia di Lammermoor, an opera of which she has been the undisputed star for over twenty-five years. (Photo: Ermete Marzoni)

"Or tutti sorgete, ministri infernali." A demonic Lady Macbeth, **Leyla Gencer** has represented the difficult Verdi character better than any other soprano since Callas. The photo comes from a performance on April 8, 1969 at the Rome Opera, with Bruno Bartoletti conducting and De Lullo directing, scenes by Pizzi. (Historic Archives of the Rome Opera Theater)

This is a historical photo. It depicts **Anton Dermota** during the interval of The Magic Flute at the Vienna Opera which went on stage on the January 24, 1982. On that occasion Dermota sang the role of Tamino, which he had been singing for over thinty years, for the last time. (Photo: G. Zerbes. Vienna)

On the preceding page: **Luciano Pavarotti**, without doubt the most famous tenor on the current world opera scene. Here he sings in Tosca with **Raina Kabaivanska**, at the Rome Opera Theater 1990.

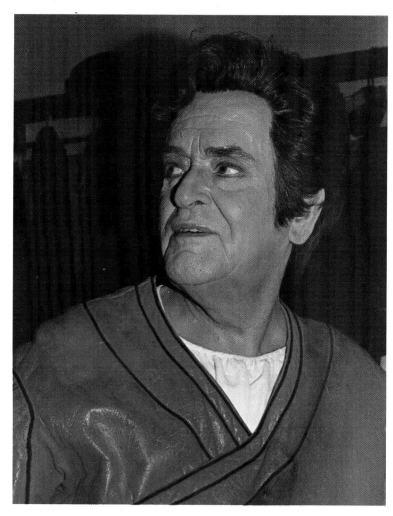

Carreras, yes or no? On one hand his passion and incomparable polish, on the other forced high notes and little interpretative imagination. The public is divided over the Spanish tenor as it was years ago over Di Stefano. In the photo are **José Carreras** and **Galia Savova** during Tosca at Ravenna, 1981.

"An actor who sings, rather than a singer who acts", is the motto of **José Cura** (here, in another scene from Aida, 1999), who pays more attention to the development of an extremely meticulous stage presence than to the evolution of a method of singing that can hardly be called orthodox. (Fondazione Arena di Verona. Photo: Gianfranco Fainello)

Leo Nucci with **Placido Domingo** in I Pagliacci (1995). Years of experience have guaranteed Nucci a knowledge of his profession that few can boast, and which have taught him a thousand theatrical stratagems to overcome virtually any emergency situation. (Fondazione Arena di Verona. Photo: Gianfranco Fainello)

Veriano Luchetti *in one of his favorite roles: that of Macduff*
in Verdi's opera, Macbeth.
(Photo: L. Romano, Archives of the San Carlo Theater, Naples)

*Another picture of **Cecilia Gasdia** and **Andrea Bocelli** in L'Amico Fritz (2001). Astute and musically well-prepared, Gasdia has a wide repertoire ranging from Monteverdi, Vivaldi, Handel, Rossini, Mozart, Bellini and Donizetti to Verdi, Mascagni and Puccini. (Fondazione Arena di Verona. Photo: Gianfranco Fainello)*

__Viorica Cortez__ (Carmen) and __Veriano Luchetti__ (Don José) at the Arena of Verona. (Photo: Passerini)

Rockwell Blake and
Leo Nucci in Il Barbiere
di Siviglia *at Modena. The
American tenor always
performs the difficult aria
"Cessa di piu resistere" in
the finale, which is usually
cut. (Photo: Arletti)*

Francisco Araiza in a
1985 version of Traviata
in Houston.

Salvatore Licitra again in Il Trovatore (2001).
Licitra made a striking debut in 1998 at the Verona
Arena in Ballo in Maschera, for which he was hailed
as a "new Pavarotti". (Fondazione Arena di Verona.
Photo: Gianfranco Fainello)

Under the austere tunic of Ferrando in Donizetti's La Favorita, **Alfredo Kraus** sings the aria "Spirto gentil" which contains a famous, frightening high c´´. However, as we well know, the tenor from the Canary Isles did not fear the top of the pentagram: we need only listen to how he launched his high c´´ and d´´ 's with bravura.

Kraus, looking like Prince Charming from a fairy tale. Actually, the elegance and composure of the famous tenor feared very few comparisons in the twentieth century.

The three great tenors — **Pavarotti**, **Carreras** and **Domingo** — on stage together in a concert destined to make history in the annals of opera; at the Terme di Caracalla in Rome, July 1990. (Photo: C.M. Falsini)

Mario Del Monaco had the habit of designing his own magnificent costumes for Otello. He was also known for his love of fur coats, luxury cars, and beautiful women. A real "divo".

There is no doubt about *Placido Domingo*'s ability as an actor, nor his complete command of the stage. He is an artist of rare musicality and intelligence; however, he has never resolved certain technical problems. Here we see him in his costume for Andrea Chénier during a production at Vienna in May 1981.

Nicola Martinucci (Calaf) and
Cecilia Gasdia (Liù) in Verona,
during one of the many Turandot
performances of the Italian tenor.
Martinucci is known for his
penetrating voice and his reliability in
some of the most difficult repertories.
(Photo: G. Passerini)

Giuseppe Giacomini as Dick
Johnson in The Girl of the Golden
West. After a difficult beginning and
some inconsistent results, Giacomini
has gained a position as one of the
best spinto tenors of his generation.
(Photo: De Rota)

Mario Del Monaco *as Andrea Chénier. (Photo. Sedqe Le Planq)*

*A scene from the film of Otello, produced by Canon, with the direction of Zeffirelli. Otello (**Domingo**) tenderly embraces Desdemona (**Katia Ricciarelli**) during the duet "Già nella notte densa." (Photo: I.O. Ronald)*

Peter Dvorsky *as Edgardo in a film version of* Lucia di Lammermoor *in 1983. The Czechoslovakian tenor has distinguished himself over the last years as an excellent interpreter of lyric roles, with a few excursions into* lirico-spinto *parts (Manon Lescaut, Adriana Lecouvreur, and even Forza del Destino and Aida).*

Placido Domingo
during the "Esultate."
Domingo has removed
the verist encrustations
that had covered the
difficult part of the Moor
for over a century, and
high-lighted the lyrical
aspect. However, the
Spanish tenor lacks
confidence on the high
notes – the ace card for
any self-respecting
Otello. (Otello. Direction,
F. Zeffirelli; Production,
Canon. Photo: P. Ronald)

José Carreras in the
role of Radames (Aida,
1995). By virtue of his
silken timbre and clear
enunciation, this Spanish
tenor has often been
compared with Giuseppe
Di Stefano (Ente Lirico
Arena di Verona. Photo:
Gianfranco Fainello)

Graziella Sciutti in the Rossini role of Donna Fiorilla in Turco in Italia. *(Giandonato Crico Collection)*

*Dallas, 1982, **Ruth Welting** in the "Mad Scene" of Lucia di Lammermoor. (Photo: H Kuper)*

Raina Kabaivanska *in* Butterfly, *a favorite opera of the Bulgarian singer, who, however, always claims that the definitions of Verist Singer or Puccini Singer are too limiting. In her repertory, in fact, are Donizetti's* Fausta, *Spontini's* La Vestale, *and Verdi's* I Vespri Siciliani.

The beautiful **Katia Ricciarelli** (Desdemona) in the second act of the film Otello, directed by Franco Zeffirelli and produced by Cannon.

Sparkling eyes, silk-ribboned bonnet, parasol: **Editha Gruberova** is an ideal Zerbinetta, performing often in Vienna and Salzburg. In the Mozart arias she reaches g´´, singing the highest notes without any apparent effort.

Gruberova is an astral Queen of the Night in a version of Magic Flute at Vienna in 1977.

The exquisite, mature femininity of **Sena Jurinac**, for over thirty-five years a mainstay of the Vienna Opera (Staatsoper). This is a portrait of her in one of the roles played in her later years – the Marschallin in Der Rosenkavalier. (Photo: Fayer)

The ritual of the autograph: **Gwyneth Jones**, a highly esteemed Wagner and Strauss singer, photographed in her dressing room after a concert at the RAI in Rome. (Photo: Giandonato Crico)

After a career lasting more than forty years, **Leonie Rysanek** was still an extraordinary interpreter of dramatic roles. The photo portrays her in the role of Chrysothemis in Richard Strauss' opera Elektra. Rysanek sang the main role for a film version, whilst later in her career she also sang Clytemnestra. (Photo: Dresse)

Tosca is the character most closely identified with **Raina Kabaivanska**. She endows this role with a complete emotional participation so irresistible that the audience bursts into spontaneous applause even after a simple phrase such as "Io piango" (I cry) in Act I. In Act II Raina renders "Vissi d'arte" in the authentic belcanto tradition, producing extraordinary emotional shadings without even glancing at the orchestra conductor.

Talented **Lella Cuberli** in Handel's Orlando at La Fenice Theater, Venice, in 1985. Miss Cuberli has always shown a stylistic authority and phrasing which have made her indispensable in the belcanto renaissance (operas by Handel, Rossini, the comic Neapolitan works, and even Bellini and Donizetti). (Historic Archives of La Fenice Theater of Venice)

At the end of her recital at the Teatro Malibran at Venice in 1981, **Joan Sutherland** smiles at the well-deserved applause. The first lessons of the great soprano were with her mother, an ex-mezzo who had studied with a student of Matilde Marchesi, legendary teacher of Melba, Eames and Calvé. (Giandonato Crico Collection)

Beverly Sills, an elegant Norina in Don Pasquale by Donizetti. When she retired fom the stage in 1980, she had over seventy different roles in her repertoire, which she performed using an almost exaggerated belcanto style. Her "madness" in Lucia was a firework display which found a worthy competitor only in Joan Sutherland. The Assedio di Corinto at an excited La Scala in 1969 is considered a milestone in the history of Rossini interpretations. As for the mythical version of Donizetti's Roberto Devereux at the New York City Opera, the audience were more than once on their feet during the performance, giving Sills an ovation which few of her predecessors had enjoyed. (Metropolitan Opera Guild. Collection Oreste Musella)

*After the tension of the performance **Lucia Popp** has a happy smile for her admirers. A Mozart and Strauss specialist, she was particularly loved by the Vienna Opera public. (Photo: Giandonato Crico)*

Kiri Te Kanawa *in one of her most famous roles; Arabella, by Richard Strauss. The nickname "Arabellissima" was coined for Lisa Della Casa but has been revived to refer to Kiri. (Giandonato Crico Collection)*

*The unmatched elegance of **Elizabeth Schwarzkopf** in the role of the Countess in Capriccio by Richard Strauss. (Photo: Fayer, Vienna)*

Montserrat Caballé and **José Carreras** in Tosca, Ravenna, 1981.

*A famous Lucia: **June Anderson**, who is also successfully involved in the revival of Rossini's serious operas. (Photo: Tabocchini)*

*On the opposite page: **Ghena Dimitrova** during Turandot presented at the San Carlo Opera in Naples. (Historic Archives of the San Carlo Theater, Naples)*

__Eva Marton__ in the candid gown of Brünnhilde. Besides her Wagnerian and Strauss repertoire, Marton sings many Puccini and verist roles. (Giandonato Crico Collection)

Agnes Baltsa and **Thomas Allen** in
Il Barbiere di Siviglia *(Photo: C. Barda)*

Renato Bruson with **Jeanine Altmeyer** in Verdi's Macbeth, *Bruson's favorite role. It is the scene of the appearance*
of Banquo's ghost. (Historic Archives of the San Carlo Theater of Naples. Photo: L. Romano)

Leyla Gencer looking extremely elegant in her costume for the opera Prova di un'Opera Seria by Gnecco, which she performed at La Fenice in Venice. It was her last operatic appearance. It is an opera well-suited to Gencer, an artist who is at once ironic and intelligent, ever-ready to criticize her fellow singers, even the most famous. (Historic Archives of La Fenice Theater, Venice)

Among the many roles interpreted by Caballé there is also Armida, an opera by Gluck, requiring an enormous commitment in acting and in expressive declamation.

The Hungarian soprano, **Eva Marton** as Turandot. She and the Bulgarian soprano **Ghena Dimitrova** have been the best interpreters of this role. (Oreste Musella Collection)

Tosca lost in prayer. **Montserrat Caballé** particularly loves this character, even if her vocal style is far from that required for the verist repertory Her "Vissi d'arte", for example, sung completely in a heavenly pianissimo, lacked the internal fire of Tebaldi, Callas, Olivero and Kabaivanska.

Sesto Bruscantini (Falstaff) amiably courts Raina Kabaivanska (Alice) during a staging of the Verdi masterpiece in Naples. Despite his intelligent and refined interpretation of the chubby knight, the baritone has had few opportunities to perform it. (Historic Archives of the San Carlo Theater of Naples. Photo: L. Romano)

The role of Ford in Falstaff allies perfectly with the vocality of Leo Nucci. After a long apprenticeship, this likeable singer is now established world-wide. (Historic Archives of the San Carlo Opera Theater of Naples. Photo. L. Romano)

The favorite opera of **Lucia Valentini-Terrani** was Cenerentola, performed in all the world's major opera houses. One of the most interesting and amusing productions is that by Ponnelle. (Historic Archives of the Teatro Comunale of Bologna)

*The intensely dramatic expression of **Fiorenza Cossotto** in the role of Azucena, sung for over twenty-five years in all the most important theaters. (Photo: A. Tabocchini)*

Isabella (**Marilyn Horne**) and her "boys" in L'Italiana in Algeri by Rossini, for years her favorite role. (Historic Archives of La Fenice Theater, Venice. Photo: G. Ariciand M.E. Smith)

On the opposite page: **Renato Bruson** in Nabucco (2000). The ace up Bruson's sleeve, so to speak, is his noble, measured emission, his mezzevoci, impeccable legato and his refusal to overact or play to the gallery. (Fondazione Arena di Verona. Photo: Gianfranco Fainello)

Piero Cappuccilli sings Nabucco at the Teatro Ducale at Parma, the Regio being closed for restoration. Almost all this Trieste baritone's greatest colleagues recognise that he is a master of breathing technique. (Historic Archives of the Teatro Regio of Parma. Photo: Montacchini)

Giuseppe Taddei. Thanks to his strong ties with Austria and his interpretative gifts, Taddei has linked his name to many, many Mozart performances, thus holding high the Italian flag in this repertory, with the help of Sesto Bruscantini and Rolando Panerai.

Cecilia Bartoli (Rosina) and *Alfonso Antoniozzi* (Don Bartolo) in Il Barbiere di Siviglia. (Photo A. Arletti)

Ruggero Raimondi in Il Barbiere di Siviglia (1996). This bass-baritone cuts an elegant figure on stage and participates in the drama with the passion and virtuosity of a great movie star. (Fondazione Arena di Verona. Photo: Gianfranco Fainello)

A group photo of Italiana in Algeri *put on at Venice: from the right* **Domenico Trimarchi** *(Taddeo),* **Samuel Ramey** *(***Mustafa***) and* **Marilyn Horne** *(Isabella). (Historic Archives of La Fenice Theater, Venice. Photo: G. Arici and M. E. Smith)*

The 1982-83 season. It is the climax of Rossini's Semiramide: *an opera which was hardly ever performed, it was monopolised by the tandem Sutherland-Home and is now more popular than* Bohème, *and within the vocal reach of all the best belcanto singers of today. In the photo we can see* **Lucia Valentini-Terrani** *whilst she is being crowned at the end of the opera. (Historic Archives of the Teatro Verdi of Trieste)*

Marcelo Alvarez and *Leo Nucci* in the version of Rigoletto staged at the Verona Arena in 2001. (Fondazione Arena di Verona. Photo: Gianfranco Fainello)

Enzo Dara sings "Miei rampolli femminini" in Cenerentola (Rossini). His execution of the aria "Sia qualunque delle figlie" is almost unique for his verbal precision and speed. (Historic Archives of the Teatro Comunale of Bologna)

of the injustice of the recording industry, her greatest performances are not on record. Many memorable Gencer evenings have, however, been preserved on "pirate" recordings, for which we should be grateful.

Montserrat Caballé's Silver Song

Montserrat Caballé (Barcelona 1933) is on a similar, though not identical, level to that of Gencer. The rare polish and clear timbre of her voice, the pearly glow of her *pianissimi*, and her light and delicate emission make her singing ideal for Bellini and Donizetti, where ecstatic, plaintive passages dominate the score. For such a sweet, seductive timbre the Verdi and Verist repertory should be beyond reach, yet, thanks to her perfect technique, the Spanish singer has performed here, there and everywhere the roles of *Tosca*, *Adriana Lecouvreur*, *Forza del Destino*, *Bohème*, and even *Turandot* (the title role), giving her audiences unforgettable moments (remember the *messa di voce* at the beginning of Leonora's aria "Pace, pace, mio Dio" and her rendition of "Poveri fiori" in *Adriana*, a magic string of *filati* notes). However, her vocal characteristics are not strictly in keeping with the dramatic nature of these roles.

In Rossini and Handel, too, which she has often performed (*Semiramide*, *Julius Caesar*), she can put to good use her gift for fast vocalization and her sound technical backing to produce every kind of embellishment; but we are also aware of the limits of a singing technique which lays too much emphasis on beauty of tone and *pianissimi*. Caballé is particularly at fault in this respect. To eliminate from Rossini the *agilità di forza* and replace it with vocal acrobatics performed in *mezzavoce* or falsetto is to deny the vocal style of the composer. Caballé's best years were from 1956 until 1976, and her most unforgettable performances have been from the early Romantic period: Donizetti's *Lucrezia Borgia*, *Roberto Devereux*, and above all *Maria Stuarda*. Who could forget her performances in Rome in 1970? And she was, of course, a great Norma; it will be diffi-

January 1982, after Liù, **Caballé** attempted the perilous role of Turandot, managing to create a credible character, thanks to her excellent technique and interpretative intelligence. (Archives of L'Opera of Nice)

"Questo è il bacio di Tosca!" **Caballé** has just plunged a knife into the unfortunate Scarpia (the baritone **Juan Pons**) during a performance in April, 1980. The Spanish soprano is highly esteemed in France. (Archives of L'Opéra of Nice)

A fairy-tale Lucia with **Renata Scotto**, **Renato Bruson** (Enrico) and **Luciano Pavarotti** (Edgardo). The orchestra was conducted by Bruno Bartoletti, the director was Aldo Vassallo, scenes and costumes were by Franco Zeffirelli. It was staged in April, 1968. The photo shows a moment during the famous sextet, "Chi mi frena." (Historic Archives of the Teatro Massimo of Palermo. Photo: Allotta)

cult to equal her open-air performance at the Festival of Orange in 1973.

After 1976 a marked decline began: her high notes became metallic; she no longer pronounced the words in the difficult passages; her attack of the high notes became too flute-like; and she took blatant refuge in *filatura* and extremely long breaths to compensate for these shortcomings.

What is more, Caballé has never excelled in artistic discipline, often skipping rehearsals and forgetting (or changing) the words. (What a mess she made in that *Barbiere* at Nice in 1980).

Side by side with her operatic work, the Spanish soprano has a noteworthy concert activity achieving extraordinary results in Richard Strauss' Lieder music.

After the Callas comet, **Renata Scotto** (Savona 1933) was the next embodiment of the *soprano drammatico di agilità*. She started in 1952 in *Traviata* and sang in all the major theaters, in a wide repertory which gradually extended from her original parts in *Lucia*, *Sonnambula*, *Rigoletto* and *Elisir d'Amore* to *Norma*, *Ballo in Maschera*, *Tosca*, *Macbeth*, *Nabucco* and *Manon Lescaut*, with sometimes questionable results. The most important factor of Scotto's talent is her extreme stylistic accuracy, her ability to find the right color for every phrase and the correct expressive nuance. In addition to this virtue, the Italian artist adds a solid technique which allows her to use trills and fluid vocalizing, intense *mezzevoci*, and an extension reaching to high e''' flat (though launched a little insecurely).

These gifts remained almost intact until halfway through the seventies when her voice began to show the strain of far too ambitious a repertoire. The high register paid the greatest price, becoming wobbly and screeching, though her characterizations became ever more refined

Renata Scotto sings Sonnambula in Rome in 1960. One of her great passions was to put herself in spiritual contact with the great divas of the past, such as Giuditta Pasta and Maria Malibran, perhaps with the secret intent of receiving some precious advice from them. (Historic Archives of the Rome Opera Theater. Photo: Oscar Savio)

December, 1968. An enchanting edition of Bellni's La Straniera, sung by **Renata Scotto** *(center),* **Renato Cioni** *(left), and the baritone* **Domenico Trimarchi** *(right). (Historic Archives of the Teatro Massimo of Palermo. Photo: Allotta)*

Renata Scotto *and* **Alberto Rinaldi** *(Sharpless) — a baritone of success in the Rossini and eighteenth century repertory — in a 1975 production of Puccini's* Butterfly. *Scotto was at the time in open dispute with the Italian opera theaters, guilty of bad organization and a lack of respect for artists; so she almost always sings elsewhere, especially at the Metropolitan in New York, where she has performed in an impressive variety of roles. (Historic Archives of the Rome Opera Theater)*

Beverly Sills *as Maria Stuarda, one of the many belcanto operas she helped revive internationally.*

(for instance, her wonderful Elena in *Vespri Siciliani* at the Florence May Festival in 1978, or her *Manon Lescaut* at the Metropolitan with Domingo, sung with great passion, but none of the verist-style exaggerations).

Three other sopranos rightly belong to the list of the truly great belcanto singers. All three are American. The first is **Beverly Sills** (Brooklyn, New York 1929), who sang from 1946 to 1981 in a wide repertory that saw her triumph in *Lucia*, *Traviata*, *Manon*, *Puritani* and *Thaïs*, until she crowned her successes with a magnificent performance of Rossini's *Assedio di Corinto* at La Scala in 1969. Sills' vocal technique originates from the mythical school of Mathilde Marchesi, one of the most famous teachers at the turn of the twentieth century. It is a vocality which privileges an intricate coloratura, pyrotechnics, tight trilling and spectacular *cadenze*, while timbre and uniformity take second place. This gave rise to her noted virtuoso ability, which compensated for a lack of vocal beauty. Sill's renderings were, therefore, technically masterful (as can be heard from her recording of *Lucia* with Schippers), but sometimes lacking in expressiveness.

Sills can be considered the worthy heir of Lily Pons for her confidence in the coloratura passages and her prodigious technique.

The next generation includes **June Anderson** (Boston 1952) and **Lella Cuberli** (Austin, Texas 1945), both with well-educated voices,

ideal for certain belcanto roles, re-presented in a philological key in the mid-seventies and for the following decade.

Anderson, after her debuts as Lucia, Sonnambula and Traviata, pushed herself a little beyond her natural limits, adding to her repertoire *Norma*, *Trovatore*, *Luisa Miller*, with results that were not always entirely satisfactory.

Cuberli, though having a less attractive voice than that of her colleague, has administered her natural talents more wisely, concentrating on works by Handal, Mozart and Rossini. However, Anderson's career has in the long run proved to be the more important, having included more record making and performances in more of the major opera houses.

The Callas Imitators

The "after Callas" era has seen a whole series of victims sacrificed on the altar of operatic melodramma: from **Elena Souliotis** (Athens 1943), exceptional in the early years of her career as Abigaille, Lady Macbeth, Norma, Gioconda, but eventually overcome by an impossibly grueling amount of work (she made her debut in Nabucco at only twenty years of age); to **Anita Cerquetti** (Montecorsaro, Macerata 1929), gifted with one of the most beautiful timbres ever and perfect emission, who sprung to fame when she stepped in for Callas in Rome, during the famous Norma interrupted after the first act. Cerquetti, who was active for some ten years practically without respite (performing *Vespri Siciliani*, *Aida*, *Ballo in Maschera*, *Norma*, *Nabucco*), retired suddenly from the stage in the early sixties, apparently for health reasons.

More stable, though somewhat disorganized, was the career of **Teresa Stratas,** (Toronto 1938), famous as Violetta in Zeffirelli's film-opera. Stratas seemed to have a special feeling for each role, was an excellent actress and has never hidden the fact that she took her inspiration from Maria Callas.

Equally brief, though intense, was the climb to notoriety of **Silvia Sass** (Budapest 1951). Gifted with a naturally lyrical voice, Sass has deliberately altered the timbre of her voice in order to be able to tackle more dramatic roles. Her performances include *Traviata*, *Macbeth* and *Tosca*, in which she has exhibited not only her singing talent but also a magnificent silhouette.

Cecilia Gasdia (Verona 1960), astute and extremely well-prepared, was launched into the limelight of some of the major theaters at an extremely early age (*Luisa Miller* at Florence in

1981, *Anna Bolena* at La Scala the following year, *Traviata* with Kleiber in 1984). Her voice is soft and delicate, not particularly extended, sure in the use of filature, while on stage Cecilia moves with confidence (Nedda, Rosina, Suzel and even Tosca). Her repertoire has ranged from Monteverdi, Vivaldi, Handel, Rossini, Mozart, Bellini and Donizetti to Verdi, Mascagni and Puccini, and includes oratorio and concert performances.

Cecilia Gasdia *off-stage during a performance of* Il Barbiere di Siviglia *(1996). (Fondazione Arena di Verona. Photo: Gianfranco Fainello)*

Other Famous Sopranos

After our chapter dedicated to the greatest sopranos of this century we have added this table which includes the names of other sopranos worthy of mention. Beside each name we have included the main titles in her repertory and a brief note on her vocal characteristics and career.

NAME	BASIC REPERTORY	REMARKS
Ackté, Aïno (1876-1944) Dramatic	Wagner, Strauss	A singer-actress of strong temperament and a luminous, powerful voice. She wrote an opera libretto and autobiographies (1925, 1935)
Augér, Arleen (1939-1993) Coloratura	Handel, Mozart, oratorio and cantatas	Flexible, musical, clear and penetrating timbre
Baillie, Dame Isobel (1895-1983) Lyric	Oratorio, cantatas, Lieder, and chamber songs	One of the most important English recital singers of the century. She wrote an autobiography in 1982
Benackova, Gabriela (1947) *Lirico spinto*	Smetana, Dvorak, Puccini	Lovely vocal color, well projected voice. A sensitive interpreter of the late Romantic and Verist repertory
Collier, Marie (1926-1971) *Lirico spinto*	*Tosca, Butterfly, Jenufa,* contemporary operas	One of the best and most moving actresses of the opera stage; she was the first Hecuba in Tippett's *King Priam*
Cruz-Romo, Gilda (1940) *Lirico spinto*	*Aida, Forza del Destino, Ernani, Luisa Miller, Otello*	Good natural qualities, good phrasing, excellent stage presence with, however, some technical difficulties and a limited extension in the high register
Curtin, Phyllis (C. Smith, 1922) Light lyric	Mozart, contemporary composers	A refined and sensitive singer of Mozart and of many twentieth century works
Dobbs, Mattiwilda (1925) Coloratura	Lucia, Rosina, Gilda, Olympia	One of the first colored singers to understake a splendid international career
Dvorakova, Ludmila (1923) *Lirico spinto*	Wagner, Strauss, Smetana, Dvorak	A good Wagner interpreter although more for her imposing presence on stage than for her vocal virtues
Gayer, Catherine (1937) Coloratura	Verdi, Donizetti, contemporary operas	Flexible and extended voice, pleasant stage presence; she was in the inaugural performances of Nono's *Intolleranza,* Dallapiccola's *Ulisse,* and several other operas of the twentieth century
Goltz, Christel (1912) Dramatic	Wagner, Strauss, contemporary operas	Extraordinary power and extension, intense actress. First interpreter of Orff's *Antigonae* and of Liebermann's *Penelope*
Gomez, Jill (1942) Lyric	Mozart, English and Spanish opera, contemporary works	A well-prepared musician with a notable stage talent
Harwood, Elizabeth (1938-1990) Light lyric	Mozart, Musetta in *Bohème,* operetta by Lehár and Johann Strauss	She had a brilliant start, with world-wide success and many recordings; but technical problems and too much work unfortunately cut short her career
Hidalgo, Elvira de (1892-1980) Coloratura	Gilda, Rosina, Lucia, Amina, Norina	Liberty style nightingale for the first quarter of the twentieth century; she was a much-appreciated teacher. Her most famous student was Maria Callas
Kniplova, Nadezda (N. Pokorna, 1932) *Lirico spinto*	Wagner, Strauss, Smetana, Dvorak	An intense dramatic actress with an incisive voice
Kubiak, Teresa (1937) *Lirico spinto*	Puccini, Mussorgsky, Tchaikovsky	One of the most interesting artists to come from Poland during twentieth century. A voice of a lovely color. Excellent on stage
Kupper, Annelies (1906-1988) Lyric	Mozart, C.M. von Weber, contemporary works	A specialist in the role of the countess in *The Marriage of Figaro;* first interpreter in 1950 of *Die Liebe der Danae* by Richard Strauss

Lazlo, Magda (1919) Lyric	Kodaly, Bartok, contemporary operas	She was the first to perform Cressida in Walton's *Troilus and Cressida* and Dallapiccola's *Il Prigioniero*
Lear, Evelyn (E. Schulman; 1928) *Lirico spinto*	Mozart, Strauss, Berg, contemporary operas	A refined and intelligent interpreter, with wide interests and catholic tastes. Wife of the baritone Thomas Stewart
Lenya, Lotte (Karoline Whilhelmine Blamauer; 1898-1981) Light lyric	Weill	A singer-actress of great talent. She married Kurt Weill and became the sublime interpreter of his music. She was the first Jenny in *Die Dreigroschenoper*, and Anna in *Die Sieben Todsünden*
Lindholm, Berit (F. Jonsson; 1934) Dramatic	Wagner, Strauss	One of the most important Wagner singers of the seventies
Lott, Felicity (1947) Lyric	Mozart, Strauss, French operas, Lieder	One of the most refined singers. Specialist in the role of the Mozart Countess and in *Arabella*. Excellent Lieder singer
Martin, Janis (1939) *Lirico spinto*	Wagner, Berg	She started singing as a soprano in 1971 after having first been a mezzosoprano. However, she always had some problems in the very high register
Masterson, Valerie (1937) Light lyric	Handel, Mozart, English operetta, contemporary operas	A well-prepared musician with a lovely vocal color. Excellent in the operas of Benjamin Britten
Mastilovi´c, Danica (1933) Dramatic	*Turandot*, *The Ring*, *Die Frau*, *Elektra*	One of the most powerful and voluminous voices ever heard in a theater. Her intonation and expressive variety were, however, lacking
Mesplé, Mady (1931) Light lyric	French operas and operettas. Chamber music repertory	A small voice with a vibrato resembling a goat's bleat; nonetheless, she was a very musical and much appreciated singer; extremely good in French operetta
Migenes-Johnson, Julia (1945) Lyric	American Music Halls, Concerts	Became famous with Rosi's film of *Carmen* in 1984. Though her voice is not special, she is a superb actress
Neblett, Carol (1946) *Lirico spinto*	Contemporary opera. Puccini	Specialist in the role of Minnie (*Girl of the Golden West*). A singer-actress of exceptional natural gifts
Neway, Patricia (1919) *Lirico spinto*	Contemporary operas	A notable dramatic talent. The first interpreter of *The Consul* and of *Maria Golovin*, both by Menotti
Pilarczyk, Helga (1925) *Lirico spinto*	Contemporary operas	A great interpreter of twentieth century operas: Berg, Schönberg, Henze, Krenek
Robin, Mado (1918-1960) Coloratura	Gilda, Lucia, Amina, Lakmé, Olympia, Queen of the Night	The highest voice that has ever existed, capable of reaching high d´´´´ flat!
Slobodskaia, Ode (1888-1970) Lyric	Tchaikovsky, Glinka, Mussorgsky, Stravinsky	The first performer of Stravinsky's *Mavra*. She lived for many years in London where she was also noted as a great star of operetta
Svobodová-Janku, Hana (1940-1995) Dramatic	*Turandot*, Brünnhilde, *Elektra*, Czechoslovakian operas	A voice of steel, with a beautiful low register
Tinsley, Pauline (1928) *Lirico spinto*	*Macbeth*, *Nabucco*, *Turandot*	A singer who was under-valued by the critics though she possessed a voice of power, vibrant in the high register
Vaness, Carol (1952) Lyric	Mozart, Gluck, Verdi	A favorite of Riccardo Muti, she is a fair interpreter of Donna Anna, Elettra in *Idomeneo*, but with precise limits of extension
Varady, Julia (1941) *Lirico spinto*	Mozart, Verdi, Strauss, contemporary operas	An extended voice of fine color, used with intelligence and good taste. She married the baritone Dietrich Fischer-Dieskau
Vaughan, Elizabeth (1936) *Lirico spinto*	Verdi, Puccini	An popular interpreter of *Madama Butterfly* in Anglo-Saxon countries

Vyvyan, Jennifer (1925-1974) Lyric	Handel, Britten	Among the most refined of English singers; a favorite of Benjamin Britten
Watson, Claire (C. Mc Lamore; 1927-1986) Lyric	Mozart, Strauss	A voice with a lovely timbre, supported by an excellent technique, and by an intense acting skill
Watson, Lillian Light lyric	Mozart, English and German operettas	A specialist in the roles of the *soubrette*

The Baritones

The Baritone Voice: Extension and Phonation

The extension of a typical baritone voice goes from G or G flat up to high a´. Of course, these limits can be exceeded both in the low and in the high notes; Benvenuto Franci and (more recently) Sherrill Milnes, Leo Nucci and Piero Cappuccilli are all baritones who have a high c´´ in their range.

A correct baritone phonation requires extended chest resonances up to c´, then passing into head resonances. To achieve this technique a singer must in part relinquish artificially darkened sound and acquire some more tenor-like inflexions and colorings. For this reason many baritones over the last decades have considered the old rules of phonation almost a *diminutio*, preferring to push their chest voice up to e´, as this increases vocal power and volume; but the high notes become harsher and forced, and the *mezzavoce* becomes difficult.

Baritone Categories in the Twentieth Century

Observing the wide range of characteristics of the baritone voice in the twentieth century, the following divisions can be made: the Verdi baritone (both lyric and dramatic), with a clear and vibrant timbre, a sufficiently extended and agile voice, soft and delicate in moments of pathos, and incisive in the dramatic passages; the *vilain* baritone – the "bad guy" of the verist repertory (Alfio, Scarpia, Tonio), who produces a malevolent, menacing sound; the *grand seigneur* baritone (the German *Kavalierbariton*), noble and refined, suited to the parts of kings and emperors in Bellini, Donizetti, the early Verdi (Don Carlo in *Ernani*) and Richard Strauss (the Count in *Capriccio*); the *Heldenbariton* of Wagner's operas (Telramund in *Lohengrin*, Kurwenal in *Tristan und Isolde*, Gunther in *Götterdammerung*), who has a powerful, robust voice; the *Spielbariton* or the *Buffo*, who is the comic element with a clear and flexible voice, suited to interpret parts such as Papageno, Figaro, Dandini, and all the other comic roles in the eighteenth and nineteenth century operas which were originally written for the basses or for the *concordant*.

THE VERDI BARITONES OF THE TWENTIETH CENTURY

The first in this glorious series is the great **Giuseppe Kaschmann** (Lussimpiccolo, Istria 1850 – Rome 1925), who had an extraordinarily long and much honored career. Thanks to a top school of singing applied to a rich, harmonic timbre (which was spoiled only by an annoying *vibrato stretto*) and to an innate musicality, he was able to sing an extremely wide repertoire: from *La Favorita* (in which he made his debut in 1876 at Turin) to *Don Carlos, Lucia* and *Forza del Destino*, distinguishing himself from 1892 on as a worthy Wagnerian performer. He was the only Italian to be admitted into the Bayreuth "temple".

His career ended in 1921, with Cimarosa's opera *Le Astuzie Femminili* in Rome. During later years Kaschmann also dedicated himself to comic opera, producing a fantastic Don Bartolo (*Barbiere*) and Don Pasquale.

In Kaschmann's case, as with so many other singers from 1900-1920, the recordings we have contradict everything his critics claimed for

Giuseppe Kaschmann *in a photo taken on July 1, 1892, when he interpreted Amfortas in* Parsifal *in Bayreuth. He was present at the opening of the Opera Theater in Zagreb (1870, Mislav by Zajc) and the inauguration of the Metropolitan of New York (1883, Lucia). (Historic Archives of the Rome Opera Theater)*

skills. He was active from 1889, when he made his debut in Spontini's *Vestale*, until 1933, when he sang for the last time at the Metropolitan. He was a greater actor than singer, but his technique always allowed him to respect the dynamics established by the composers, from feather-like *pianissimi* to his fluid legato. Amongst his most successful performances were *Ernani, Faust, Carmen, Falstaff, Aida, Don Giovanni* and *Tosca*. He performed many of these works with Caruso at the Met.

Titta Ruffo (whose real name was Ruffo Titta, Pisa 1877 – Florence 1953) exhibited noteworthy vocal power, using his facial cavities to the utmost to make his high notes more penetrating. (His high g´´s and a´´s thundered across auditoriums, thrilling the audience).

His debut took place in Rome, as the Herald in *Lohengrin*; but soon the ideal parts for this great singer became Rigoletto, Scarpia, the Conte di Luna, Figaro, Renato in *Ballo in Maschera*, Gérard and Hamlet. It was in this last opera, by Thomas, that he achieved total identification with his character, especially in the "Toast". At the end of the aria, Ruffo was in the habit of adding a long *cadenza* which he would perform all in one breath. Note after note his voice would streak

him. In his recording of "Oh de' verd'anni miei," made when he was just over fifty, his singing appears tremulous and anti-musical.

A penetrating voice and precision of phrasing were the principal features of **Pasquale Amato** (Naples 1878 – New York 1942). He was an authentic Verdi champion. He made his debut in his native city playing Germont in *Traviata* in 1900, and from then on Verdi was his favorite composer, followed by some of the most prominent Verists. His phrasing was varied and eloquent in *Rigoletto, Falstaff, Ballo in Maschera, Tosca, Gioconda* and *Pagliacci*. In these operas he showed an almost tenor-like extension in the high notes and a soft, smooth emission worthy of the best belcanto traditions. What is more, he was a formidable actor, dominating the stage completely. About 1920 a certain tiredness could be heard in his voice, partly caused by a delicate kidney operation; but Amato continued to sing until 1933-34. His last performance took place at the Chicago Opera.

Antonio Scotti (Sarno, Naples 1866 – Naples 1936) had authentic vocal and acting

Very popular in the United States, **Pasquale Amato** *taught from 1935 on at the University of Louisiana, gaining the esteem and affection of many students. (Historic Archives of the Rome Opera Theater)*

Antonio Scotti, in Mozart's Don Giovanni. He played Whether in London and New York's Metropolitan, being the first to perform many important baritone roles, among them Scarpia and Sharpless.

(Manoppello, Pescara 1882), who studied with Cotogni; **Mathieu Ahlersmeyer** (Cologne 1896 – Garmisch 1979), a great Macbeth; **Apollo Granforte** (Legnago, Verona 1886 – Gorgonzola, Milan 1975), a thundering voice with a splendid timbre; **Mario Ancona** (Leghorn 1860 – Florence 1931), the first Silvio in *I Pagliacci*, an opera in which he would later become legendary as Tonio; **Joseph Schwarz** (Riga 1880 – Berlin 1926), a noteworthy Rigoletto, and one of the few interpreters of the time who was able to respect what was written by the composers without exaggerating; **Eugenio Giraldoni** (Marseille 1871 – Helsinki 1924), the first Scarpia at Rome and at La Scala, famous as Gérard in *Andrea Chénier*; **Enrico Nani** (Rome 1873 – 1940), an excellent Nabucco; **Mario Basiola** (Annico, Cremona 1892 – 1965), renowned as Iago and Amonasro; the great **Giuseppe Danise** (Naples 1883 – New York 1963), a voice which was robust, flexible, and expressive; **Giovanni**

An eloquent expression by **Riccardo Stracciari** in Verdi's Rigoletto. During the years 1920-1940 he played Figaro more than nine hundred times, sharing public favor with Ruffo and De Lucia.

across the pentagram, from low to high, with penetrating impetus and a dizzying ring.

In the long run, however, those unnatural nasal sounds present in every one of his performances robbed Ruffo's voice of its stylistic qualities and led to a precocious decline.

He retired in 1931, performing *Tosca* and *Hamlet* in Buenos Aires; but at this point the fantastic *cadenza* could no longer be finished in only one breath.

Considering his amazing capacity and his highly successful career, it follows that Titta Ruffo constituted a fundamental turning point in the history of the baritone voice in the twentieth century. After the light, almost tenor-like, baritones of the nineteenth century, we began to encounter singers with a wide and powerful central range, very different from any tenor model. From the twenties onwards no one could deny the incomparable polish of the great Titta.

Despite the fact that many turn-of-the-century baritones have not been well served by their recordings (many of which are quite colorless and show very little respect for the value of the musical notes) we would like to mention the most important among them: **Adolfo Pacini**

John Charles Thomas *as Germont in Verdi's* La Traviata.

Inghilleri (Porto Empedocle, Sicily 1894 – Milan 1959); **Emilio Ghirardini** (Ferrara 1884 – Nervi, Genoa 1965); **Dinh Gilly** (Algeria 1877 – London 1940), much sought after as Amonasro; **John Charles Thomas** (Meyersdale, Virginia 1891 – Apple Valley, California 1960), who was a wonderful Germont at the Met during the thirties; **Armand Crabbe** (Brussels 1883 – 1947); **Giacomo Rimini** (Verona 1888 – Chicago 1952); **Denis Noble** (Bristol 1899 – Spain 1966); **Jean Noté** (Tournai, Belgium 1859 – Brussels 1922), famous as Rigoletto; **Willi Domgraf-Fassbaender** (Aachen 1897 – Nuremberg 1978), an exceptional singer-actor who performed in a wide repertoire.

"All'idea di quel metallo"
Figaro (*Barbiere*): Riccardo Stracciari

By virtue of his correct singing style, the weight and richness of his timbre, and his great acting skills, **Riccardo Stracciari** (Casalecchio, Bologna 1875 – Rome 1955) was one of the greatest baritones of the twentieth century: an incomparable Figaro, Rigoletto and Germont.

This goes to show that, with a solid technique and a sense of moderation and vocal composure, a singer can preserve his voice for decades. Indeed, Stracciari began to sing in 1899 and continued until 1944 when he retired with a memorable *Traviata* at the Teatro Sociale of Como. We can admire his perfect legato and his exemplary breath distribution in the recording of Don Carlo's aria from *Ernani* "Oh de' verd'anni miei," which concludes with a rounded, penetrating a´ flat.

In his favorite role of Figaro (heard in the recording, of course) we cannot help but be amazed at the variety of his expressions and above all at the super-fast "patter" in the recitatives, which was great fun to listen to as well as being part of the art of a virtuoso. His "All'idea di quel metallo" remains famous.

One of Stracciari's students was **Sándor Svéd** (Budapest 1906 – 1979). He was among the most correct and incisive singers of the thirties and forties, famous for the beauty of his timbre and smoothness of emission in operas such as *Rigoletto*, *Ballo in Maschera* and *Trovatore*, but he performed in the French and Wagnerian repertory as well.

Stabile – A Legendary Falstaff

Another baritone of immense importance was **Mariano Stabile** (Palermo 1888 – Milan 1968), who sang for over half a century and was the greatest Falstaff ever known. He sang this role about one thousand two hundred times, starting in 1921-22, when he performed it at La Scala under the baton of Toscanini, after having meticulously prepared the part with the famous conductor. Even the phrase "Due fagiani, un'acciuga" in the first act was tried over and over again (apparently seventy times!) to obtain the right inflexion, accent and color.

Apart from the corpulent knight, Stabile included in his repertory a sinuous Iago, Figaro, the sheriff Rance, Gérard, Don Giovanni, Don Alfonso and Prosdocimo in *Turco in Italia* (revived in Rome in 1950 for the first time in the twentieth century).

His success derived, above all, from his perfect acting, which was studied in the minutest detail, like an authentic *comédien*, and from the extreme flexibility of his voice, neither beautiful nor powerful, but able to exhibit a wide series of nuances. Whenever he pronounced the phrase "Vado a farmi bello" in the second act of *Falstaff* with a whisper of a voice, ambiguous and enchanting, Stabile won a warm applause from the audience.

Another exceptional stage presence was **Lawrence Tibbett** (Bakersfield, California 1896

Mariano Stabile, taken during the first act of Falstaff which opened the 1952-53 season of the Rome Opera. Stella, Elmo, Silveri, Lazzari and Neri sang with him. On the podium, Franco Capuana. Even putting on his make-up, Stabile took great care, as can be seen from by this photo. (Historic Archives of the Rome Opera Theater Photo: Savio)

– New York 1960), who made his debut in 1923 at the Metropolitan, but was truly launched when he performed an exceptional Ford in *Falstaff* during the 1925 season, with Scotti in the title role. The audience acclaimed the young singer at length, awarding him an unprecedented triumph.

From that moment Tibbett's career went from one success to another: Amonasro, Scarpia, Iago, Simon Boccanegra, Rigoletto, roles which require enormous effort were resolved with ease, good high notes, a smooth emission, and the right shadings for every phrase. He sang at the Metropolitan until 1950, idolized by the public.

Leonard Warren (New York 1911 – 1960), Tibbett's heir, did his advanced studies at the famous school of De Luca, from whom he learnt all the secrets of the classical belcanto style. In January 1935 he made his debut at the Metropolitan as Paolo in *Simon Boccanegra*, with Tibbett in the leading role. And, exactly as had occurred ten years earlier for his illustrious colleague, Warren was an immediate success. With his wide and pliant voice, which easily executed the high notes and the *mezzevoci*, and his very long breaths, the American baritone took on key roles such as Rigoletto, Macbeth, Conte di Luna, Simon, Don Carlo in *Forza del Destino*, Tonio in *I Pagliacci*, Iago, and even *Falstaff*; the

Leonard Warren *in the title role of Verdi's* Macbeth.

Metropolitan public acclaimed him time and again. He died on stage at the Metropolitan after having sung "Urna fatale" in *Forza del Destino*.

Another baritone who specialized in Verdi was **Aldo Protti** (Cremona 1920 – 1995), an excellent Rigoletto, Iago, Amonasro and Don Alvaro but also renowned as Gérard, Tonio and Barnaba. He was active from the fifties until his death, caused by complications after a delicate operation, thanks to his excellent technical ability and extraordinary natural talent (extension, uniformity over the entire range, sculptured phrasing).

Both these baritones are to be remembered for their correct emission, robust voices and stylistic fidelity to the Verdi repertoire.

The singular artistic progress of **Paolo Silveri** (Ofena, L'Aquila 1913 – Rome 2001), a vigorous Verdi baritone from 1943 until 1959, began after he started as a bass at Rome (1939-43). In 1959 he attempted to rise to the tenor range, without great success, making a debut as Otello in Dublin. In 1960 Silveri wisely returned to the baritone class.

These exhausting vocal ups and downs were only made possible by the Italian singer's hardy physique. During his best years he had a warm,

The Metropolitan's "best loved" singer during many performances, **Lawrence Tibbet** *interpreted numerous first-ever* prime. *He was also a silver screen actor. (Historic Archives of the Rome Opera Theater)*

robust and slightly melancholic voice, thus he was an excellent Conte di Luna, Simon Boccanegra, Iago, Scarpia, Gérard, Germont and Rigoletto, and a singer who was able to obey all the expressive signs on the scores.

Giuseppe Valdengo (Turin 1914), a complete musician and a sensitive, refined artist, first qualified as an oboe and cor anglais player, before turning to opera. He made his singing debut as Sharpless at Alessandria in 1936. Among his favorite roles were Germont, Tonio, Figaro, Riccardo in *Puritani*, Rigoletto, but, above all, Jago, Amonasro and Falstaff, which he perfected and sung under the baton of Toscanini for NBC. The few but significant records that he made underline his excellent technical preparation, his intelligent use of *mezzetinte*, his varied, carefully balanced phrasing.

Also worthy of mention are **Mario Zanasi** (Bologna 1927), celebrated Gérmont (together with Callas in London in 1958) and performer of seventeen Verdi operas; **Enzo Mascherini** (Florence 1911 – Leghorn 1981), who sang at La Scala from 1941 to 1955 (he also sang Macbeth with De Sabata in 1952); **Robert Merrill** (New York 1917), Gérmont and Renato with Toscanini for NBC, a voice of iron and a great actor, he was still making concert performances in the early nineteen-nineties; **Anselmo Colzani** (Budrio, Bologna 1918), a specialist in the role of Don Carlo in *Forza del Destino*, highly sought after by all the major American opera houses, despite strong competition; **Mario Sereni** (Perugia 1928), Italian star of the Met for twenty years from 1957, impeccable performer of *Ernani*, *Trovatore*, *Traviata*, *Butterfly*, *Don Carlos*, thanks to the beauty of his tone-color and his measured phrasing; **Giorgio Zancanaro** (Verona 1939), much loved in Germany and Austria, a specialist in the roles of Renato and Conte di Luna by virtue of his excellent emission, even though his acting is somewhat bland and at times even affected. During the nineties the Russian singer **Vladimir Chernov** (Krasnojarsk 1953) arrived on the scene, well-supported by his record company. His voice is reminiscent of that of the great Bastianini, his diction excellent, his adherence to style a little less so; he has achieved particular success as Conte di Luna. The American **Thomas Hampson** (Elkharst, Indiana 1955), successful in a vast repertoire, versatile and keen to tackle all sorts of different roles, has been hailed as the successor of Sherril Milnes at the New York Metropolitan, though he has not yet succeeded in establishing his name as a true Verdi baritone. His voice is soft, well-emitted, extended (even up to the over-emphasized c in the *cadenza* from Rossini's *Barbiere di Siviglia),* but reveals shades of belcanto more typical of the comic baritone. Famous as Malatesta, Figaro, but also as Oneghin, Werther (in the baritone version composed by Massenet for Battistini), Hamlet, Amfortas, Atanaele, his interests further extend to musical comedy and Leider. Hampson is also a fine singing teacher and musicologist, and has established an institution for the safeguarding of America's musical heritage.

Juan Pons (Palma de Mallorca 1946) began his singing career as second bass and then went on to take the leading role in *Falstaff* at La Scala in the early eighties. He has since built up a solid reputation world-wide, thanks to his generous, well-extended voice, capable of ranging throughout the entire baritone repertoire, with a particular preference for the roles of Scarpia, Gérmont, Nabucco, Gianni Schicchi and Tonio in *Pagliacci*. Pons has also made numerous records, though his voice (characterized by a *vibrato* and certain guttural sounds typical of Spanish singers) is more effective live than on record.

Rapidly rising to fame is another Spanish singer, **Carlos Alvarez** (1966), whose sturdy, well-controlled voice enables him to give excellent performances in roles such as Rigoletto, Gérmont and King Alfonso in *La Favorita*. The Roman singer **Carlo Guelfi** (1958) has also made a name for himself, and is today one of the most sought-after Verdi baritones of the latest generation. Gifted with a clear voice, lacking a little in resonance perhaps, well-sustained emission, his repertoire includes *Rigoletto*, *Trovatore*, *Don Carlos* and *Otello*, performed with success even in huge open spaces such as the Verona Arena.

The Misunderstood Baritone: Ettore Bastianini

Ettore Bastianini (Siena 1922 – Sirmione, Brescia 1967) was another baritone who began singing as a bass (as Colline in *Bohème* in Ravenna, 1945) and then went on to sing as a baritone from 1952 onwards. A thick, rich timbre, a seductive manner and an amiable stage presence: these were the best characteristics of this Italian artist, who died prematurely in 1967, after the first tragic signs of his illness had forced him to abandon the stage in 1965.

The Italian critics, however, were never kind towards this meritorious singer. He was always accused of singing everything at full voice (but what a voice!), of technical shortcomings in the *passaggio* from center to high range, and of thus being stylistically inadequate in many of his roles. These claims do have some truth; but they ignore Bastianini's huge popular success in such operas as *Trovatore, Ballo in Maschera, Ernani, Don Carlos* (with von Karajan at Salzburg in 1958), *Forza del Destino, Traviata* (with Callas and Di Stefano in Visconti's legendary production at La Scala in 1955) not forgetting his important performances of *Mazepa, Eugene Onegin* in 1954, and the revivals of *Pirata* and *Poliuto* (with Callas).

Cornell MacNeil (Minneapolis 1922) was on stage in all the world's major theaters for over forty years, distinguishing himself not only for his admirable technique but also for his great acting skills, especially evident in the parts of Scarpia, Iago and Gérmont.

During his best years, 1955-70, the American baritone exhibited a measured singing line, being easily able to sustain the long legato passages of the Verdi arias, diminishing and reinforcing the sounds with an authentic *mezzavoce* and tenor-like high notes (up to high b´ flat in the finale of Gusman's *cabaletta* in *Alzira* in Rome in 1967). His most successful characterizations were those of Rigoletto,

Don Carlo in *Ernani,* Nabucco, Amonasro, Rance, and the above- mentioned Scarpia, Iago and Gérmont, roles which he took on in later years.

It should be added that, right from the start, MacNeil's voice tended to wobble over the *passaggio*: this mattered less in a young, fresh voice, but it proved fatal when he was older. If this problem had been resolved in time, he would not have had to rely solely on his acting skills; he would have been able to continue launching high notes and modulating his voice as he pleased.

The list of great contemporary American baritones must include the name of **Sherrill Milnes** (Downers Grove, Illinois 1935). He started in 1963, but was "launched" in 1965 when he sang the part of Valentin in *Faust* at the Met.

Thanks to his dramatic talent on stage and particular vocal qualities (a tenor extension on the high notes, *mezzevoci*, intense, careful phrasing), Milnes is a worthy successor of Warren and Tibbett, having achieved considerable success in *Rigoletto, Trovatore, Traviata, Ballo in Maschera, Macbeth, Forza del Destino, Simon Boccanegra, Otello,* not to mention *Tosca, Fanciulla del West, Don Giovanni* and Thomas's *Hamlet* (revived in Chicago in 1990), and in an infinity of other roles. In the late nineties he added *Falstaff* to his repertoire and intensified his activity in yet another long-standing interest, publishing. Moreover, he has put virtually his entire repertoire on record (of particular interest is his splendid interpretation of Massenet's *Thäis* together with Sills and conducted by Maazel, and of *La Fanciulla del West* conducted by Mehta).

Cappuccilli: Nature plus Technique

Piero Cappuccilli (Trieste 1926) will be remembered as the most technically complete baritone of his generation. His superb breath control, his famous legato, the uniformity and resonance of his voice and his extension have been envied and copied by many of his famous colleagues, above all by Pavarotti, who has no qualms in admitting the superiority of Cappuccilli's technique.

Cappuccilli sang with amazing regularity for over forty years, having made his debut in 1956 at the Teatro Nuovo in Milan in *Pagliacci*. But his rise to fame was a long one. There was strong competition throughout the entire repertoire from some fine singers. Moreover, his early acting tended to be a little bland, at times even monotonous. From 1971 on, when he was the

Ettore Bastianini, *in dark jacket in the center, with some friends and colleagues: from left* **Renata Tebaldi**, **Giulietta Simionato** *and* **Franco Corelli**, *all singing in* Adriana Lecouvreur. *To put together such a galaxy of stars today (and even more so for Adriana) is unthinkable: in forming a cast nowadays one aims at a good lead singer and a reasonably valid partner. The lack of authentic voices just does not allow for a full cast of four "giants" like these in the photo. (Historic Archives of the San Carlo Opera of Naples)*

Cornell MacNeil *in the role of Baron Scarpia, in a version of* Tosca *performed at the splendid Sferisterio in Macerata, 1979.*

Side by side during a recording session, **Sherill Milnes** *left, and the tenor* **Nicolai Gedda**. *Milnes is very active in the recording world. (Historic Archives of EMI. Photo: P. Wilson)*

Ettore Bastianini *in* Lucia, *in the role of Lord Ashton. Inexplicably, this artist from Tuscany has been severely attacked by the Italian critics, who, it seems, have forgotten the current disastrous state of the Italian baritone school. At the time of Bastianini (and this is the truth!), there was too much competition: Bechi, Gobbi, Taddei, Silveri, Protti, MacNeil, Mascherini, Guelfi, Panerai, and many others. (Historic Archives of La Fenice Theater Venice)*

Ettore Bastianini *in the role of Count di Luna in* Il Trovatore.

protagonist of a memorable version of *Simon Boccanegra* and of *Macbeth* under Strehler's direction, the artist reached his vocal and acting maturity, and began the second, glorious, part of his career. For twenty years he obtained worldwide triumphs as Rigoletto, Iago, Amonasro, Macbeth, Simon Boccanegra, and also in the lesser known role of Ezio in *Attila*, where he was acclaimed for his tenor-like b´ flats at the end of the *cabaletta* "È gettata la mia sorte," which never failed to excite the audience. His career, still at its height in the nineties, was suddenly cut short by a terrible road accident, which Cappuccilli miraculously survived but not without suffering severe injuries. After returning to the stage in *Aida*, *Pagliacci* and concerts, he devoted himself to teaching.

Figaro is a role not frequently sung by **Cappuccilli**, perhaps because it contains too many patter passages. In the photo the artist is involved in singing a high note, with Rosina, the mezzo-soprano **Alicia Nafé**. This performance was in 1982. (Historic Archives of the Opera Theater of Pretoria)

Aida: under the baton of von Karajan, gathered such famous names as **Cappuccilli** (Amonasro), Freni (Aida), Horne (Amneris), Ghiaurov (Ramfis), and Carreras (Radames). (Historic Archives of the Salzburg Festival)

Simon Boccanegra was taken on tour to Japan by La Scala. The role of the Doge has been thoroughly studied over the years by **Cappuccilli,** supported in the photo by **Freni** and the tenor **Luchetti**. (Bunka Kaikan. Tokyo. September, 1982)

THE *VILAIN* BARITONES
OF THE TWENTIETH CENTURY

The more malevolent and shady the character, the more the powerful voice of **Benvenuto Franci** (Pienza, Siena 1891 – Rome 1985) seemed to be at home. It was ideal for "bad guy" roles, such as those of Iago, Rance, Barnaba or Scarpia. He was in his full vocal glory during the twenties and thirties, and whilst vocalizing could easily emit a high c″ worthy of a tenor, maintaining a singular homogeneity between the registers.

What was amazing about **Domenico Viglione-Borghese** (Mondovì 1877 – Milan 1957) was the enormous volume of his voice and his fiery accent, especially in the parts of the sheriff in *Fanciulla del West*, Barnaba, Iago and Amonasro.

Andrea Mongelli (Bari 1901 – Rome 1970) had a less attractive timbre, but such a powerful high f′ that it permitted him to thunder as Rance, Gérard, Scarpia and Amonasro.

An elegant and refined Don Carlo in Verdi's Ernani, **Gino Bechi**. This singer played in many successful films, in which he was obviously exploited for the sound track. A light little song remains famous in the Bechi version: "Vieni, c'e una strada nel bosco" (Come, there's a path in the woods). (Historic Archives of the Rome Opera Theater)

Benvenuto Franci in Guglielmo Tell. His performances in London of Scarpia, Rigoletto, and Gérard, often with Jentza, signalled an epoch. (Historic Archives of the Rome Opera Theater)

Cesare Formichi (Rome 1883 – 1949) made his operatic debut at the Teatro San Carlo of Naples in 1911, revealing a torrential voice, ideal for the *vilain* baritone roles: Iago, Klingsor in *Parsifal*, Barnaba.

Another huge voice was that of **Antenore Reali** (Verona 1897 – Milan 1960), whom we can admire in his recording of *Il Tabarro* with Clara Petrella.

Gino Bechi (Florence 1913 – 1993) was not a *vilain* in the strict sense of the word, having played during the course of his career many different roles, not always of the natural-verist type.

Right from his debut (in *Traviata* at Empoli in 1936) his vocal ductility and extension were stunning, and, when necessary, he performed interminable *filature* and high notes up to a′. His physical presence did the rest, and the baritone from Tuscany dominated the stage as Amonasro, Rigoletto, Nabucco, Figaro, Iago and even Falstaff (under the baton of De Sabata, with the La Scala company at London in 1950).

Bechi's golden years were from 1936 to 1950, though he continued singing until 1965. His voice rang throughout the theater full and resonant, characterized by the nasal sound of certain notes (as though he wanted to make his characters seem more evil and his high notes more penetrating). He tended to overdo the *fermate* (he was renowned for his interminable "Dio m'esaudì" in *Traviata* and the phrase "Pietà signori, pietà" from *Rigoletto*) and his intonation was not always perfect. Nonetheless, he always managed to impassion the audience, with a charisma that few, if any, other baritones have possessed. He then began teaching, but with inconsistent results, and participated enthusiastically in singing competitions and master classes world-wide until his death, with the same verve and sarcasm so typical of Tuscans.

"Three Cops and a Carriage..." (Scarpia)

Tito Gobbi (Bassano del Grappa 1913 – Rome 1984) had a huge repertoire (consisting of more than one hundred operas) and a career even longer than that of Bechi: he made his singing debut as Count Rodolfo (*Sonnambula*), a bass part, at Gubbio in 1936; his official debut as a baritone came in 1938 at the Teatro Adriano of Rome in *Traviata*.

During the first part of his career (1936-56) he displayed a voice which, though not powerful, had a lovely timbre, smooth and delicate in the *mezzavoce*, flexible in the legato; this talent was aided by noteworthy intelligence and stage presence. With rare style and musicality he played Figaro, Rigoletto, Wozzek, Rodrigo (*Don Carlos*) Iago, Tonio, Gianni Schicchi, Scarpia, Falstaff, Simon Boccanegra, Don Giovanni and Michele (*Tabarro*). However, he had serious problems in placing high notes, which were always approached with incorrect positioning in the facial mask and seemed closer to a scream than to a sung note. It would be too easy and, for that matter, unjust to keep harping on this point, considering that the second part of Gobbi's career (1956-1976) was seriously damaged by his problems in the upper register. What was exceptional about the Venetian baritone was his ability to enter into the psychology of a character, studying the era and its customs with attention to both the historic and musical background of the opera being performed. To this meticulous preparation,

Gobbi in Leoncavallo's Pagliacci. With a glance, a small smirk, a gesture, Gobbi succeeded in making his character come alive. (Historic Archives of the Rome Opera Theater Photo: Oscar Savio)

The role of Renato in Ballo in Maschera, a role **Gobbi** did not really like; and yet just look at the proud nobility he displays in this photo. (Historic Archive of EMI)

Gobbi added formidable make-up and costuming and a fantastic stage presence, moving before his audience with the skill of a great actor.

It would be difficult to find a more cynical Baron Scarpia, a falser Iago, a shrewder Schicchi, a more malicious Tonio than those offered by Gobbi for decades in theaters all over the world. As Scarpia, his gesture of running his goose-feather pen down Tosca's arm just after having used it to write Cavaradossi's sentence would make the audience shiver with disgust.

As the Doge in *Simon Boccanegra* Gobbi knew instead how to be noble and profoundly human, finding moving shadings and accents in the death scene. His Figaro was an amiable rascal, his Falstaff an aristocratic rogue, while his Don Giovanni was exuberant and proud. He also sang this part at Salzburg with Furtwängler.

Right up until 1976, when Gobbi sang his last Falstaff in Germany, he was one of the public's best loved and most acclaimed artists.

*And here is that friendly rogue, Gianni Schicchi, to whom **Gobbi** gave a special voice – "yellow," the baritone described it. (Historic Archives of the Rome Opera Theater Photo: Oscar Savio)*

*In the gallery of characters made unforgettable by **Tito Gobbi** we must justly insert his cruel and introspective Michele of Il Tabarro. (Historic Archives of the Rome Opera Theater. Photo: Oscar Savio)*

*December 26, 1960. **Mario Del Monaco** and **Tito Gobbi** in Verdi's Otello, conducted in Rome by Franco Capuano. The darts of the Italian music critics were aimed at Gobbi, just as at Bastianini – criticism that can never darken the memories left by these two truly great artists. (Historic Archives of the Rome Opera Theater. Photo: Oscar Savio)*

Guelfi strikes the poor *Corelli* without pity in Allegra's opera Romulus. Whether for their voices or for their physique, both singers were perfectly suited to the roles of mythical heroes. (Historic Archives of the Rome Opera Theater. Photo: Oscar Savio)

Cyclone Guelfi

In his *Voci parallele*, Lauri Volpi calls **Giangiacomo Guelfi's** (Rome 1924) voice "a veritable foghorn"; and one cannot disagree, considering its power and volume. After his debut in 1950 as Rigoletto, he won the Spoleto Experimental Theater competition, and then his career took off with some well-defined roles: Ezio in *Attila*, Rance in *Girl of the Golden West*, Macbeth, Gianciotto in *Francesca da Rimini*, Amonasro in *Aida*, Telramund in *Lohengrin*, and Scarpia in *Tosca*.

However, we must not think of Guelfi's voice as a sort of hurricane or a machine for huge sounds. His memorable interpretation of the

A memorable performance of I Due Foscari (Verdi) given at La Fenice Theater of Venice on December 26, 1957. The leading performers were **Giangiacomo Guelfi** (Doge), left in the photo; at the center is Maestro Serafin, and to the right **Leyla Gencer** (Lucrezia) and **Mirto Picchi** (Jacopo Foscari). The evening was a triumph, thanks to their vibrant performances. (Historic Archives of La Fenice Theater of Venice. Photo: Giacomelli)

Doge Foscari in the revival of Verdi's opera in 1957 under the baton of Tullio Serafin (La Fenice Theater, Venice) demonstrated that he used *mezzavoce* and soft singing to effect: bending his voice to the dictates of the score, his rich timbre assumed melancholy inflections that were very moving.

Obviously, the weight of his voice and his incisive accent made him ideal for the *vilain* roles, first amongst which Puccini's sheriff. Yet it is also true that his premature vocal fatigue was due to his excessive use of bombastic resonances and of sounds which were forcibly widened, which he achieved without ever lightening his voice, as is technically necessary.

Other baritones of recent years include **Matteo Manuguerra** (Tunisi 1924 – Montpellier 1998), gifted with an ample, mellow voice, who became a baritone at the age of thirty-seven having begun his career as a tenor. He achieved world-wide success especially in the last years of his life, at the Met. **Louis Quilico** (Montreal 1929 – 2000) also had a long-lasting association with the famous American opera house (from 1971 on) singing a wide repertoire, thanks to excellent vocal characteristics, though his style and phrasing were somewhat less refined. **Ingvar Wixell** (Lulea, Sweden 1931) was frequently engaged to perform Scarpia during the eighties, though his voice was not particularly suited to this role (clear timbre, limited volume). The French baritone **Alain Fondary** (Bagnolet, Paris 1932) and the Italian **Silvano Carroli** (Venice 1939) were both gifted with an authentic baritone voice as regards color, volume and extension, especially suited to the roles of Scarpia, Nabucco, Jack Rance, which they have performed on numerous occasions outdoors (Verona Arena, Orange, Caracalla) and in the world's major theaters. Carrol performed Scarpia in Jonathan Miller's famous version at Florence, set during the Fascist era.

Excellent vocal characteristics belong also to **Bruno Pola** (Rovereto 1943) and the younger **Paolo Gavanelli** (Alcamo, Trapani 1959), who have both succeeded in creating a far from secondary niche for themselves at an international level, thanks to a solid professional ability.

THE *GRAND SEIGNEUR* BARITONES

*An elderly but still formidable **De Luca** performs with **Martinelli** and the blond **Maria Jeritza**, accompanied at the piano by Arturo Toscanini. A memorable concert!*

Three Aces:
De Luca, Galeffi, Tagliabue

Giuseppe De Luca (Rome 1878 – New York 1950) made his stage debut in 1897 at Piacenza, singing Valentine in *Faust*. His beginning in provincial theaters saw him performing, above all, comic parts, and secondary ones at that: Lescaut, Silvio (*Pagliacci*), Marcello (*Bohème*); and then he took part in the first performance of *Adriana Lecouvreur* (Milan 1902), creating a magnificent Michonnet. It was the big turning point in his career. He was signed up by all the major theaters year after year in a wide selection of operas (*Favorita, Puritani, Rigoletto, Traviata, Barbiere, Don Pasquale, Tosca, Aida, Mastersingers of Nuremberg, Butterfly*), always with great success.

He was impeccable in style, refined in phrasing, and possessed a controlled and fluid emission which he put to the service of a clear tenor-like timbre. De Luca can be considered the first *grand seigneur* baritone of the twentieth century. Due to the quality of his technique and his aristocratic acting, he managed to confer nobility even to more violent parts such as

Amonasro, Barnaba, Scarpia, or Beckmesser in *Mastersingers*. He also demonstrated a great variety of nuances in his favorite characters: Rigoletto, Figaro, Gérmont, Rodrigo and Malatesta (*Don Pasquale*).

After having sung over one hundred different opera roles, and having allowed himself the luxury of performing *Rigoletto* when he was over seventy, he celebrated his golden jubilee in 1947 with a legendary concert at the Town Hall of New York. In his recording of the Figaro-Rosina duet, together with Lily Pons, made in 1940, he continues to amaze his listeners with a voice as clear as when he first began.

De Luca never had a very powerful voice, quite the opposite, he was often obliged to avoid the extreme high notes with clever tricks. Nonetheless, he was a great singer and a good teacher, always full of advice for young singers.

While a lyric tendency was immediately apparent in De Luca's singing, this was not true for **Carlo Galeffi** (Malamocco, Venice 1884 – Rome 1961), who exhibited great vocal volume

*A fine photo of **Carlo Galeffi**, Rigoletto of outstanding talent. (Historic Archives of the Rome Opera Theater)*

and a certain arrogance right from the start of his career, especially when he sang Amonasro, Scarpia, Escamillo and Tonio.

He made his debut in 1889 in a minor part in *Forza del Destino*, followed by sporadic performances of *Lucia*, *Pagliacci* and *Rigoletto* in Rome. His excellent vocal placement, his musicality and his sensitivity as an artist enabled him to evolve towards a greater softness and poise in his singing, until he reached a truly stylized and noble singing technique.

He was the first to perform some of Mascagni's compositions (*Amica*, *Parisina*, *Isabeau*), the role of Fanuel in Boito's *Nerone*, Manfredo in Montemezzi's *L'Amore di Tre Re*, and he also gave the first performance of Amfortas in Italy and the first Schicchi in Europe. However, his greatest roles, between 1910 and the mid-fifties, were *Rigoletto*, *Nabucco*, *Guglielmo Tell*, *Ballo in Maschera*, *Simon Boccanegra*, and especially the aristocratic roles of Rodrigo and Carlo V (*Ernani*), not forgetting his woeful *Boris Godunov*, sung under the guidance of Arturo Toscanini.

Carlo Tagliabue (Mariano Comense 1898 – Monza 1978) took on De Luca's and Galeffi's inheritance, demonstrating that class and a refined technique can enable a singer to remain on stage for decades without feeling the weight of a wide repertoire or the passing of the years. The Italian baritone, in fact, sang from 1922 (when he debuted in *Loreley* at Lodi) until 1958, when he decided to retire while still in full possession of his vocal abilities.

With his heavy, rich, but flexible and smooth voice, Tagliabue was an excellent King Alfonso in *La Favorita*, Don Carlos in *Forza del Destino*, Germont, Rigoletto, Conte di Luna, Riccardo in *Puritani*, Gérard, Scarpia and Enrico in *Lucia*, allowing us to admire the beauty of his authentic legato, his full *mezzavoce*, never falsetto, and his class.

Good Old Sir John

For various reasons the artistic activity of **Giuseppe Taddei** (Genoa 1916) has a hint of the miraculous: a career lasting over sixty years (from 1936 when he made his debut at Rome as the Herald in *Lohengrin*, to *Gianni Schicchi* and *Elisir d'Amore* performed in 1999!), almost ten thousand performances and more than 140 different roles.

Taddei began singing almost at birth. At the age of fourteen he was imitating the great baritones at small operatic gatherings and made his debut as an Ogre in the operatic version of *Puss in Boots*. During singing lessons with his

Carlo Tagliabue (Rigoletto) with the soprano **Dolores Wilson** (Gilda) in a performance during the 1950-51 season at La Fenice, Venice. (Historic Archives of La Fenice, Venice. Photo: Giacomelli)

teacher, Giuseppina Lusso, he flatly refused to vocalize but would burst into song in the famous arias straight away: his was a voice born for opera. From 1946, after a tragic period as a prisoner of war in a German concentration camp, the young baritone was launched in the opera theaters of Austria and immediately signed up, practically "adopted", by the Vienna Staatsoper, the theater in which Taddei sang without respite from 1946 to 1992, adored by both audiences and conductors alike. Here, he gave historical performances of *Le nozze di Figaro* with Böhm, *Tosca* and *Othello* with Karajan and *Simon Boccanera* with Abbado in 1989.

His voice had a rare tone-color and has often, without any exaggeration, been compared to the smooth and velvety *cavata* of a cello, a full-bodied sound, emitted with technical expertise. Taddei also possessed an innate ability for imaginative interpretation, succeeding in finding the right vocal expression (accents, coloring and inflexions), the right make-up, stage movements and characterization for each role.

It is obvious that with all these gifts his repertoire could be nothing but wide and varied and, in fact, included over fifty parts: from his splendid Mozart (Figaro, Leporello, Papageno and Guglielmo in *Così Fan Tutte*) to his indomitable Falstaff, the role with which he celebrated his golden jubilee at the Metropolitan, with James

Giuseppe Taddei, *Dulcamara in Elisir d'Amore staged in Florence in 1984. To the right we can recognise* **Luciana Serra** *and* **Alfredo Kraus**. *(Historic Archives of the Teatro Comunale of Florence. Photo: Marchiori)*

Taddei-*Dulcamara triumphantly demonstrates his miraculous elixir – does the secret of his extraordinary artistic longevity lie in that magic bottle? (Historic Archives of the Rome Opera Theater. Photo: Reale)*

Falstaff, 1982: for his new Salzburg production von Karajan called on **Giuseppe Taddei**, **Rolando Panerai**, **Raina Kabaivanska**, **Francesco Aralza** *and* **Christa Ludwig**. *It was an enormous success, captured on disc by Deutsche Grammophon. (Historic Archives of the Salzburg Festival. Photo: Weber)*

A fine portrait of **Giuseppe Taddei** *as Germont.*

Levine conducting, under the direction of Franco Zeffirelli; from his mature Verdi (*Macbeth, Rigoletto, Traviata, Vespri Siciliani, Simon Boccanegra, Otello*) to the most important Verist roles, including among the many Scarpia, Tonio, Schicchi and Gérard. His performances were all marked by incisive phrasing and a variety of shadings.

But there have been other roles that have played an important part over the span of Taddei's long career: his poetical and lovable Hans Sachs in *The Mastersingers*, his shady and somber Flying Dutchman, his Prince Igor, and his unforgettable Eugene Onegin.

The last stage appearances of this indomitable lion included Tosca and Falstaff recorded for Italian Radio in 1997-98; *Elisir d'Amore* in Japan and *Gianni Schicchi* in 1999; not to mention umpteen concerts held the world over (the latest in March 2000 at Osaka and Tokyo!).

The Class of Renato Bruson

Renato Bruson (Ganze, Padua 1936) has inherited a part of Taddei's noble phrasing and rich timbre. Thanks to his assiduous studies with his teacher Fava Ceriati, and to his long apprenticeship in Donizetti and Verdi's early works, the Venetian singer is able to modulate his voice very well, obtaining *smorzature* and an extremely gentle legato. From 1975 until today, following his initial dedication to memorable revivals of early romantic operas such as *Maria di Rohan, Il Pirata, Masnadieri, Linda di Chamounix, Caterina Cornaro*), Bruson has intensified his involvement with Verdi's greatest characters (Macbeth, Simone, Doge Foscari, Don Carlo, Rigoletto, Marquis of Posa, Germont, Miller, Jago, Falstaff) and has enlarged his repertoire to include *Andrea Chénier, Tosca, Don Giovanni* (he made his debut in Bonn in 1984), confirm-

Renato Bruson *in* I Masnadieri *by Verdi, presented in Rome on 25 November, 1972. For at least a decade during the sixties, although taking part in many important productions, Bruson was virtually ignored by the critics and the recording industry. (Historic archives of the Rome Opera)*

Two great singer-actors, **Renato Bruson** (Germont) and **Raina Kabaivanska** (Violetta), in the second act of Traviata, Macerata, 1984. (Photo: A. Tabocchini)

ing his superb expressive ability and class. Bruson's trump card is his noble, measured emission, his *mezzevoci*, his impeccable legato and the total absence of histrionics. His voice always sounds homogeneous in the middle register, perhaps less confident on the high and low notes. His stage presence is most impressive, as can be seen from his impersonations of the old Doge Foscari, the insinuating Iago, at last played according to Verdi's intentions.

Leo Nucci and the New Era

With **Leo Nucci** (Castiglion de' Pepoli, Bologna 1942) a new era of international stars has opened. It is the era of records, of digital technology, of large companies that manage the destiny of opera in the world and of television that establishes the precepts. The opera singer, in order to achieve success, need not necessarily shatter windows with the power of his voice; he must know how to act on stage, he must be musical and confident, be able to jump from one plane to another without a moment of respite. This, in brief, is a portrait of Leo Nucci: his voice is not exceptional but used with intelligence and very extensive (he began his studies as a tenor); it is accompanied by rare acting skills, and can tackle a vast repertoire which, after a brilliant debut, singing Figaro at Spoleto

in 1967, has gradually been concentrated on Nucci's favorite composer, Verdi. Nucci has virtually become identified with Rigoletto, a role he has sung in all of the world's major theaters. He is unequalled in the *cabalette*, and in the *strette* of Verdi's operas up to the concluding top note: Nucci is unrivalled on the g´s and high notes which often conclude the master scenes of *Forza del Destino*, *Luisa Miller*, *Ballo in Maschera*. His long preparation, first with the La Scala chorus and then with small provincial theaters, has provided both invaluable experience and a knowledge of the trade that few can boast, and has enabled Nucci to remedy with a thousand theatrical stratagems all manner of emergency situations.

The more recent generations of baritones include **Gino Quilico** (New York 1955), son of the famous Louis, who, after a brilliant start to his career in the French and Italian repertoires, has failed to find his ideal speciality (his best results have been as Figaro and Malatesta); **Paolo Coni** (Perugia 1957), a sensitive and intelligent performer of many of Donizetti's belcanto roles, but less successful for technical reasons in Verdi; **Roberto Frontali** (Rome 1958) and **Roberto Servile** (Genoa 1957), both of whom have a good technique and interesting natural talent, especially suited to Mozart and belcanto in general, but less so to the dramatic repertoire; the Russian **Dimitri Hvorostovsky**

(Krasnojarsk 1962), star of the recording industry, endowed with a voice of unexceptional volume but beautiful color, specially suited to the role of Onegin and also to early Verdi operas; the American **Dwayne Croft**, new star of the Met in the late nineties, gifted with a beautifully colored, penetrating voice (he made an excellent Figaro in Barbiere and Marquis of Posa) and a tall, slim physique.

Heldenbariton: The Wagnerian Baritones of the Twentieth Century

Heading the list of best performers of the difficult Wagnerian baritone parts in the twentieth century is **Anton van Rooy** (Rotterdam 1870 – Munich 1932), a most profound and vocally gifted Wotan, Sachs and Kurwenald in the years between 1891 and 1914. For having sung Amfortas in the *prima assoluta* of *Parsifal* at New York in 1903, violating Wagner's dictate that forbade the opera being performed outside Bayreuth, he was banned from the "sacred city" until 1913.

Leo Nucci again, during a pause in the performance of Il Barbiere di Siviglia staged in 1996. (Fondazione Arena di Verona. Photo: Gianfranco Fainello)

Leo Nucci in Rigoletto (2001), a role he has sung in all the world's major opera theaters. (Fondazione Arena di Verona. Photo: Gianfranco Fainello)

Friedrich Schorr (Nagyvàrad 1888 – Farmington, Connecticut 1953) can be considered the heir of van Rooy, for he was the greatest Wotan, Sachs and Flying Dutchman from 1920 until 1940. His recordings reveal a rich, warm timbre, a particularly incisive voice in the dramatic passages and caressing *mezzevoci*.

Rudolf Bockelmann (Luneburg 1892 – Dresden 1958) also proved exceptional in the most perilous Wagnerian parts, singing between 1923 and 1945 and rivaling Schorr. Because of his Nazi tendencies he had to interrupt his career in the immediate post-war period, dedicating his time to teaching singing.

A group of eminent performers populate the beginning of the twentieth century; **Leopold Demuth** (Brunn 1861 – Czernowitz 1910); **Friedrich Weidemann** (Ratzeburg in Holstein 1871 – Vienna 1919), who took part in many first performances at Vienna (*Elektra* in 1909, *Pélleas* in 1910, *Der Rosenkavalier* in 1911) and was also a Mozart specialist; **Martial Singher** (Oloron, Pyrénées 1904 – S. Barbara, California 1990) was an excellent Amfortas; **José Beck-**

mans (Liège 1897 – Vichy 1987), whose repertoire was limitless (more than 300 operas!), was most applauded as Kurwenald (*Tristan*) and Wotan, especially in his performances at the Opera Theater of Monte Carlo.

Emil Schipper (Vienna 1882 – 1957), the first Barak in *Die Frau ohne Schatten* in 1919, was an acclaimed Wagnerian baritone until 1938.

Herbert Janssen (Cologne 1895 – New York 1965) had a smooth and well-modulated voice. It was particularly suited to noble and melancholy characters like Wolfram (*Tannhäuser*) and Amfortas (*Parsifal*). He sang from 1924 until 1951 in Germany, America and England, specializing above all in one role: that of Kothner in *The Mastersingers*.

Heinrich Schlusnus (Braubach 1888 – Frankfurt 1952) and his follower, **Josef Metternich** (Hermulheim, Cologne 1915) are best remembered for their important work in promoting Verdi in Germany (the Verdi revival began there in 1930); but their interest in Wagner must not be forgotten either. Metternich, in particular, proved to be a truly diabolical Telramond.

Paul Schöffler (Dresden 1897 – Amersham, Buckinghamshire 1977) was one of the most complete baritones in every sense, singing between 1926 and 1965. He had a rich, well-emitted voice which extended from a warm, low register to easy, penetrating high notes. He was very musical and respected with absolute precision every expressive sign left by the composer, be it Mozart, Wagner or Richard Strauss. Schöffler became famous for his interpretations of Sachs, the Flying Dutchman, Jochanaan (*Salome*), Don Pizzarro (*Fidelio*), Figaro and the Count in *The Marriage of Figaro*, and Don Giovanni.

One of the greatest German singer-actors ever was **Erich Kunz** (Vienna 1909-1995). The Vienna State Opera audience was able to continue applauding him into the eighties, when the elderly singer would still perform small parts, always demonstrating his extraordinary acting gifts and his mastery of "spoken-song".

He made his debut 1933 as Osmino (a *basso-profondo* part) but the roles which were most suited to his flexible and amiable voice were Papageno, the sarcastic Beckmesser and the extrovert Leporello, roles he sang frequently at Salzburg, Vienna, New York, London, and in Italy.

Amongst the most aristocratic singers belonging to the generation following Schöffler, was **Eberhard Wächter** (Vienna 1929 – 1992), still singing at the beginning of the nineteen-eighties, though with evident vocal deterioration.

The historic, matchless Papageno of **Erich Kunz**, a master of "Sprechgesang"; a likeable, dynamic actor, and much-loved favorite at the Vienna Staatsoper. (Historic Archives of the Rome Opera Theater)

In the period from 1950 until 1960 he was one of the most acclaimed performers of Amfortas, and, in the Verdi repertory, of Renato and Rodrigo. Under the guidance of the greatest conductors, he was also a Count Almaviva and a Don Giovanni of rare scenic and vocal talent.

King Dietrich I

The uncontested king of the German baritones is **Dietrich Fischer-Dieskau** (Berlin 1925), whose extraordinary career stretched from 1947, when he made his debut at Freiburg as a soloist in Brahms' *Deutsche Requiem*, to his last concert in Berlin in the mid-nineties, when he decided to retire after having sung symbolically the fugue from Falstaff ("Tutto nel mondo è burla"). His voice was not particularly wide or powerful, but exceptionally flexible and well-extended (from low E to high b′), capable of penetrating the profoundest meaning of a score, be it Bach, Handel, Mozart, Verdi, Wagner, Strauss, or the entire Lieder repertory, which he performed with particular interpretative intelligence and musicality.

Thanks to his perfect Italian pronunciation, which is easier to understand than that sung by many Italians, Fischer-Dieskau was able to include Falstaff, Rigoletto, Iago, Rodrigo, Renato, Sharpless, Scarpia, Gérmont and Guglielmo Tell in his repertoire, finding for each opera the right inflexion, coloring and dramatic definition.

Amongst his best characterizations were his elegant Mandryka in *Arabella,* his noble Wolfram in *Tannhäuser,* his sorrowful Amfortas in *Parsifal,* his poetic Sachs in *The Mastersingers,* and his unsurpassable performance of the Count in the *Marriage of Figaro.*

The extraordinary artistic story of Fischer-Dieskau, apart from his vocal contribution to the history of opera singing (which is often easily overlooked), is summed up in the definition "musician-singer", that is, in his capacity to follow the directions given by the composer, always respecting, never exceeding, what was written on the score.

In conclusion, here are some other noteworthy singers who have performed in the world's most important theaters: **Hermann Prey** (Berlin 1929 – Krailling, Baviera 1998), an exceptional Beckmesser, an acclaimed Figaro (both in Mozart and in Rossini), and a much appreciated Lieder singer, even though his specific vocal limitations prevented him from including Verdi and the Italian romantics in his repertoire. **Walter Berry** (Vienna 1929-2000), excellent in the Mozart roles of Leporello, Don Alfonso, Papageno, Guglielmo and Figaro, and the Wagner roles of Klingsor, Wotan and Telramond, executing all these parts with great stage ability and vocal confidence. One of his best portrayals of the later years of his cereer is that of Barak in Richard Strauss' *Die Frau ohne Schatten.* The Englishman **Norman Bailey** (Birmingham 1933) has been a Wotan par excellence at the Sadler's Wells company of London; but he is also much acclaimed in the roles of Pizzaro, Gunter, Hans Sachs, and Kutuzov in *War and Peace.* **Donald McIntyre** (Auckland, New Zealand 1934) is an acclaimed Wagnerian baritone (Wotan, Kingsor, Amfortas) at Covent Garden. **Thomas Stewart** (S. Saba, Texas 1928) is a stable member of the Deutsche Oper of Berlin and also performs at Bayreuth in the parts of Wotan, the Flying Dutchman and Amfortas. His voice is smooth and well projected and his acting is equally good.

Reinforcing the ranks of contemporary German repertory baritones are the solid, flexible voices of **Bernd Weikl** (Vienna 1942) and **Wolfgang Brendel** (Munich 1947), both of whom are excellent singers and gifted actors. Brendel reaches high b′ without effort in chest voice (*Carmina Burana*) with a beautiful timbre. He performs Papageno, Wolfram, Figaro, Renato and Silvio in *Pagliacci,* principally in Munich. The only criticism that could be made of his performances is that they are sometimes a little uncommitted.

Weikl is more dynamic and spirited: his Doctor Falke in Johann Strauss' *Die Fledermaus* is great fun, and punctually repeated each New Year at Vienna; another of his regular roles is that of Belcore in *L'Elisir d'Amore.* Strangely enough, though Weikl has a voice with a beautiful timbre and achieves a good extension, he fails to accomplish a credible Gérmont or Figaro (Rossini). He exaggerates too much, and abuses the high notes. On the other hand, his perform-

Dietrich Fischer-Dieskau.

ances in *Eugene Onegin*, *The Mastersingers* (Hans Sachs) and *Parsifal* (Amfortas) are excellent, and there he demonstrates a noble phrasing and fidelity to style.

Another excellent northern talent is **John Bröcheler** (Vaals, Holland 1945), who did his master studies in Paris under Pierre Bernac. Singing mainly in the United States and German opera houses, he is best known for his participations in *Don Giovanni*, *Arabella*, *Parsifal* and *Elektra*. He is justly acclaimed for a voice characterized by its magnificent polish and powerful sound.

Proposed by Abbado for a number of important Mozart productions, **Bryn Terfel** (Port Kmadog, Wales 1965) and **Simon Keenlyside** have both proved to possess excellent stylistic and acting abilities; Terfel in particular has an attractive, full-bodied timbre and a natural talent for the Italian repertoire (in 2000 he made his debut in *Falstaff* in London). Another highly popular singer is **Olaf Bär** (Dresden 1957), famous as the Count in *Nozze di Figaro*, but better on record than on stage, by virtue of some rather evident vocal limitations.

THE COMIC BARITONE IN ITALIAN COMIC OPERA AND MOZART

In the difficult art of farce a singer must be able to unite vocal gifts (agility, extension and speedy patter) with stage talent. He needs to be having good fun himself, to be able to make us have fun. Apart from the great Taddei, who was included with the *grand seigneur* baritones,

Rightly famous, the Figaro of **Bruscantini**, *here photographed during a performance at Parma for the 1966-67 season. (Historic Archives of the Teatro Regio of Parma. Photo: Montacchini)*

another master of the comic genre was **Sesto Bruscantini** (Porto Civitanova, Macerata 1919), though he interpreted other roles from the baritone repertory with equal success: Riccardo (*Puritani*), Rodrigo (*Don Carlos*), Simon Boccanegra, Gérmont, Scarpia, Falstaff, Rigoletto and Atanaele (*Thaïs*). In these operas the intelligent Italian singer succeeded in substituting the arrogance and exaggeration of many bad performers with a knowing use of *mezzevoci*, varied accents, and imaginative and stylized phrasing of great class.

Certainly, Bruscantini's voice found fertile ground in the comic repertory right from his start in 1949 (Don Geronimo in *Matrimonio Segreto* at La Scala). He never hammed his acting by inserting jokes of dubious or bad taste. Instead he followed a moderate line founded on the correct use of recitative and authentic virtuosity. In later years, Sesto Bruscantini triumphed as Dulcamara, Don Pasquale, Don Bartolo in *Barbiere* and Don Alfonso in *Così Fan Tutte*, giving genuine singing lessons to many of his younger colleagues.

Of the younger generation **Bruno Praticò** (Aosta 1958) excels as one of the most refined comic bass baritones, adhering strongly to the Bruscantini and Dara tradition. His voice, though of limited volume, is ductile and extensive, and has enabled Praticò to successfully take on roles from Rossini and Donizetti operas, earning particular acclaim as Don Bartolo, Dulcamara and in the main comic roles. His teacher was the famous baritone Valdegno.

Bruscantini's heritage has instead passed to

two of his pupils, **Roberto De Candia** (Bisceglie, Bari 1968) and **Alfonso Antoniozzi** (Viterbo 1964), both dedicated to the comic genre, though with different vocal characteristics and manner of interpretation. Antoniozzi has the more impressive stage presence, while De Candia lays stronger emphasis on his singing, though he has yet to reach the heights of his illustrious teacher.

At the beginning of the twentieth century there were many comic baritones on the stage worthy of a mention here, such as **Jean Périer** (Paris 1869 – Nevilly 1954), who sang the French and Mozart repertoires; **André Pernet** (Rambersville 1894 – Paris 1966), an acclaimed Don Giovanni; **Francisco d'Andrade** (Lisbon 1859 – Berlin 1921), who performed a legendary Don Giovanni until 1919; **Alfred Jerger** (Brünn 1889 – Vienna 1976), a perfect Mozart singer performing mainly at Salzburg; **John Forsell** (Stockholm 1868 – 1941), who taught Jussi Björling and Set Svanholm; **Gerhard Hüsch** (Hanover 1901 – Munich 1984), an excellent Papageno; **John Brownlee** (Geelong, Australia 1900 – New York 1959), a grand Don Giovanni and Guglielmo in the version of *Così Fan Tutte* conducted by Busch; **Lucien Fugère** (Paris 1848 – 1935), a legendary interpreter of the now little performed French *comique* repertoire, as was **Maurice Renaud** (Bordeaux 1861 – Paris 1933), one of the most extraordinary personalities of the French school, as can be heard, luckily, from his recordings.

Lucien Fugère performed from 1870 to 1933, when he once again sang as Bartolo in *Barbiere* at the Trianon-Lyrique in Paris. He remains one of the mythical interpreters of the French lyric and comic repertory, especially known for his performances as the Duc de Longueville in Messager's *La Basoche*. Further accolades attended his highly entertaining interpretations of Leporello, Falstaff and Papageno.

Maurice Renaud started his career in Brussels in 1884. After his acclaimed performances in Paris, London, Berlin, at La Scala and the Met, he was nicknamed "the French Battistini." As a singer-actor his niche in history is secure, and he is still remembered for his crystal clear diction and his interpretative creativity, particularly when he played Méphistophélès in *La Damnation de Faust*, a role he also sang in a noteworthy 1902 production at La Scala, with Toscanini conducting. His was a wide-ranging repertory, including Iago, Don Alfonso, Don Giovanni, Scarpia, Rigoletto, Figaro and Germont. His final performance was in a Paris production of Offenbach's *Monsieur Choufleuri*.

At a somewhat later date **Michel Dens** (Roubaix 1911) and **Renato Capecchi** (Cairo

Francisco d'Andrade is Don Giovanni beside the legendary *Lilli Lehmann*'s Donna Anna.

1923 – Milan 1998) came to international attention. Dens specialized in the role of Figaro in *Barbiere* but had a wide repertory and a long career, singing until the end of the nineteen-eighties. Capecchi made his debut in Reggio Emilia in 1949 and was still singing in the early nineties, though almost exclusively in the United States. An excellent singer-actor, he could range from the dramatic parts of Iago, Ashton (*Lucia di Lammermoor*) or Amonasro to a wide variety of comic and brilliant roles, such as Figaro, Leporello, Dr. Bartolo, Falstaff and Dulcamara, not to mention the contemporary repertory. Among his most famous characterizations were Ford and Fra Melitone (*Forza del Destino*).

In our historic overview, we cannot skip names such as **Alberto Rinaldi** (Rome 1939) and **Richard Stilwell** (St. Louis 1942). Rinaldi has made his name in particular in Germany, Austria and England, and is especially noted for his performances as Dandini, Ford, Figaro and Malatesta. Stilwell boasts a wide repertory,

Gabriel Bacquier *as Coppelius in Offenbach's* Les Contes d'Hoffmann. *He became internationally known in a variety of roles, including those of Scarpia* (Tosca) *and Boris Godunov.*

ranging from Monteverdi to Britten. He is renowned as Pelléas and the Count (*The Marriage of Figaro*).

Next, is a brief highlight of the career of **Gabriel Bacquier** (Béziers 1924). He has been on stage since 1949, offering a repertory that includes operettas as well as opera. Gifted with a full, yet pliant voice, he began his career alternating between a series of Mozart roles (the Count of Almaviva, Don Alfonso, Leporello, Don Giovanni) and the more dramatic parts of Iago, Scarpia and Marcello *(Bohème)*. In the nineties he began to devote his talent to comic roles, from Don Pasquale to Gianni Schicchi and from Sancho Panza (Massenet's *Don Quixote)* to Falstaff, performing with exuberant verve.

English-speaking countries were the main province of **Sir Geraint Evans** (Pontypridd, Wales 1922 – Aberystwyth, Wales 1992). He was a regular performer at Covent Garden from 1948 to 1984 when he bid farewell to the stage in his final Dulcamara *(Elisir d'Amore)*. The characters best suited to his intelligent interpretations were Beckmesser (*The Mastersingers)*, Papageno, Leporello, Mr. Flint *(Billy Budd* by Benjamin Britten), Falstaff and Figaro (Mozart). After his retirement he became active in stage direction, working in various American theaters and with the Welsh National Opera.

There is no disputing the fact that **Thomas Allen** (Seaham, Durham 1944) ranks as one of today's top international stars. Starting out in London in 1969 as Figaro in *Barbiere,* he has developed an extensive and eclectic repertory. His well-positioned voice is very smooth, with a good extension and beautiful color. And his acting talents contribute to his success, particularly in the noble roles of Eugene Onegin, Pélléas, the Count in *The Marriage of Figaro*, Valentin in *Faust* and Don Giovanni (La Scala production, 1987). Since 1973 he has taken part regularly in the annual Glyndebourne Festival, where he has sung almost all his favorite roles.

Derek Hammond-Strand (London 1929) studied with Husch and is memorable for his performance in roles such as Melitone, Bartolo and the sacristan in *Tosca,* but he has also achieved success as Alberich and Beckmesser. **Zoltán Kélémen** (Budapest 1933 – Zurich 1979) was a specialist in the part of Alberich, singing at Bayreuth, Salzburg and the Metropolitan. The English singer **John Shirley Quirk** (Liverpool 1931) was an excellent and refined performer in a wide repertoire ranging from Purcell to Mozart, but he also included the contemporary English composers, and oratorio. Sweden's **Hakan Hagegard** (Karlstaf, Sweden 1945) was Papageno in Ingmar Bergman's film *The Magic Flute.* **Benjamin Luxon** (Redruth 1937) has been on stage at Covent Garden since 1972 and applauded as the Conte d'Almaviva, Don Giovanni, Eisenstein in *Die Fledermaus,* and in *Eugene Onegin.* **Giorgio Gatti** (Poggio a Caiano, Florence 1948) performs a vast repertoire that ranges from Monteverdi to an infinity of eighteenth century Neapolitan songs, to Mozart, Rossini, Donizetti, Verdi, Puccini (Sharpless, the Sacristan, Ping), all accomplished with a blend of verve and moderation.

Rolando the Indomitable

Rolando Panerai (Campi Bisenzio, Florence 1924) is another illustrious veteran of the opera stage (he made his debut in *Werther*, in Florence, 1947) who developed a wide and demanding repertoire. Showing an uncommon vocal dexterity and resistance, he has been able to sing *Trovatore, Favorita, Puritani, Rigoletto* and *Bohème* and also Don *Pasquale, Mosè, Barbiere, Cenerentola, Così Fan Tutte* (both as Guglielmo and Alfonso) and many twentieth-century operas (Hindemith, Prokofiev and Turchi). The results have not always been successful, occasional slips of intonation and an exaggerated use of additional high notes have been noticed. This is especially true of his per-

Rolando Panerai *in* Gianni Schicchi, *singing with* **Cecilia Gasdia** *(Lauretta) and* **Alberto Cupido** *(Rinuccio). The spoken final of Schicchi "Ditemi voi signori" aroused an enormous response from the Florentine audience when Panerai declaimed it with a genuine Tuscan accent. (Historic Archives of the Teatro Comunale of Florence. Photo: Marchiori)*

formances in Verdi and in the romantic operas on the whole, whereas in comic opera Panerai has always communicated high spirits, amiability and good taste, being perfectly at his ease as Dulcamara, Malatesta, Don Alfonso, Leporello, Taddeo (*Italiana in Algeri*) and Figaro. He has totally identified himself with one role: that of Ford in *Falstaff*, of which he was Karajan's favorite interpreter for over thirty years.

Reflecting the destiny of other vocal categories, later generations of comic baritones have included many personalities of undeniable talent, but none on a par with the "prodigies" of the past. Here are some: **Claudio Desderi** (Alessandria 1943), who has become something of a myth in English-speaking countries (thanks in part to his long-standing cooperation with Abbado, Muti and other famous conductors),

applauded more for his dramatic talent in Mozart, Rossini and Donizetti, than for his unexceptional vocal qualities; **Alessandro Corbelli** (Turin 1952), former pupil of Valdegno, specializing in Mozart and Rossini, a stylistically correct singer, gifted with a voice of excellent color but of a less attractive timbre; **Lucio Gallo** (Taranto 1959), initially engaged to sing Mozart (he gave interesting performances in *Così Fan Tutte* conducted by Harnoncourt and as Leporello in Vienna in 1990, with Abbado), but who later extended his repertoire to comprise more dramatic roles, including a rather unconvincing Scarpia in *Tosca*, far too formal and lacking the necessary dramatic weight; **Pietro Spagnoli** (Rome 1964), an intelligent and well-prepared bass-baritone of great elegance, who is most careful in his choice of repertoire.

Other Famous Baritones

Concluding the chapter dedicated to the top baritones of the twentieth century, here is a list of other singers no less worthy of a mention. Beside each name we have gived the principal titles in his repertoire and a brief note on his vocal characteristics and career.

NAME	BASIC REPERTORY	REMARKS
Blanc, Ernest (1923) *Grand Seigneur* Baritone	French repertory. (Massenet, Bizet, Saint-Saëns)	An intense voice of beautiful color, smooth emission
Bösch, Christian (1941) *Spiel Bariton*	Mozart, J. Strauss, Lehár, Offenbach	An agile and self-possessed actor. His voice was neither particularly powerful nor extended. An excellent Papageno
Glossop, Peter (1928) Verdi Baritone	*Otello, Ernani, Forza del Destino, Ballo in Maschera, Traviata, Rigoletto*	An appreciated interpreter in the Verdi roles, especially in England. His voice was a little harsh but he had good stage talent
Gramm, Donald (D. Gramsch; 1927-1983) Bass Baritone	Mozart, Rossini, contemporary operas	A first rate singer-actor, with scenic verve and interesting vocal gifts
Hemsley, Thomas (1927) Comic Baritone	Wagner, Britten, contemporary operas	Specialist in the role of Beckmesser; first interpreter of Demetrius in *A Midsummer Night's Dream*
Herinex, Raimund (1927) Bass Baritone	Wagner, Verdi, Puccini, Massenet, contemporary operas	A wide and diverse repertory. The first performer of works by Maxwell Davies, Williamson, Henze, Tippett
Hynninen, Jorma (1941) Comic Baritone	Mozart, Verdi, contemporary Finnish operas	A refined and intelligent artist with a vast repertoire
Kraus, Otakar (1909-1980) Bass Baritone	Wagner, Stravinsky, Britten, Walton	Specialized in the role of Alberich; linked for many seasons with Covent Garden; singer in many first-ever performances. An esteemed teacher: among his students Robert Lloyd, Gwynne Howell, Elizabeth Connell
Kusche, Benno (1916) Comic Baritone	Wagner, Strauss, operetta	A talented character actor in opera and German operetta. The first interpreter of Orff's *Antigonae*
Leiferkus, Sergei (1946) *Grand Seigneur* Baritone	Verdi, Tchaikovsky, Mussorssky, Rimsky-Korsakov	One of the best Russian singers of recent generations. A complete artist, possessing a rich, well-placed voice
Lisitsian, Pavel (1911) Verdi Baritone	Verdi, Russian repertory	The first Russian artist to be invited to the Metropolitan of New York in 1960. Great natural gifts and dramatic talent
Massard, Robert (1925) *Grand Seigneur* Baritone	French operas	Excellent singer-actor. Specialist in the roles of Escamillo and Valentino (*Faust*)
Mazurok, Juri (1931) Verdi Baritone	Verdi, Tchaikovsky, Rimsky-Korsakov, Russian repertory	A voice of a lovely color emitted with a skillful technique; however, he is rather static on stage and monotonous in his phrasing
Nimsgern, Siegmund (1940) *Vilain* Baritone	Verdi, Wagner, Strauss, contemporary repertory	A singer-actor of note, much appreciated by directors and famous orchestra conductors. His voice presents some technical blanks
Nissen, Hans Hermann (1893-1980) Bass Baritone	Wagner, Strauss	Specialist in the roles of Wotan and Hans Sachs in the period between the two world wars. His voice was velvety and technically perfect
Paskalis, Kostas (1929) Verdi Baritone	Verdi, contemporary operas	A great actor and sensitive interpreter, despite occasional slips in intonation, specializing in the roles of Macbeth and Rigoletto

Reardon, John (1930-1988) Comic Baritone	Opera and operetta (English), contemporary repertory	An American artist with a very wide repertory. Often asked to work in films and on television
Roich, Günther (1921-1988) Comic Baritone	Contemporary operas	Famous in the part of Dr. Schön (*Lulu* by Schönberg) and in many other contemporary roles
Rothmüller, Marko (1908) Verdi Baritone	Verdi, contemporary operas	Much appreciated in *Wozzek* by Berg and for other rarely staged operas. Noted for his considerable on-stage ability and the lovely color of his voice
Souzay, Gérard (G. Tisserand, 1920) *Grand Seigneur* Baritone	French repertory, Lieder and chamber songs	A fine and intelligent performer of the Chamber Music repertory
Uppmann, Theodore (1920) Comic Baritone	Mozart, contemporary English and American operas	Much applauded in America as Papageno and as Pelléas. The first interpreter in America of Britten's *Billy Budd* and of Bernstein's A *Quiet Place*

Marian Anderson, *one of the first black solo artists to establish a name for herself on the concert stage.*

The Mezzo-Sopranos

The Mezzo-Soprano Voice: Extension and Phonation

The mezzo-soprano voice lies between the contralto and the soprano. The extension goes from a to a´´ but can be stretched from g to b´´ or even high c´´´. The same is true of the contralto, the lowest female voice, which is characterized by a greater volume and a darker timbre.

Up until the middle of the nineteenth century the term "mezzo-soprano" was not in use, as only various classes of contralto existed. With the advent of the Romantic School and the consequent extension of the tessitura, there arose a need for a true mezzo-soprano: from the classic role of the soprano's rival (Amneris in *Aida*) to the principal role (Leonora in *Favorita*), from the dreamy Mignon to the sensual Carmen, from the high singing Valentine in *Les Huguenots* to the deep, low La Cieca in *La Gioconda*. In Germany there exists a traditional division between the *dramatischer Alt*, or dramatic mezzo-soprano, characterized by a solid, incisive voice (Erda in the *Ring*) and the *komischer Alt*, the comic mezzo-soprano, whose voice is more extended and agile (Frau Reich in *The Merry Wives of Windsor*, by Nicolai).

The subdivision of the mezzo-soprano and contralto voices in the twentieth century must be based on each individual singer's repertoire, as the many definitions that exist for the tenor and soprano voice (light, lyric, dramatic, etc.) do not exist in this category.

However the mezzo-soprano repertory can be divided thus: the Romantic Italian and French works (Donizetti, Verdi, Thomas, Massenet); the Verist repertory (the Young Italian School and French Naturalism); the German repertory (Wagner, Richard Strauss) and the Russian repertoire (the Group of Five, Tchaikovsky, Shostakovich).

THE ITALIAN AND FRENCH ROMANTIC REPERTOIRE

Our roster opens with **Margarete Matzenauer** (Temesvàr 1881 – Van Nuys, California 1963), described by Lauri-Volpi as "a bewitching voice." Her debut was made in 1901, as Puck in Weber's *Oberon*; but it was not long before the public could applaud her vibrant interpretations of Azucena, Amneris, Laura (*Gioconda*), *Orfeo* (Gluck), Delilah, Fidès (*Le Prophète*), her wonderful Wagnerian performances, and her soprano performances (Isolde, Kundry, Ortrude, Brünnhilde).

From Monaco to New York, from London to Paris, from Bayreuth to Buenos Aires, Matzenauer was acclaimed for her exceptional voice, with its rich timbre, perfect polish, rare extension, uniformity in all the registers, power and penetration. These gifts were sustained by a fluid and smooth technique of vocal projection, worthy of a great singer. Strangely, her recordings do not pay her justice.

After 1914 she sang chiefly in contralto roles, including Kostelnicka in the American première of *Jenufa*, and Eboli in the first Met performance.

Her farewell to the stage took place in 1934, at the Lewisohn Stadium in New York, with a last performance of *Samson and Delilah*.

Fanny Anitùa (Durango 1887 – Mexico City 1968) studied in her homeland but did advanced studies in Rome, and made her debut at the Teatro Nazionale (Gluck's *Orfeo*) in 1910. The statuesque Mexican must have made quite an impression when she entered on stage with her imposing physique and voice. From 1910 until 1939 she sang regularly in Italy, America and in Latin-American theaters, bas-

*The celebrated contralto **Fanny Anitua**, with a proud stance, in the center of the back row, surrounded by her partners in a formidable Il Barbiere di Siviglia produced in Parma on March 11, 1916. Standing, at left, **Nazzareno De Angelis** (Basilio) and at right, **Umberto Macnez** (Fiorello); seated at left is **Giuseppe Kaschmann** (Bartolo); at center **Amilcare Zanella** (Almaviva); and at the right **Carlo Galeffi** (Figaro). They were celebrating the centenary of Rossini's opera. (Historic Archives of the Teatro Regio of Parma)*

ing her repertoire on *Trovatore, Ballo in Maschera* (Ulrica), *Orfeo, Aida, Samson and Delilah*, and singing the role of Etra in the first-ever performance of Pizzetti's *Fedra*. Her voice was renowned for its extension and vigor, both in the high and low notes, sustained by a moderate agility.

Two authentic, truly talented Verdi contraltos were **Elvira Casazza** (Ferrara 1887 – Milan 1965) and **Cloe Elmo** (Lecce 1910 – Ankara 1962). Casazza created the role of Jaele in Pizzetti's opera *Debora and Jaele* (La Scala, 1922), and had low notes which sounded like those of a baritone. Cloe Elmo was an unforgettable Azucena, Quickly and Ulrica, vocally uniform and penetrating over her entire wide range.

And we must not omit the gifted, but unfortunate **Kathleen Ferrier** (Higher Walton, Lancashire 1912 – London 1953) who died of cancer at the height of a great career. The terrain favored by her warm, velvety, smooth voice was not that of opera (even if she often sang Gluck's *Orfeo* and a single *Carmen*) but Lied and oratorio, with a special preference for Mahler. Her version of the *Lied von der Erde* and the *Kindertotenlieder*, under the baton of the great Bruno Walter, is an example of a refined and sensitive art. She was unique for the depth of her dramatic interpretations and the pure beauty of her vocal timbre. Her fatal illness prevented her from completing her series of Covent Garden performance, as Gluck's *Orpheus*, 1953.

Upon completion of her studies, **Gabriella Besanzoni** (Rome 1888 – 1962) seemed destined for a brilliant career as a coloratura soprano; but she soon realized that she was more suited to the dramatic soprano and mezzo-soprano tessitura. This drastic change in no way damaged her general voice placement, proving what a fine voice this Roman singer had. Her low notes were solid and generous, her high notes luminous and penetrating and her character fiery. With such qualities, Besanzoni could be nothing less than a magnificent Amneris, Orfeo, Carmen, Isabella (*Italiana in Algeri*) and Cenerentola, revealing tremendous versatility. She was adored by the Latin-American public, especially in Argentina; but she also gained extraordinary success in Italy and New York, often performing with Caruso.

Rarely in the twentieth century have we had the opportunity of hearing a more powerful or extended voice than that of **Sigrid Onegin** (Elisabeth Elfriede Emilie Hoffmann; Stockholm 1889 – Magliaso, Lugano 1943), who always chose just the right vocal style for every one of her performances.

During the period from 1912 (when she made her debut in *Carmen* at Stuttgart) until 1934, she performed in Germany, London and

*Here is **Elvira Casazza** in an heroic pose, interpreting the role she made famous – Debora in* Debora and Jaele, *an opera by Pizzetti. In the part of Jaele was the magnificent soprano Giulia Tess; Arturo Toscanini conducted.*

Gabriella Besanzoni *as Carmen. After her beginnings as a coloratura soprano, she starred in Viterbo in 1911 as Adalgisa in* Norma. *(Historic Archives of the Rome Opera Theater)*

New York over a wide repertoire: *Orfeo, Le Prophète, Don Carlos* (Eboli), *Macbeth, The Ring,* the role of Brangäne in *Tristan,* and Dryad in the first performance of Strauss' *Ariadne auf Naxos*.

Perhaps the recordings of the time do not do her justice, as is true of most of her contemporaries. However, having said that, her interpretative style in Eboli's "Canzone del Velo" and in the aria from *La Favorita* is indeed questionable.

Marian Anderson (Philadelphia 1897 – Portland, Oregon 1993) is worthy of a special mention. Despite the problems caused by racial discrimination in the United States, she managed to triumph at the Metropolitan in 1955 as Ulrica in *Un Ballo in Maschera*. Anderson was famous for the incredible uniformity and depth of her voice throughout its range. She was excellent in Lieder and specialized in Spirituals.

Though she held her first concert in 1925, her career moved slowly and had to overcome many great difficulties; and it was only in the following decade that she gained recognition in Europe and Australia. Miss Anderson later gave an historic concert at the Lincoln Memorial in

Risë Stevens, *a Met star from 1938 on, especially cherished as Carmen. She also acted in films (including* Going My Way *with Bing Crosby, 1944).*

1944), endowed with a well-colored, uniform voice and a formidable temperament; the contralto **Luisa Bertana** (Quilmes, Buenos Aires 1898-1933), chosen by Toscanini as Preziosilla and Adalgisa; **Louise Homer** (Pittsburgh 1871 – Winter Park, Florida 1947), a famous Amneris, Orfeo, Adalgisa and Laura in *Gioconda*; **Florica Cristoforeanu** (Rimnim-Sarat, Rumania 1887 – Rio de Janeiro 1960); **Aurora Buades** (Valencia 1895 – Florence 1965), a diva of the Latin-American theaters; **Maria Capuana** (Fano, Pesaro 1891 – Cagliari 1955), mostly engaged in the Wagner repertory but famous also as Amneris; **Marie Delna** (Meudon 1875 – Paris 1932); **Maria Gay** (Barcelona 1879 – New York 1943), wife of the tenor Zenatello, with whom she formed a historic couple in *Carmen* and *Aida*; **Marthe Chenal** (S. Maurice, Paris 1881 – 1947). At only thirteen years of age **Gladys Swarthout** (Deepwater, Missouri 1904 – Florence 1969) was already singing solo in church. She made her debut in 1924 in Chicago as Pastorello in *Tosca* and was a splen-

Ebe Stignani *in Gluck's Orfeo, a role which she tackled with a large and powerful voice and, above all, her refined stylistic gifts. (Historic Archives of the Rome Opera Theater Photo: Camuzi)*

Washington, D.C. before 75,000 people, including President Franklin Delano Roosevelt, who was her great friend and admirer.

After her memorable Ulrica at the Met, she made frequent appearances in all the major theaters, exhibiting her splendid talent. In 1965 she retired after an extraordinarily successful worldwide tour.

Here are some other famous mezzo-sopranos performing in the Italian repertory in the early years of the twentieth century: **Louise Kirkby-Lunn** (Manchester 1873 – St. John's Wood 1930), who sang, with notes as fixed as those of a train whistle, at the Metropolitan and Covent Garden; **Dame Clara Butt** (Southwick, Sussex 1873 – North Stoke 1936), famed for her cavernous low notes; **Margarethe Arndt-Ober** (Berlin 1885 – Bad Sachsa 1971), famous as Eboli, Amneris and Azucena despite evident vocal limits in the high register; **Irene Minghini-Cattaneo** (Lugo di Romagna 1892 – Rimini

*Carmen is being instructed; and the diva, **Giulietta Simionato**, listens to the conductor, Herbert von Karajan - an artistic duo linked to many splendid productions. (Historic Archives of La Fenice Theater. Venice)*

*Smiling and radiant in the dress of Cinderella, here is **Giulietta Simionato** in a photo from 1955. (Historic Archives of the Rome Opera Theater. Photo: Reale)*

did Carmen and Mignon. She also starred in several American films, among which *Champagne Waltz*. **Edith Coates** (Lincoln 1908-1983) worked regularly in the London theaters from 1931 until 1963, and was famous as Auntie in *Peter Grimes*; **Pia Tassinari** (Faenza 1909-1995) began as a lyric soprano, then from the forties on became a sensitive and refined performer of mezzo-soprano roles (Carmen, Charlotte); **Eugenia Zareska** (Rava Ruska 1910) sang in the Mozart repertory and became a famed Carmen at Covent Garden. Additional names are **Rosette Anday** (Budapest 1903 – Vienna 1977) and **Blanche Deschamps Jehin** (Lyon 1857 – Paris 1923), an exceptional performer in the French repertory with many premiere performances to her credit (Lalo's *Le Roi d'Ys*, Charpentier's *Louise* and the first performance of Saint-Saëns' *Samson and Delilah* in Paris).

The following generation saw the emergence of stars such as **Irene Dalis** (San José, California 1925), who successfully performed in a wide-reaching repertoire; **Grace Hoffmann** (Goldie Hoffmann; Cleveland 1925), famous as Eboli, Brangäne and Kundry in the American and German theaters; **Kerstin Meyer** (Stockholm 1928), a singer-actress of talent and sensitivity who performed in many contemporary operas; **Anna Pollak** (Manchester 1912), who studied with Joan Cross; **Monica Sinclair** (Somerset 1926), who often sang with Joan Sutherland, but showed evident vocal and stylistic limits; **Rosalind Elias** (Lowell, Massachusetts 1929), a regular performer at the Metropolitan, as was **Mignon Dunn** (Memphis, Tennessee 1928); **Viorica Cortez** (Bucium, Rumania 1935), **Rita Gorr** (Ghent, Belgium 1926), whose repertoire was wide and demanding; **Risë Stevens** (New York 1913), who sang from 1936 to 1964 in a large number of roles, but particularly favoring those of Carmen and Orfeo. In conclusion, **Nan Merriman** (Pittsburgh 1920); **Miriam Pirazzini** (Vicenza 1918), a famous Azucena, Laura and Preziosilla; **Alicia Nafé** (Buenos Aires 1948); **Josephine Veasey** (London 1930); **Oralia Dominguez** (San Luis Potosì, Mexico 1927); **Jean Madeira** (Centralia, Illinois 1918 – Providence, New York 1972), a splendid Delilah, Carmen and Ulrica; and finally **Nadine Denize** (Rouen 1943).

Ebe Stignani: Her Voice had the Sound of a Stradivarius

One of the greatest Italian singers ever was **Ebe Stignani** (Naples 1903 – Imola 1974), the Verdi mezzo-soprano par excellence. After her

Fedora Barbieri, *a Carmen of great beauty and explosive vitality.*

debut at the San Carlo Theater of Naples in 1925 (as Amneris in *Aida*), she frequently sang the roles of Amneris, Adalgisa (*Norma*), Eboli, Laura (*Gioconda*), Leonora (*Favorita*), Azucena, Ulrica and Santuzza, giving to these characters a vocal polish and luminosity of unsurpassable beauty.

Her timbre was rich and limpid, completely controlled by her breathing and an authentically belcanto technique, which assured her well-rounded and homogeneous notes, an impeccable legato, and cutting high notes that reached up to high c‴ (as could be heard in her performances of *L'Italiana in Algeri*, *Cenerentola*, *Mosè*, and even her *Semiramide* at Florence). Her generous and monumental phrasing, supported by her clear enunciation, could be fully appreciated in Gluck's *Orfeo*, where Stignani's voice was at its natural best. She retired from the stage in 1958 still in excellent vocal form, following her last illustrious performances of *Ballo in Maschera*, *Trovatore*, and *Aida*. Her farewell appearance was as Azucena, London, Drury Lane, 1958.

Happily Ever After...

A long period of apprenticeship preceded the brilliant international success of **Giulietta Simionato** (Forlì 1910). She first sang in Pizzetti's *Orseolo* at the age of twenty-five, but her big break came only in 1947, after several acclaimed performances of *Così Fan Tutte* (Dorabella) and *Mignon*. It had been a long but useful training, which had helped her refine not only

her vocal art but also her scenic style and acting skills without straining her voice with overwork.

In many respects Simionato preceded the advent of the Rossini *contralto d'agilità*, such as Marilyn Horne, singing in some important revivals (*Semiramide* with Joan Sutherland, 1962, at La Scala, *Tancredi*, *Barbiere*, *Cenerentola*, *Italiana in Algeri*). In these performances she demonstrated an excellent use of florid singing, fluid vocalizing, precise trilling and tasteful variations. These gifts were rare indeed among the mezzo-sopranos active in the pioneering years of the Rossini renaissance.

Her warm and flexible voice, governed by a refined technique and style, permitted Simionato to perform in many operas: from the legendary *Anna Bolena* (La Scala 1957) with Maria Callas to *Norma* and *Favorita*; from *Aida* to *Trovatore*; from *Carmen* to *Don Carlos*; from Handel's *Julius Caesar* to *Les Huguenots* (as Valentina). In this last opera her death scene was simply amazing. More than for her vocal power, Simionato was admirable for her sense of moderation and vocal adaptability in every kind of opera, be it belcanto or *verismo*. Her disci-

Regina Resnik *as Clytemnestra in* Elektra. *She was the Baroness in the premiere of Barber's* Vanessa, *1955, and Claire in the first U.S. performance of Einem's* Der Besuch der alten Dame, *1972.*

pline and technical confidence allowed her to sing magnificently for over thirty years. (Her farewell performance: Piccola Scala, Servilia in *La Clemenza di Tito*, 1966).

The voice of **Fedora Barbieri** (Trieste 1920) was greater in volume and power, but less stylized than that of Simionato. Fedora was unforgettable as Quickly in Verdi's *Falstaff*. It will be difficult to hear such full and resonant low g´s again: the truth is that the many "Reverenza!" and "Silenzio, silenzio" sung by this Italian mezzo-soprano were so powerful because they rested on the *poitrinés*, that is, on an artificially enlarged sound which in the long run undermines the uniformity of the registers. In fact, already at the end of the fifties, after fifteen years of exacting work (she made her debut in 1940 at Florence singing Fidalma in *Matrimonio Segreto* one day and Azucena in *Trovatore* the next), inequalities and harsh sounds began to show in her voice, due to vocal stress and the inability to lighten her notes.

The beauty of her timbre and her acting ability made Barbieri one of the most important interpreters of the roles of Azucena, Ulrica, Delilah, Amneris, Carmen, Orfeo, and the Leonora of Gusman; but she also performed as Isabella in *Italiana in Algeri* and Cenerentola (though with precise stylistic limits). Her amiable Quickly (which she continued to sing throughout the seventies) has become legendary, for her temperament in this part will be difficult to equal. But she also made a splendid Madelon in *Andrea Chénier* at Vienna in the 1982 season, where some of her old talent could still be heard. She sang at Buenos Aires, Colón, 1947; Covent Garden, 1950, 1957-58 as Azucena, Eboli and Amneris; New York, Met, 1950-54, 1956-57, 1967-68, making her debut as Eboli on the opening night of Bing's management.

After having begun her career as a soprano in New York in 1942 singing Lady Macbeth, **Regina Resnik** (New York 1922) decided to change range towards the second half of the fifties, when she began to have serious difficulties in performing dramatic soprano roles. She studied the part of Amneris for a whole year, then made her debut as a mezzo-soprano at the Metropolitan, singing Marina in *Boris*. With time, there followed Azucena, Carmen, Ulrica, Quickly, Clytemnestra and roles from a considerable number of contemporary works, all distinguished by her inborn stage presence and her warm, solid voice. Despite vocal impairment Resnik continued to appear on American stages for a long time (in 1982 she was much applauded as the Countess in Tchaikovsky's *Queen of Spades*), always affectionately received by her audience.

The Voice-Instrument of Fiorenza Cossotto

Ebe Stignani's heir is **Fiorenza Cossotto** (Crescentino, Vercelli 1935), gifted with a "voice-instrument" of a golden timbre, vibrant and incisive in the high register, delicate in the *mezzavoce*, renowned also for her passionate phrasing and acting. She made her debut in Milan in 1957, as Matilde in Poulenc's *Dialogues des Carmelites*, which she performed with the typical characteristics of the mezzo-soprano *acuto* and with perfect vocal placement, formed in the school of Ettore Campogalliani. In 1962 she played the difficult part of Urbano in *Les Huguenots* at La Scala, revealing a noteworthy virtuosity and a unique extension. These gifts would later allow her to sing Rossini, Handel, Bellini and Donizetti.

Soon, Cossotto began to appear in the more

Fiorenza Cossotto in her phenomenal interpretation of Eboli. We especially remember the exceptional evening in Rome at the RAI at the beginning of the sixties: on the podium, Schippers; Ghiaurov (Filippo II), Cappuccilli (Rodrigo), Prevedi (Don Carlos), Zylis-Gara (Elisabetta) and Cossotto, unforgettable in the aria "O don fatale," long-applauded by the audience. (Historic Archives of the Salzburg Festival. Photo: Rabanus)

difficult mezzo-soprano roles, triumphing as Amneris, Eboli, Santuzza, Azucena, Leonora, and as the Princess de Bouillon in *Adriana Lecouvreur*, which is perhaps her very best interpretation.

Though we may regret that her excessive dedication to *Aida* and *Adriana* was made at the expense of a more assiduous approach to the belcanto repertoire, it cannot be denied that Cossotto's vigorous performances of "Anatema su voi!" and "Acerba voluttà" will long be remembered by her audiences.

Two Illustrious Rivals

It is difficult to classify the ambiguous voices of **Shirley Verrett** (New Orleans 1931) and **Grace Bumbry** (Saint Louis, Missouri 1937), both of which fluctuate between the dramatic soprano register and that of the mezzo-soprano. Bumbry sang as a soprano (Tosca, Abigaille, Gioconda, Aida) with unsuccessful results, and on occasions Verrett, too (Norma, Amelia in *Ballo in Maschera*). Under the circumstances, it is probably better to consider these two excellent artists as mezzo-sopranos, whose natural extension in the high register (both reach high c´´´ sharp, and Verrett even rises to d´´´) does not mean that they are immune to the damage caused by a constant, punishing change of tessitura, especially difficult in the delicate *passaggio* area.

Compared with her rival, Shirley Verrett, the more gentle and aristocratic of the two singers, shows a greater aptitude for florid singing, to the point that she was able to overcome the arduous Rossini parts (*Mosè*, *Assedio di Corinto* and Rosina's aria, which she often sang in recital) and chose for her favorite encore the difficult "Alleluja" from Mozart's motet "Exultate, jubilate". Amongst the best renderings of this American artist are Carmen, Lady Macbeth, Elisabetta in *Maria Stuarda*, Delilah, and Dido in Berlioz' *Les Troyens*; she also has a noteworthy Lieder activity. At her peak she was a truly great artist, and a fine and most accomplished actress.

Grace Bumbry has a more fiery temperament and incisive phrasing. Thus her Carmen and her sensual Eboli become somewhat wild characters, who are, nonetheless, capable of languid sweetness in the more relaxed, melodic moments. Among Bumbry's best characterizations are Salome and Amneris, which also offer her the opportunity to use to fine advantage her magnificent figure.

Interestingly, these two illustrious rivals faced each other at close range in a concert organized in America in 1984, which was later repeated, when the two singers alternated soprano and

*The splendid **Shirley Verrett** photographed during a memorable recital held at the Rome Opera in April, 1986. Right from the beginning of her career, Verrett has dedicated a large part of her activity to the concert platform, achieving a series of uncontested successes. (Photo: Annamaria Bemardini)*

*Dressed like this, **Grace Bumbry** has little difficulty in showing off her curvaceous figure. She is Carmen in Rome in March, 1970: directed by Bolchi, with scenes by Guttuso. (Historic Archives of the Rome Opera Theater)*

Recording Verdi's Don Carlos *for EMI: chatting are* **Shirley Verrett**, *left, and* **Montserrat Caballé**, *respectively Eboli and Elisabetta di Valois. Verrett had a voice of large extension and agility enabling her to dominate with confidence a very wide repertory. (Giandonato Crico Collection)*

mezzo-soprano arias, then sang together the duets from *Norma, Anna Bolena* and *Gioconda*, concluding with the duet between Norma and Adalgisa "Sì, fino all'ore estreme".

Born in the same year, **Tatiana Troyanos** (New York 1938 – 1993) and **Yvonne Minton** (Sydney 1938) both achieved a good reputation in many international theaters. Troyanos alternated belcanto roles (Ariodante, Adalgisa, Julius Caesar, Seymour in *Anna Bolena*, Sesto in *Clemenza di Tito*), which she sometimes tackled with a little too much zeal, and romantic roles (Charlotte, Amneris, Carmen, Preziosilla, and Marina in *Boris*), verist parts (Santuzza), Wagnerian roles (Kundry, Venus in *Tannhäuser*), Strauss works (Octavian in *Der Rosenkavalier*, the Composer in *Ariadne auf Naxos*), and even modern pieces (she was the first to sing in Penderecki's grueling opera *The Devils of Loudon* at Hamburg in 1969). Her voice was full and powerful, extending up to c‴, and agile, though she needed to exercise strict psychological control on her exuberant temperament. With her sudden death, American audiences lost one of their favorite opera singers.

Yvonne Minton is more moderate and observant of the expressive possibilities of each role she undertakes. She is well-known as Brangäne, Orfeo, Octavian, Dorabella, and is also a worthy performer of Lieder.

Agnes Baltsa (Lefkas, Greece 1944) undertakes a repertory ranging from Mozart (Cherubino, Dorabella) and Gluck (Orfeo) to Rossini (Rosina, Cenerentola, Isabella), Bellini (Romeo), Donizetti (Elisabetta in *Maria Stuarda*), Verdi (Eboli and Amneris), Bizet (Carmen), Massenet (Thérèse, Hérodiade) and Strauss (the Composer in *Ariadne auf Naxos*,

Octavian in *Der Rosenkavalier*). Baltsa brings to these roles a well-timbred voice, sweet and velvety, a considerable agility and extension (she has easy, penetrating high notes) and an elegant stage presence. She was one of von Karajan's

Radiant and beautiful **Shirley Verrett** *as Carmen, in the early sixties. (Giandonato Crico Collection)*

favorite artists, and he often invited her to sing at the Salzburg Festival, and included her in all his major recordings. In addition to her operatic activity, the Greek artist (who was already a gifted pianist at the age of seven) often performs in Lieder and concert recitals.

Agnes Baltsa was still performing a full program in the nineties, having extended her repertoire to include the roles of Delilah, Azucena, Fides in Meyerbeer's *The Prophet* and Fedora, and singing mainly at the Vienna Opera House.

After beginning her career in the belcanto repertoire, especially Rossini's, **Luciana d'Intino** (S.Vito al Tagliamento, Pordenone 1959) has shown talent, sustained by a fine voice color and admirable style, for Verdi, too, giving excellent performances as Eboli, Preziosilla, Amneris.

The voice of the American **Dolora Zajick** (Reno, Nevada 1952) can only be described as bursting forth, with meteoric high notes and powerful chest voice. For the range of her repertoire and her physical resistance, she could well be considered as the rightful heir of Fiorenza Cossotto. After her debut as Azucena in 1986 at San Francisco, she has never looked back, triumphing worldwide in all the main Verdi roles (including the soprano role of Lady Macbeth) but above all as Amneris, Eboli and Azucena.

The immensely attractive vocal and physical characteristics of **Denyce Graves** have made her the Carmen of the nineties. As is true of most colored mezzo-sopranos, the timbre of her voice is quite enchanting, though at times a little husky and opaque, characteristics that have tended to limit her repertoire.

The Verist Mezzo-Soprano

Given the prevalence of the Verist style during the first fifty years of the twentieth century, the temptation is to include many singers who were not truly verist (in voice type or in repertoire) but who were dragged along by the fashion of the time. However, we will name just one, the greatest mezzo-soprano in the verist

Carmen of the nineteen-nineties. **Denyce Graves** *in the 1995 staging of this opera at the Verona Arena. (Fondazione Arena di Verona. Photo: Gianfranco Fainello).*

repertory and the French *lyrique*: **Gianna Pederzini** (Vò di Avio, Trento 1900 – Rome 1988). She studied with De Lucia in Naples, and made her debut in Messina in 1923 as Preziosilla in *Forza del Destino*.

Right at the start Pederzini demonstrated a fine virtuoso talent, distinguishing herself in operas by Rossini (*Conte Ory, Barbiere, Italiana in Algeri*), Flotow (*Martha*), Bellini (*Norma*), Meyerbeer (*Les Huguenots* as the Page), and accompanying her vocal arabesques with spicy acting skills. Thanks to her uncommon vocal gifts and her innate dramatic nature she was soon able to include *Aida, Adriana Lecouvreur, Carmen, Fedora, Cavalleria, Werther* and *Mignon* in her repertoire, and create powerful characterizations in *The Queen of Spades*, Menotti's *The Medium*, Bloch's *Macbeth*; in addition she took part in the premiere performance of Poulenc's *Dialogues des Carmélites* at La Scala in 1957.

Milan, Rome, London, Buenos Aires, Paris, Berlin, Barcelona are all cities in which, between 1923 and the end of the fifties, Gianna Pederzini triumphed, dominating the stage with a rare artistic intelligence and personal charm.

January 19, 1958. **Gianna Pederzini** *and* **Nicola Rossi-Lemeni** *in the version of* Macbeth *composed by Bloch; an absolute innovation for Rome. (Historic Archives of the Rome Opera Theater. Photo: Oscar Savio)*

The Belcanto Mezzo-Soprano and the *Contralto d'Agilità*

Conchita Supervia (Barcelona 1895 – London 1936) was the forerunner of the great *mezzo-soprani d'agilità*. She made her debut at Buenos Aires in 1910 (*Los Amantes de Teruel* by Bréton), and by 1914 was already able to perform the parts of Rosina, Isabella and Cenerentola with correct vocal style and virtuosity. In 1925 she had an extraordinary success in *L'Italiana in Algeri* at Turin conducted by Vittorio Gui, but most of the world's great theaters had the opportunity of applauding Supervia in her Rossini performances.

Nor did this singer limit her career to the composer from Pesaro. She was also an excellent *Carmen*, Octavian in *Der Rosenkavalier* and Cherubino, uniting vocal talent and a bright and entertaining stage presence.

Jennie Tourel (St. Petersburg 1900 – New York 1973) became the first mezzo-soprano to sing Rosina at the Met in 1945. She included Cenerentola, Adalgisa, Mignon and Carmen in her repertoire. Tourel was much respected by great conductors like Toscanini and Bernstein for her musicality and style, even though her

Gianna Pederzini *in* Carmen, *one of her favorite roles.*
(Historic Archives of La Fenice Theater, Venice. Photo: Giacomelli)

voice was not extraordinarily gifted. In 1973, not long before her death, she played the Marquise in the *Fille du Régiment* in Chicago.

A Lady-like Carmen

After the decisive "lessons" in Rossini given to mezzo-sopranos by Simionato and to sopranos by Callas, it was **Teresa Berganza** (Madrid 1935) who then carried on the "good work" in Mozart and Rossini operas, highlighting correct technique and style. Her voice has never been powerful, nor particularly extended, but her timbre is beautiful, and equal in all the registers; she is fluid in vocalization, smooth in legato, able and imaginative in her use of shading. She made her debut many years ago in 1955, with a concert at the Ateneo of Madrid; but her career really took off after her performances at the Festival at Aix-en-Provence in 1957, when she sang Dorabella in *Così fan Tutte*. Teresa Berganza immediately displayed her skill as an extraordinarily refined stylist, and went on to perform many of the most important parts in eighteenth and nineteenth century opera:

Isabella, Rosina, Isolier in *Le Comte Ory*, Cenerentola, Zerlina, Cherubino, Dorabella; and she has even managed to restore the difficult role of Carmen to its *opéra-comique* origins, ridding it of useless exaggerations and respecting Bizet's music in every detail.

She was still singing in the late nineties, though only in concert performances, her voice intact and showing all the qualities that first made her famous.

Belcanto Marilyn

Marilyn Horne (Bradford, Pennsylvania 1929) is the only true Handel/Rossini *contralto d'agilità* of the twentieth century, capable of making the lower female voice obey the belcanto requirements of these two composers, to push it up into perilous *tessiture* and into impossible acrobatics, to turn it into a "voice-instrument", an instrument expressing the deepest emotions.

This exceptional voice did not develop thanks to some famous teacher, but springs rather from her father's encouragement and her own strict

*Poor Cinderella (**Teresa Berganza**) is pulled away by Don Magnifico (**Paolo Montarsolo**) under the gaze of Dandini (**Renato Capecchi**). (Historic Archives of the Teatro Comunale of Florence. Photo: Marchiori)*

An unequalled star of many productions of Cenerentola *and* Il Barbiere di Siviglia, **Teresa Berganza** *has even brought Rosina to the screen.*

self-discipline. Initially, Horne alternated performances as a soprano (Maria in *Wozzek*, San Francisco, 1960, Marie in *Fille du Régiment*, San Francisco, 1962, and even Minnie in *The Girl of the Golden West*) with those of a mezzo-soprano (*Cenerentola*, Los Angeles, 1956; *Carmen*, San Francisco, 1961; Arsace in *Semiramide*, New York, 1964), where she demonstrated her extremely fluid emission and her gifts as a virtuoso.

She gradually increased her Rossini repertory, with enormous success (*Barbiere* at Florence, 1967; *Italiana in Algeri* at the RAI in Turin in 1968; Neocle in *Assedio di Corinto* at La Scala in 1969) putting her best qualities on show. Hers is a velvety timbre (obtained by a skillful use of

poitrinée technique which has not harmed the uniformity of her registers), and an amazing ability for all the belcanto requisites (tight trills, fast vocalization, *roulades*, *messe di voce* and *canto di sbalzo*), qualities Marilyn has developed thanks to a unique way of singing in the throat in the center register and a perfect use of breath on every note.

Horne also displays great exuberance and incisiveness in the long recitatives *en travesti* (trousers) roles (Vivaldi's Arsace, Calbo, Malcolm, Falliero, Neocle, Tancredi, Orlando, and Handel's Rinaldo and Orlando) which remind us of the incredible *castrati* of past centuries (as far as we can judge from contemporary accounts).

After the lesson scene, **Marilyn Horne** *receives the warm applause of the audience at Macerata during a performance in 1980. In place of the rondo written by Rossini, she revived a custom of many prima donnas of the past, and inserted a scene taken from another Rossini opera (in this case,* Tancredi*) and, on the request of the public, she gave, without accompaniment, an encore of an American song by Stephen Foster.*

Amongst her most memorable performances are her historical *Semiramide* in duo with Joan Sutherland, Handel's *Rinaldo* at Houston in 1975 (with the acrobatic aria "Or la tromba in suon festante", where she competed with a solo trumpet, a feat worthy of Farinelli!), and Handel's *Orlando* in Venice in 1985.

However, her performances outside the belcanto repertory were not so successful, as evident from her weak Amneris at Salzburg, where she was almost always covered by von Karajan's powerful orchestra; or from her exaggerated *Carmen* in Macerata (1982), which by the end of the opera had become so blatantly coarse that it compromised even her fascinating renderings of the solo arias ("Habanera," "Seguedilla" and "Chanson bohème"). Following a number of performances of *Italiana in Algeri* in London, of Arsace in *Semiramide* and Quickly in *Falstaff* at the Metrolpolitan in the late nineties, Marilyn retired from the stage, though she still gives highly popular recitals.

The Heartbeats of Tancredi

Italy's answer to Marilyn Horne was *contralto d'agilità* **Lucia Valentini-Terrani** (Padua 1946 – Seattle 1998). She studied with Iris Adami-Corradetti, and won the Rossini competition held by the RAI in the early seventies.

She made her debut as Cenerentola during the 1968-69 season at Brescia. The role always remained dear to this artist, and provided her with the opportunity to display her warm, burnished timbre, together with her exceptional technical gifts.

As prescribed by the best manuals, Valentini-Terrani had an extremely agile execution, the notes fluctuating on her breath, uniformly over all the registers, from the low to the high, thanks to her good voice placement. She had a few problems in the passage between her middle and lower registers, which sounded slightly "out-of-focus", and she did not attack the high notes forcefully enough. Nonetheless, Lucia was a singer of rare talent, an ideal interpreter of Isabella, Malcolm (*Donna del Lago*), Cenerentola, Arsace and Tancredi, roles she rendered, not with Horne's absolute confidence, perhaps, but with the audacity and style of a real *diva*.

Thanks to her smooth emission, pure timbre, and variety of vocal shadings, Valentini-Terrani was more than able to include some French *lyrique* roles in her repertoire: Charlotte in *Werther*, Mignon, Dulcinée in *Don Quichotte*, and Carmen (which she sang for the first time in Bonn in 1986) with noteworthy results. She

rendered the part of Marina in *Boris Godunov* surprisingly well and was also an excellent Lieder and concert performer, often singing Verdi's *Requiem*, Beethoven's *Ninth Symphony*, Mahler's symphonies and Lieder, and Brahms' *German Requiem*.

Towards the end of the eighties, Valentini-Terrani's voice began to show signs of fatigue, and she consequently decided to cut down her stage appearances, and to concentrate in the main on her favorite roles of Isabella and Cinderella, but at the same time increasing her Lieder activity. Her debut in Offenbach's *Grande-Duchesse de Gérolstein* at the Martina Franca Festival was her last personal success on stage, before she sadly died of leukaemia.

Dame Janet Baker (Hatfield, Yorkshire 1933) gave her farewell to the stage in 1982 after a final series of performances of the operas that had made her world-famous: Gluck's *Alceste* and *Orfeo*, and Donizetti's *Maria Stuarda*, roles which she performed respectively at Covent Garden, the English National Opera and the Glyndebourne Festival, the theaters most familiar to her.

Baker made her debut at Edinburgh in 1960, and soon after specialized in Handel's operas and oratorio. As time went on her repertory expanded to include Purcell, Britten, Lully, Haydn, Mozart, Gluck, Berlioz, Monteverdi, Richard Strauss (Octavian in *Der Rosenkavalier*), Bellini (Romeo in *Capuleti e Montecchi*) and Donizetti (Maria in *Maria Stuarda*, in which she lowered the tone). All these different roles and styles were approached with great musicality and intelligence, making use of a well-educated, smooth and flexible voice. She perhaps showed a certain coldness and lack of imagination in her singing of Handel's belcanto repertory, where, under the guidance of competent conductors, she could have added lively variations in the *da capo*, and thus made her characterizations more vibrant and more philologically correct.

A brief mention is due to another English mezzo-soprano, **Carolyn Watkinson** (Preston 1949), who specialized in the Baroque repertory (Rameau's *Hippolyte et Aricie*, *Ariodante*, *Incoronazione di Poppea*), often working with prestigious companies such as La Grande Écurie et la Chambre du Roi of Jean-Claude Malgloire.

Thanks to her very special style and charm, **Frederica von Stade** (Sommerville, New Jersey 1945) has made a big name for herself on the international scene, especially as a singer of Mozart (Cherubino, Annio in *Clemenza di Tito*) and Rossini (Cinderella and Rosina). She also enjoys strong backing from her recording company. She is a highly attractive figure on stage, extremely well-prepared both musically and dramatically, though her voice at times sounds sharp and lacks extension. One might be tempted to see her as a publicity stunt, were it not for her natural charm and excellent acting talent and style. Thus she triumphed at La Scala in 1986 in Debussy's *Pélleas et Melisande* and in the many other recitals she has performed world-wide. She has strong ties with the Metropolitan, where she sang yet again in 2000.

The French singer **Martine Dupuy** (Marseille 1952) played an important role during the eighties, in the rampant years of the so-called Rossini renaissance, specializing in Italy in the *en travesti* parts of Arsace, Malcolm, Romeo (Bellini's *I Capuleti e Montecchi*) and Giulio Cesare, achieving excellent results in coloratura singing, but showing precise limits in other areas due to the unpleasant color of her voice. **Anne-Sophie von Otter** (Stockholm 1955), who studied with Geoffrey Parsons in London and Erik Werba in Vienna, is gifted with greater vocal and stylistic qualities and is thus a highly competent singer of Mozart, Rossini, oratorio, Lieder and even the masterpieces of Richard Strauss (she is particularly famous for her performance of Oktavian in the version of *Rosenkavalier* conducted by Carlos Kleiber). Her many records bear witness to her versatility in a repertoire ranging from Bach to the songs of Weill.

Stylistically perfect, **Bernadette Manca di Nissa** (Cagliari 1954) has made a name for herself internationally in the *contralto d'agilità* roles of Handel, Mozart and Rossini, though still grappling with a problem or two in the high register. Even greater success has been achieved by **Jennifer Larmore** (Atlanta, Georgia 1958), who has taken over from Marilyn Horne in the roles of Isabella, Rosina and Cinderella, and in many of Handel's operas. She is an attractive, self-confident figure on stage, gifted with an extensive voice, especially efficient in the high register, but encountering some problems with the center and lower notes. The latest generation of singers includes three new Rossini voices of particular interest: **Sonia Ganassi** (Parma 1966), **Gloria Scalchi** (Trieste 1956) and **Daniela Barcellona** (Trieste 1969). Sonia, who gave a startling performance as Rosina in the *Barbiere di Siviglia* directed by Verdone at the Rome Opera House, has made a rapid climb to fame, giving excellent performances as Isabella, Cinderella, Adalgisa and Maffio Orsini, revealing a full, pleasantly colored voice, well able to cope with coloratura demands and confident in the high register, and an attractive stage presence. Gloria Scalchi, a typical *mezzosoprano*

acuto but nonetheless capable of producing a powerful chest voice to cope with the low notes, has included in her repertoire not only Rossini, but also Leonora in *Favorita*, Azucena and Carmen, relying, however, more on the clarity of her high register, than on her acting, which is always rather bland. Daniela Barcellona, tall as a maypole, has proved to be a formidable belcanto singer, especially in Rossini operas, but the power and extension of her voice strongly suggest future possibilities as a Verdi singer.

And it is in the Verdi repertoire that we find **Elisabetta Fiorillo** (Naples 1957), a highly acclaimed performer of *Trovatore*, *Aida* and *Don Carlos*, and **Violeta Urmana,** who puts her solid, well-extended voice to excellent use in the classical mezzo-soprano repertory, ranging from Verdi to Wagner and Mascagni (one of her favorite roles is Santuzza in *Cavalleria*).

Martine Dupuy *(Romeo) in Bellini's* Capuleti e Montecchi. *(Photo: E. Bisaza,. Verona)*

The Myth of Cecilia Bartoli

During the nineties, the major American, Japanese and German record selling stores filled their windows with posters of Cecilia Bartoli (Rome 1966). Some depicted her in a black leather jacket on a motorbike, others as a femme fatale, or casually poised beside her pianist or conductor. A perfect publicity stunt organized on behalf of the latest newcomer to the international opera world: an attractive brunette, with a captivating smile, precocious musical talent (she was barely nineteen when she sang in Paris in a concert, conducted by Prêtre, in memory of Maria Callas), not to mention her talent for flamenco dancing, in short, miles away from the customary opera singer clichés. Added to this, were her scrupulous musical preparation, her naturally extensive, agile voice and her wise choice of composers: Handel, Mozart (especially Despina), some Rossini operas (*Barbiere, Cinderella, Italiana in Algeri, Conte Ory*), plus chamber music and oratorio. There were all the ingredients to justify an authentic boom, above all in the United States and Germany. But also for her to be hailed as the heir to Teresa Berganza and Marilyn Horne. However, Cecilia's voice, when not enhanced by microphones and recording studios, is less effective live on stage. It is a small voice, not sufficiently penetrating, slightly guttural in the low register. Consequently, while her live appearances are rare, she makes frequent concert appearances and has cut many records.

THE MEZZO-SOPRANO IN THE GERMAN REPERTORY

Although chronologically she belongs more to the nineteenth century than to the twentieth, **Ernestine Schumann-Heink** (E. Rössler; Lieben, Prague 1861 – Hollywood 1936) can be considered as the historical beginning of the German dramatic mezzo-sopranos of the twentieth century, as her career stretched from 1816 until 1932: at seventy-one years of age she still managed to sing Erda in *Siegfried*. She had almost a hundred and fifty different roles in her repertory, thus showing an incomparable versatility. Her great voice flow, which reached up to a high b´´, splendidly suited the difficult Wagnerian roles (Brangäne, Ortrud, Erda, Fricka, Waltraute), and in particular the part of Clytemnestra (Richard Strauss' *Elektra*), of which Ernestine was the first performer at Dresden in 1909.

She sang light music, acted in a film (*Here's to Romance*, 1935), and made a recording of Maffio Orsini's "Brindisi" (Donizetti's *Lucrezia Borgia*) in a belcanto version that included an excellent tight trill.

Karin Branzell (Maria Branzell; Stockholm 1891 – Altadena, California 1974) was also a wonderful *dramatischer Alt* in the Wagner repertory. She sang from 1912 until 1944, mostly at the New York Metropolitan, gaining notable successes in *Die Walküre, Lohengrin*, and *Tristan und Isolde*, and as Amneris and Azucena, too. However (according to Lauri Volpi in his book *Voci Parallele*, and he was a "live" witness) Branzell was far less at ease in the Italian *cantabile* and legato. Her robust voice was better suited to Wagnerian declamation; and her recordings confirm the opinion of the great tenor.

And we must not forget **Marie Goetze** (Berlin 1865 – 1922), who was an historic performer of Strauss at Berlin; **Kerstin Thorborg** (Venjan, Sweden 1896 – Stockholm 1970), who had a beautifully polished timbre which she put at the service of such roles as Ortrud, Brangäne, Fricka and Eglantine in Weber's opera *Euryanthe*; and **Maria Olszewska** (Ludwigsschwaige, Bavaria 1892 – Klagenfurt 1969), a famous Wagnerian singer in Germany, who sang at Covent Garden from 1924 until 1932, and at the Met from 1932 until 1935.

Belonging to the next generation, **Margarete Frida Klose** (Berlin 1902-1968) sang from 1925 to 1961. A noble contralto, gifted with a singularly charming timbre enhanced by unique technical skill, she was one of the best performers of *Orfeo, Tristan und Isolde* (Brangäne), *Lohengrin* (Ortrud), *Salome* (Herodias), and *Elektra* (Clytemnestra) in the post World War One period. She took part in the "live" recordings of *The Ring* made by the RAI in 1953, singing Erda and Waltraute under Furwängler's magical baton.

We should also mention **Elisabeth Höngen** (Gevelsberg, Westphalia 1906 – Vienna 1997); **Hildegard Rössel-Majdan** (Moosbierbaum, Austria 1921); **Hertha Töpper** (Graz 1924); **Ira Malaniuk** (Stanislav, Ukraine 1923); **Marga**

Blanche Thebom *in the title role of Bizet's* Carmen. *She was at the Met from 1944 to 1967, and sang the role of Dido in London's first complete performance of Berlioz's* Les Troyens. *(Covent Garden, 1957)*

Höffgen (Müllheim, Baden 1921); **Maureen Forrester** (Montreal 1930); and **Birgit Finnilä** (Falkenberg, Sweden 1931).

No list would be complete without **Blanche Thebom** (Monessen, Pennsylvania 1918), who studied in New York with Matzenauer and Edyth Walker. For more than twenty years she cast a splendid figure in all the major American opera houses. Protagonist of the 1955 American premiere of Stravinsky's *The Rake's Progress*, she was also famous as Dido in a magnificent Covent Garden production of Berlioz' *Les Troyens*. After retiring from the stage in the mid-sixties she taught musical studies at the University of Arkansas.

The ranks of the German mezzo-sopranos gradually diminished, but we must not omit the great **Christa Ludwig** (Berlin 1924), who made her debut in 1946 at Frankfurt as Prince Orlofsky in J. Strauss's *Die Fledermaus* and retired in the early nineties. An extremely musical singer with a vast and varied repertoire, she was able to range from the typical *komischer Alt* parts (such as the above-mentioned Orlofsky or Clairon in *Capriccio*) to more dramatic and vocally exhausting roles such as Fricka, Ortrud, Kundry, Octavian, the Composer and Ariadne in *Ariadne auf Naxos*, Eboli, Lady Macbeth, Azucena, Quickly, Adalgisa (*Norma*), Dorabella, Cherubino, and Ifigenia (Gluck).

All this was made possible thanks to her admirable technique and an innate talent for the stage, which made her an excellent actress; and no one can forget her splendid Lieder and concert recitals, which earned her the respect of the world's greatest conductors.

Brigitte Fassbänder (Berlin 1939) has become Ludwig's successor. Her first basic singing lessons were given to her by her father, the famous baritone Willy Domgraf-Fassbänder. She completed her studies in her native city and in Nuremberg. From 1961 she became a regular performer in the world's major opera houses in a wide repertoire that included Mozart (Dorabella, Cherubino, Sesto), Verdi (Amneris, Azucena, the *Requiem*), Johann Strauss (*Die Fledermaus*), Wagner (*Die Walküre*), Flotow (*Martha*), Pfitzner (*Palestrina*), plus a vast Lieder and recital selection. Her best vocal characteristics were her robust and burnished timbre, her uniformity over all the registers, her extension, and her noteworthy verve, which was best displayed in the *en travesti* roles of Orlofsky and Octavian in *Der Rosenkavalier*. In 1970 she was awarded the Bavarian title of Kammersängerin. Octavian in *Der Rosenkavalier* was her debut role at Covent Garden in 1971 and at the Met in 1974.

We conclude with **Marjana Lipovsek**, who has won international acclaim in all the great Wagner roles, as Clytemnestra in *Elektra* and in a wide range of Lieder.

THE MEZZO-SOPRANO IN THE RUSSIAN REPERTORY

The historical Russian mezzo-sopranos of the twentieth century include **Sophia Preobrazhenskaya** (St. Petersburg 1904), who was a permanent member of the Kirov Opera from 1928, splendid as Martha in *Khovanshchina*, Joan of Arc and Countess in Tchaikovsky's *Queen of Spades*; the contralto **Maria lvanovna Dolina** (1868); **Zara Doluchanova** (Moscow 1918), who was able to tackle the parts of the *contralto d'agilità* with bravura as her recordings of Arsace's *cavatina* (which she graced with interminable *cadenze*) demonstrate; and **Vera Davydova** (Nishnii, Novgorod 1906).

They were all forerunners of the great **Irina Arkhipova** (Moscow 1925), who began her musical career as a hobby, taking evening lessons after her daytime work as an architect. Her debut was made at Moscow in 1954, as Liubacha in *The Tsar's Bride* by Rimsky-Korsakov, and caused a great sensation. From then on she never looked back. Thanks to her superb timbre, her luminous polish, her naturally smooth emission and her excellent technique, Arkhipova was a fantastic performer in operas by Mussorgsky, Glinka, Shostakovich and Tchaikovsky, but also a vibrant Azucena, a passionate Carmen and a singularly eloquent Eboli and Amneris. She appeared in Montreal with the Bolshoi during EXPO 1967, in San Francisco, 1972 and at Covent Garden, 1975.

Elena Obraztsova (Leningrad 1939) made her debut in 1964 as Marina in *Boris Godunov*, a part which has always suited her. In her best years her voice was powerful, reaching up to high c‴, of magnificent color, sufficiently agile and gentle in the *mezzevoci*, and generous in the low notes (even if she somewhat overdid the use of *poitriné* sounds, which tended to compromise the *passaggio* notes).

*A triple ace for the Bizet masterpiece: from left Franco Zeffirelli, director, at center, **Obraztsova**, still with her hand on her hip, and, at right, blond and heavyset, **Domingo.** Carmen was performed with great success at the Vienna State Opera under the baton of Carlos Kleiber.*

In a photo from 1946 we see the great **Sophia Preobrazenskaia** *in* The Maid of Orléans. *Her interpretation of the farewell scene and the recognition scene in the second act of Tchaikovsky's opera long-remained in the memory of her Russian audience. (Historic Archives of the Kirov Theater of Leningrad)*

From 1975 she gathered triumphs worldwide, ever enlarging her repertoire: *Carmen, Samson and Delilah, Aida, Cavalleria Rusticana, Don Car-* los, *Boris Godunov, Kovantchina, Trovatore* and *Adriana Lecouvreur*. Sometimes, pushed by her passionate temperament, she indulged in some rather unnecessary exaggerations, such as at the end of Azucena's great scene in the second act of *Trovatore* performed at San Francisco in 1975, where she concluded with a series of sobs worthy of *verismo*. Few, however, will ever be able to forget her luxuriant and voluptuous Eboli in La Scala's *Don Carlos* in 1977, or her sweet Charlotte in *Werther* at La Scala in 1976. Obraztsova made her Met debut as Amneris (*Aida*) in 1976, and her Covent Garden debut in the same role in 1985.

Another excellent mezzo-soprano of the Russian and Slav repertoires is **Alexandrina Milcheva-Nonova** (Shoumen, Bulgaria 1936), who made her debut in *Carmen* at Varna in 1961 before becoming internationally famous in a wide selection of roles (she made a splendid recording as Marina in *Boris* and also in *Kovantchina*).

Two other mezzo-sopranos began to make a name for themselves in the nineties, **Vesselina Kasarova** (1965) and, especially, **Olga Borodina** (1963). Vesselina has specialized in Rossini works and belcanto, which are particularly suited to her type of voice, more ductile and softer, though less voluminous, than that of her colleague, Olga has instead undertaken the dramatic repertoire, with remarkable results which have seen her triumph in *Carmen, Aida, Don Carlos, Samson and Delilah, Boris* and *Prince Igor* at the world's major opera houses. She also has a splendid figure and an impressive stage presence, which enhance her perfect emission and attractive voice color.

José Mardones, *as Ramfis in Verdi's Aida.*

The Bass Singer

The Bass Voice: Extension and Phonation

This is the lowest of the male voices. The extension usually ranges from F reaching up to f′, but in some exceptional cases it can stretch from C to g′. However, the amazing basses who sing in Russian choirs often reach the octave below low F, thus achieving that singular "organ-like" effect.

On the basis of vocal characteristics and repertoire, the bass voice can be sub-divided as follows. The *basso nobile* or *cantante* (the noble bass) of the Italian, French and Russian repertory (Verdi, Boito, Mussorgsky, Glinka) is the most common category. It is an ideal fusion of a smooth, rich, powerful and extended voice with superior interpretative gifts; the *basso profondo* (the German *tiefer Bass*), particularly suited to priestly, austere and sometimes mythical characters (Fafner in *Siegfried*); the comic bass (the Italian *basso buffo* and the German *komischer Bass*) is agile and fun-loving, a great actor, and a master in the art of "spoken-singing" such as that required by the parts of Dulcamara in *Elisir d'Amore*, Bartolo in *Barbiere* or Osmino in *Die Entführung aus dem Serail*; the bass-baritone (the German *Bass-Baryton*) is the type of voice which combines characteristics of the baritone (higher extension and clearer middle register) with those of the comic and noble basses; thus he fulfills the demands of roles initially conceived for "voices" in the wider sense of the word (Mozart's *Don Giovanni* is an example, which has, in the past, been sung by tenors like Garcia and Nozzari, baritones like Gobbi, Wachter and Milnes, and basses such as Pinza, Siepi and Ghiaurov); lastly there is the belcanto *basso*, which has been reincarnated by the American star Samuel Ramey, champion of the old style virtuoso, especially suited to the Handel and Rossini repertory.

Now let's give them a closer look.

THE *BASSO NOBILE* IN THE TWENTIETH CENTURY

The music world remembers the world-wide historical appearances made by **Leo Sibirjakov** (St. Petersburg 1869 – Antwerp 1942), a wonderful Pimen and Mefistofele; **Oreste Luppi** (Rome 1870 – Milan 1962); **Vittorio Arimondi** (Saluzzo 1861 – Chicago 1928), the first singer to perform Pistola in *Falstaff*; **Francesco Navarini** (Cittadella, Rome 1853 – Milan 1923), a great Silva in Ernani and Marcel in *Les Huguenots*; **Ivar Andresen** (Oslo 1896 – Stockholm 1940), an outstanding Wagner singer; **Paul Payan** (1878 – St. Juan-les-Pins, 1959); **Josef von Manowarda** (Cracow, Poland 1890 – Berlin 1942), a great Philip II, Osmin, Gurnemanz, Marke and Barak (*Die Frau ohne Schatten*) of which he was the first interpreter in 1919.

For the beauty of his timbre, his power and vocal extension governed by a perfect technique, **Marcel Journet** (Grasse, France 1867 – Vittel, Vosgi 1933) was practically unrivalled from 1891 right until the end of the twenties. These were the golden years of his long career, which eventually ended in 1932 at the Paris Opera. Thanks to his uncommon vocal gifts he was able to sing virtually everything: from the *basso profondo* roles (Baldassarre in *La Favorita*, Sparafucile in *Rigoletto*) to the most important roles of the Italian repertory (Philip II, Basilio, Mefistofele, Ramfis, Simon Mago in the inaugural performance of Boito's *Nerone* in 1924), the French repertory (Méphistophélès in Gounod's *Faust*, the Father in *Louise*) and the German repertory (the Wanderer in *The Ring*, Hans Sachs in *The Mastersingers of Nuremberg*, King Henry the Fowler in *Lohengrin*). During the last years of his career, he sang mostly baritone or

An aimiable photo of the famous bass **Marcel Journet**, who had a voice of great power and flexibility. (Historic Archives of the Rome Opera Theater Photo: G. Antico)

In a photo from 1910 we see **Feodor Shalyapin** in Boris Godunov. (Historic Archives of the Kirov Theater of Leningrad).

bass-baritone roles, still possessing an enviable extension and confidence in the high register.

He sang in London, Covent Garden, 1897-1907, 1927-28; New York, Met, 1900-1908; Paris, Opéra, 1908-31, where he was the first Fafner, Klingsor, Phanuel (*Hérodiade*), Dosifey and Sultan in *Marouf*.

Shalyapin's Thousand Voices

The legendary bass of the twentieth century is, without doubt, **Fyodor Shalyapin** (Kazan 1873 – Paris 1938), one of the most sensitive and generous artists ever to have enriched the operatic world. It was already apparent in his teenage years that the phenomenal bass had the operatic stage in his blood. He actually began his career at the age of fifteen, as a bit-part player in a traveling company.

In 1892 he made his debut at Tiflis in Dargomisky's *Rusalka*, and soon after he was offered a contract with the Leontovsky Theater of St. Petersburg, in which he first sang in 1894 in the tricky role of Bertram in Meyerbeer's *Robert le Diable*.

Devilish characters were perfectly suited to Shalyapin's impressive stage presence and acting. He was an insuperable master in the art of chiseling sound, and perfect in stage movement. He always found the right gesture, gaze and expression to help him reach the audience's heart.

Feodor Shalyapin *and* **Rosina Storchio** *in Boito's* Mefistofele.

Nazzareno De Angelis *in his favorite role as Mosè, in a photo from 1926.*

His Méphistophélès, both in Boito's and in Gounod's *Faust*, was truly terrifying: menacing, unctuous and calculating, with a range of vocal shadings that went from tenor-like *pianissimi* to amazing explosions of sound.

From 1896 until 1919 he performed in Moscow, specializing in the great Russian repertory: operas by Glinka, Mussorgsky, Rimsky-Korsakov and Tchaikovsky, each of which he studied in every dramatic detail, with an unequalled sense of analytic phrasing and expressive power. Shalyapin became famous in America, France, England and at La Scala, triumphing in his favorite operas: *Boris Godunov*, *Kovantchina*, *Mefistofele*, *Barbiere di Siviglia*, *Ivan the Terrible*, and *Prince Igor*. Often, dragged to excess by his passionate temperament, he indulged in exaggerations of dubious taste: in Basilio's aria (*Barbiere*) he was in the habit of adding the words "Ma questa è la fine del mondo" (But this is the end of the world) in a querulous voice after Rossini's "tremuoto" and "temporale", a useless and unjustified liberty. But you only needed to watch the stage movements and expressions of his Basilio to see that he was totally immersed in the part.

In fact, it was as Don Basilio that he gave his

farewell to La Scala in the 1932-33 season, whilst he retired for good in 1937 after a final *Boris Godunov* at Montecarlo.

Another amazing bass came from Poland: **Adam Didur** (Sanol, Galizia 1874 – Katowice 1946), who was only partially influenced by his national origins, and was, in fact, very close to Italian taste, style and repertory.

His debut was made in Latin America (Rio de Janeiro) in 1894. Didur sang on that continent for several years before going to Italy (where he had previously studied singing). Subsequently he performed in Warsaw; then he was employed by La Scala; and lastly he settled at the New York Metropolitan, where he sang as first bass from 1909 until 1932, thus becoming Edouard De Reszké's successor.

Thanks to his exceptional extension, his uniformity over all the registers, the beauty of his timbre and his attractive appearance, Didur was among the greatest singers of the twentieth century to interpret parts such as Marcel (*Les Huguenots*), Méphistophélès (Boito and Gounod), Ramfis, Sparafucile, Kecal (*The Bartered Bride*), Wotan, Don Basilio, Boris, and even Figaro and the Count in Mozart's *Marriage of Figaro*. Listening to his records we are able to appreciate his wonderful polish and the unique clarity of his high notes, especially in Méphistophélès' *ballata* in *Faust* ("Le veau d'or"), Basilio's *cavatina* ("La calunnia"), and in the aria from Meyerbeer's opera *Robert le Diable*.

The Devil's Trill

Nazzareno De Angelis (Rome 1881-1962) had an amazing voice in many respects: first of all it was exceptionally long-lasting, as he sang from 1903 (when he made his debut) at L'Aquila in *Linda di Chamounix*) until 1938. However, the Roman bass also possessed a very powerful voice, which was flexible and well-extended, smooth in the *mezzavoce*, robust in the low notes, and he controlled this voice with an excellent technique and vocal placement.

The legato he exhibited in the long *cantabile* passages (especially in "Celeste man placata" from Rossini's *Mosè* and in "Dormirò sol nel manto mio regal" from Verdi's *Don Carlos*) seemed more like the *cavata* of ten cellos than the sound of a human voice. As for his high notes, Bruno Barilli's description sums them up admirably: "He launched towards the audience... note after note, *roulades*, as massive and incandescent as cannon balls".

He was noble and moving in the Wagnerian roles of Wotan and Guernemanz, proud and belligerent in *Vespri Siciliani*, terrifying in

*For over twenty years, **Ezio Pinza** was the lead bass at the Metropolitan of New York. He was idolized by the public and became a legend in the role of Don Giovanni. Besides the Mozart masterpiece, he interpreted more than fifty operas.*

Mefistofele, and thundering as Oroveso in *Norma*. De Angelis made Rossini's *Mosè* his favorite role, and even managed to acquire the famous "tight trill" after assiduous study for the great scene "Eterno, immenso, incomprensibil Dio." An exploit, thankfully preserved on record, which will probably remain unequalled. He sang in all leading Italian theaters and with the Chicago Opera, 1910-11 and 1915-20.

Ezio Pinza: a Winning Don Giovanni

Another Roman bass inherited De Angelis' technical qualities (breath control, smooth and well-placed sounds, extended and penetrating high notes, and finely chiseled singing) even if he could never equal his volume. His name was **Ezio Pinza** (Fortunio Pinza; Rome 1892 – Stamford, Connecticut 1957). He also had a natural flair for drama, commanding the stage with an attractive physical appearance and the intelligence and sensitivity of a great actor.

After his debut at Soncino, Italy, in 1914, he was forced to interrupt his career during the years of the First World War, when he was a soldier for six years. In 1919 he began to sing again, this time at Florence, in the small parts of Roucher in *Andrea Chénier* and Ferrando in *Il Trovatore*. His contract with the Teatro Costanzi in Rome for the 1919-20 season at last brought him to the public's attention. Pinza sang admirably in *Forza del Destino*, *La Gioconda*, *Tristan und Isolde*, *Rigoletto*, *Aida* and *Boris Godunov* (Pimen), demonstrating talent and a fine technique.

La Scala (from 1921 until 1924), the Metro-

*Many first-ever performances of opera were entrusted to the powerful vocal qualities of **Tancredi Pasero**, such as Ghedini's Re Hassan, which we see in the photo. Other celebrated prime were Emiral (Barilli), Orseolo (Pizzetti), Gli Orazi (Porrino), Nerone (Mascagni), and Margherita da Cortona (Refice). (Historic Archives of La Fenice Theater, Venice. Photo: Giacomelli)*

politan (from 1926 until 1948) and Covent Garden (from 1930 until 1939), all the world's major theaters welcomed Pinza as their absolute favorite, right up to his Broadway performances of *South Pacific* by Rogers and Hammerstein, with which he retired from the stage in 1949.

Because of his aristocratic phrasing and his vocal qualities he emerged in the typical roles of the *basso nobile*: Fiesco, Philip II, Ramfis, Boris, Mefistofele and Oroveso; but he also managed to sing the role of Don Giovanni exceptionally well, becoming legendary in that part. Pinza, who had a repertory of more than ninety-five roles, sang *Don Giovanni* more than two hundred times, and appeared more than seven hundred and fifty times in fifty operas during his engagement with the Met.

During an evening at the Met in 1942, Pinza was performing Mozart's masterpiece, with the famous bass Kipnis in the part of Leporello. When they came to the balcony scene in which the two characters imitate each other while disguised, cheeky Kipnis began to produce funny bleating sounds (mimicking one of Pinza's personal defects), making the audience roll in their seats with laughter. Pinza, however, was not able to copy the cavernous voice of the *basso profondo*, thus losing the challenge. Apparently, the two great singers never spoke to each other again.

Tancredi Pasero (Turin 1893 – Milan 1983) completes the golden triangle of Italian basses (De Angelis and Pinza). His career embraced a long period of time and a wide repertory. He sang from 1918 (he began at Vicenza as Conte Rodolfo in *Sonnambula*) until 1953, and his voice remained miraculously intact until his death, according to many reliable witnesses.

Compared with many of his famous colleagues Pasero had neither a particularly attractive timbre nor a very powerful voice. However, he was able to make a practically unlimited use of his voice, having complete control of his vocal faculties, from his low notes to his vibrant high notes. His favorite theaters were La Scala (where he was first bass from 1926 to 1952), the Metropolitan and Covent Garden, although he often performed in other theaters the world over (including South America, Spain, Portugal).

His varied and incisive accent helped distinguish him as a Verdi bass, especially in the roles of the Padre Guardiano, Philip II, Zaccaria, Walter (*Luisa Miller*), but he also included Donizetti (*Linda di Chamounix, Lucrezia Borgia*), Bellini (*Sonnambula, Norma, Puritani*) and even Rossini (apart from his excellent and controlled Basilio, he was also an applauded Mosè and occasionally Assur in *Semiramide*, Florence 1933 and 1940). Pasero also performed memorably as Boris, Wotan, Gurnemanz, King Marke,

Mark Reizen *as Boris in 1930. What struck one most about this artist was his colossal size and his great dramatic capacity. (Historic Archives of the Kirov Theater, Leningrad)*

Caspar in *Der Freischütz*, Mefistofele, Alvise Badoero (*Gioconda*), and in some contemporary works created especially for him.

Two important Russian basses must be mentioned, even though they remained in Shalyapin's shadow. **Alexander Pirogov** (Novoselka, Rjazan 1899 – Moscow 1964) was the first bass at the Bolshoi from 1924, and was much acclaimed as Boris, Ivan, Mefistofele and Pestel in *Decabristi*, an opera by Saporin. **Mark Reizen** (Zaitsevo 1895 – Moscow 1992) made his debut in 1921 at Kharkov, and was a permanent member of the Moscow's greatest theater from 1930 onwards; he distinguished himself in the classic role of Boris, as Dositeo (*Kovantchina*) and as Gremin (*Eugene Onegin*).

A close-up of the bass **Gottlob Frick**, *a celebrated Hagen and Osmin. (Historic Archives of EMI. Photo: Fayer)*

His vocal longevity is legendary: he apparently still managed to sing in 1985 (on the occasion of his ninetieth birthday!) an entire performance of *Eugene Onegin* at the Bolshoi (in the role of Gremin).

Moving on to the great German *bassi cantabili* we find **Richard Mayr** (Henndorf, Austria 1817 – Vienna 1935), who was persuaded by Gustav Mahler to take up music instead of the medical studies he had already started. After his debut at Bayreuth in 1902 as Hagen, his career developed at Vienna (Staatsoper, 1902-35), Salzburg, London (Covent Garden, 1924-31) and New York (Met 1927-30). He always favored the principal Wagnerian roles, Leporello, Figaro (*Marriage of Figaro*), Sarastro, Barak in Strauss' *Die Frau ohne Schatten* (of which he was the first interpreter in 1919); but it was his performance of Baron Ochs in *Der Rosenkavalier* which became legendary.

Ludwig Weber (Vienna 1899 – 1974) belongs to the following generation, and sang in the theaters of Vienna, Bayreuth, London and many other German theaters from 1920 to 1960. His repertoire included Mozart, Verdi and, primarily, Wagner. He became well-known in the parts of Gurnemanz (*Parsifal*), Hagen and Daland. Thanks to his vocal flexibility and his

Josef Greindl in the role of the perfidious Hagen, and, seated, Adolf Vogel in the part of Alberich, during a scene from Götterdämmerung performed March 16, 1957 in Venice. The director was Wolfgang Wagner. (Historic Archives of La Fenice Theater, Venice. Photo: Giacomelli)

*Wagner, Die Walküre, performed in Naples in 1963. In the opera's finale, Wotan (**Hans Hotter**) is about to build a wall of fire around the sleeping Brünnhilde (the beautiful **Anja Silja**. (Historic Archives of the San Carlo Theater of Naples. Photo: Troncone)*

interpretive intelligence he was able to perform in the Lieder and oratorio fields as well.

Among the best German basses between 1930 and 1970, **Gottlob Frick** (Ölbron, Württemberg 1906 – Pforzheim 1994) deserves a mention. His voice was of a dark timbre, rich, well-extended and robust, ideal for the role of the "bad guy" in the operas of Wagner (Hagen, Hunding, Fafner) and Mozart (his Osmin in *Die Entführung aus dem Serail* has remained unforgettable). He was active from 1927 until the end of the seventies with all the main operatic companies the world over. Frick was also the protagonist of many contemporary compositions and included several Verdi roles in his repertoire, such as Padre Guardiano and Philip II, with excellent results.

From Valhalla, an Unforgettable Wotan: Hans Hotter

Hans Hotter (Offenbach 1909) was best suited to roles full of pathos. He was formed by the great school of Römer in Munich (Bavaria), a student of the mythical Jan De Reszké. His timbre, rich in harmonics and governed by a superior technique and musicality, made his renderings of the Wagnerian roles of Wotan, Hans Sachs, King Marke, Hunding, Amfortas,

Kurwenal and the Dutchman truly great and allowed him to give excellent performances in the Italian repertory (Philip II, Scarpia, Amonasro, the Grand Inquisitor) and in Lieder, especially that of Richard Strauss.

He made his debut in 1929 as the Orator in *The Magic Flute*, staged at Opava. From then on the German bass sang in Bayreuth, Munich, Vienna, Paris, Milan, New York, London, and, in Munich, took part in the first-ever performances of Richard Strauss' *Friedenstag* (1938) and *Capriccio* (1942). Even in the early nineties he was still treading the stage (as the Orator in *The Magic Flute* and in some of Berg's operas), and has been acclaimed as a living legend in German theaters and at Covent Garden.

Josef Greindl (Munich 1912 – Vienna 1993) was both an excellent actor and singer, endowed with a powerful voice and lovely low register. He first sang in 1935 and became immediately popular in the Germanic countries as Sarastro, Osmin, Hunding (*Die Walküre*), Fafner, King Marke, Daland (*Flying Dutchman*), Hagen (*Götterdammerung*), Rocco (*Fidelio*) and Sparafucile (*Rigoletto*).

We have rarely had the occasion to hear the prayer "O Isis und Osiris" (Sarastro) sung in such an aristocratic way. Greindl filled the concert halls and opera theaters with his resonant accents and vibrant voice, of which the low notes resembled powerful "organ peddles." He was exceptional in Osmino's difficult aria "Ach! Wie will Ich triumphieren", which he performed with an extraordinary verve and skill, right down to the impossibly low D, full and sonorous. Unfortunately, from 1960 on, his high register suffered strain, becoming ever harsher and wobbly. Nevertheless, Griendl was still an excellent singer-actor, creating a magnificent Moses in Schonberg's opera *Moses und Aron*. He sang his last Wotan in Paris in June 1972.

The Amiable Baron of Lerchenau: Otto Edelmann

From the end of the thirties until the early seventies the opera stage boasted the presence of one of the twentieth century's most important singer-actors in the German repertory, **Otto Edelmann** (Vienna 1916). After having completed his studies in his native city, under the guidance of the famous teacher Lierhammer

*The bass **José van Dam** as Philip II in Verdi's Don Carlos. Here he is during the aria "Ella giammai m'amo." (Historic Archives of the Opera de Nice)*

*The noble Hans Sachs of **Otto Edelmann**, a part he interpreted many times in all the world's great theaters. In particular, we wish to remember the recording made at Bayreuth in 1951 with the conducting of Herbert von Karajan. The tenor Hopf, Schwarzkopf and Erich Kunz sang together with Edelmann. (Metropolitan Opera House. Photo: Melançon)*

(his classmates were Christoff, Welitsch and Kunz), Edelmann made his debut at Gera, playing the lead role in *The Marriage of Figaro*.

From 1947 on he became a permanent member of the Vienna State Opera ensemble, and after that his career soared. New York, San Francisco, London, Bayreuth, Salzburg, Edinburgh and Milan were fundamental steps in a brilliant profession that developed under the guidance of the most eminent conductors (Furtwängler, Knappertsbusch, von Karajan, Mitropoulos, Böhm). His vocal qualities (a beautiful timbre, smooth emission, perfect legato with good extension) placed him half way between the *basso-nobile* and the German *Bass-Baryton*. His wide repertoire is proof. It swept from Mozart (Figaro, the Count, Osmin, Leporello, Publio in *La Clemenza di Tito*) and Verdi (Philip II and Falstaff) to his natural Wagner territory (Hans Sachs, Wotan, Amfortas, the Dutchman, and King Henry in *Lohengrin*) and his adored Richard Strauss (his Baron Ochs and his Waldner in *Arabella* are unforgettable). In addition to his purely vocal gifts Edelmann also displayed a refined dramatic talent, far superior to the possibilities of most opera singers.

*A typical attitude of **Boris Christoff**, in the role of Boris Godunov. His acting talent was equal to his singing. (Historic Archives of the Rome Opera Theater Photo: Oscar Savio)*

*"Le veau d'or" from Gounod's Faust, performed energetically by the great **Boris Christoff**. (Historic Archives of the Rome Opera Theater Photo: Piccagliani)*

In the roles of Hans Sach, Wotan and Ochs, he governed the stage with a variety of expressions and gestures worthy of a dedicated actor. His habit of whistling nonchalantly during the letter scene, when playing the part of surly Baron Ochs in *Der Rosenkavalier*, has remained famous; with that simple gesture, as director Hartmann noted perceptively, Edelmann expressed far more than he ever could have with words.

Another famous name was **Oskar Czerwenka** (Vocklabruck, Linz 1924 – Vienna 2000), who was a member of the Vienna State Opera for over thirty years from 1951 onwards. He was acclaimed in seventy-five different roles as well as in many concert performances. The American **Jerome Hines** (J. Heinz; Hollywood 1921) was employed by the Met from 1947 onwards and was applauded for his performances as Boris, the Grand Inquisitor, and Gurnemanz, which he even sang at Bayreuth in 1958. The English singer **Forbes Robinson** (Peter Robinson; Macclesfield 1926) was a permanent member of the Covent Garden Opera Company from 1954 onwards. He was the first to perform Don Giovanni in that theater after Sir Charles Stanley. He sang over seventy roles including Pizarro, Figaro, Boris, Swallow, and Claggart in *Billy Budd*.

The true German *basso-nobile* (with characteristics of the *Bass-Baryton*) is epitomized by **José van Dam** (Josef van Damme; Brussels 1940), who sings in French, Austrian and German theaters. He was much appreciated by von Karajan who often invited him to sing in Salzburg. His rich and velvety voice is well-extended, technically well-organized, and perfectly suited to melancholy, pensive characters such as Philip II, the Dutchman and Amfortas, but can also be adapted to Escamillo, Figaro (*The Marriage of Figaro*), Méphistophélès (*The Damnation of Faust*) and Jokanaan (*Salome*). He began at the Paris Opéra in 1961 and later sang in other major theaters, including Covent Garden (debut as Escamillo in *Carmen*, 1973).

In the twenty years from 1960 to 1980, a pre-eminent position was held by two excellent German basses, **Karl Ridderbusch** (Recklinghausen Westphalia 1932) and **Hans Sotin** (Dortmund 1939), both of whom possess a smooth and well-extended voice and an aristocratic singing style, ideal for the parts of King Marke, King Henry the Fowler, Gurnemanz, Wotan, the Flying Dutchman, Sarastro, and a few roles from the Italian repertory.

King Boris

Boris Christoff (Plovdiv 1914 – Rome 1993) was a great Bulgarian bass. Interestingly, the name "Boris" played a fundamental role in Christoff's career: it was King Boris III of Bul-

garia who awarded him the scholarship which permitted him to study singing in Italy (after the king had noticed the young singer when he was a soloist in the Gussla Choir of Sofia); and it was his superb interpretation of the role of Boris Godunov which made him famous the world over.

Thanks to the invaluable guidance of the baritone Stracciari, the Bulgarian bass was able to create a fascinating mixture between the Slav style of singing (the unmistakable *portamenti*, the slightly Byzantine-sounding accents and inflexions) with the dictates of pure Italian belcanto (perfectly placed sounds, smooth emission, use of the *mezzavoce* and of the various dynamic nuances, uniformity in the registers); he thus avoided the errors that often mar many Slav basses (high notes in the throat, harshness, exaggerations).

It was obvious that Christoff would excel in the Russian repertory. His Boris, his Ivan the Terrible, his Prince Galitsky and Konchak in *Prince Igor*, his Kochubei in *Mazeppa*, and his Ivan Susanin in *A Life for the Tsar* by Glinka were all splendid. He perfectly amalgamated power of expression, analytic phrasing, beautiful polish and a dominant stage presence.

The Verdi characters he rendered best were those of the proud Silva in *Ernani*, Attila, Fiesco in *Simon Boccanegra*, Procida in *Vespri Siciliani*; but above all, Philip II in *Don Carlos*. His King of Spain was complete in all the dramatic details indicated by Schiller and Verdi. According to the different moments in the opera, his character would become proud, melancholy, a wounded father or an important king. It was a great interpretation, which he deepened with every performance, culminating in the memorable staging in 1982 at the Teatro Regio of Parma, with a whispered "Ella giammai m'amò", which was so moving that at the end of this difficult monologue the audience burst into an interminable ovation, crowned with the spontaneous cry of "You're a marvel!". It was Christoff's farewell, the last performance of his wonderful career.

He was invited by the Metropolitan Opera in 1950, but was barred for political reasons because he was from a communist country; he sang in San Francisco and Chicago (1956-63), but never at the Metropolitan.

In Shalyapin's Footsteps

Many singers followed in Shalyapin's footsteps, two of the best being **Ivan Petrov** (Irkutsk 1920) and **Nicola Rossi Lemeni** (Constantinople 1920 – Bloomington, U.S.A. 1991).

Petrov entered the Bolshoi Opera in 1943, where he immediately proved himself to be an artist of fine vocal resources and good stage presence. He preferred Russian parts such as Dositeo in *Kovantchina*, Kochubei in *Mazeppa*, Boris, Konchak in *Prince Igor*, René in *Iolanta* by Tchaikovsky, but he also sang Don Basilio and Méphistophélès in Gounod's *Faust*.

Nicola Rossi Lemeni studied with Maestro Cusinati at Verona. He had learnt the basics from his mother, but the turning point came when he began to listen to the recordings of Shalyapin and De Angelis, who became his great models. With care and sensitivity he succeeded in learning their interpretative skills, changing his own voice to make it resemble that of his illustrious predecessors, especially that of Shalyapin. During his golden years, between 1946 and 1960, Rossi Lemeni's voice was not particularly powerful, nor extended in the low register, and with a slightly veiled timbre. But it was exceptionally flexible, adaptive to every expressive demand: from tenor-like *pianissimi* to the effects of *smorzando* and *rinforzando*, which were very moving. It was extended in the high register, right up to a penetrating high g´, agile in patter singing and rapid vocalizing passages (to the extent that he could successfully tackle the parts of Selim in Rossini's *Turco in Italia*, Don Basilio, Mosè, Don

"My dear Don Ottavio, fix your jacket if you want to be a Don Giovanni", **Nicola Rossi-Lemeni** seems to be saying to tenor **Luigi Alva,** his partner in Don Giovanni, performed at Venice on January 14, 1958. The orchestra conductor was Vittorio Gui. (Historic Archives of La Fenice Theater of Venice. Photo: Giacomelli)

Giovanni, Uberto in Pergolesi's *Serva Padrona* and Handel's *Julius Caesar*).

The Italian bass was helped by a commanding appearance, an expressive face and a natural elegance and dignity in his movements on stage. He refined his art thanks to his constant, intelligent self-control and innate musicality. Rossi Lemeni was a great Boris, Philip II, Silva, Procida, Mefistofele, Don Quichotte, Giorgio in *I Puritani*, Oroveso, Basilio; he also sang in many modern compositions, the most important of these being Pizzetti's *Assassinio nella Cattedrale*, of which he was the first interpreter in 1958 at La Scala.

A Lord of the Stage

Cesare Siepi (Milan 1919), together with Christoff, was the last legendary representative of the *basso nobile* school.

Siepi's unusually long career is a clear example of superior class and vocal technique. Siepi made his debut at Schio, near Venice, in 1941, singing Sparafucile in *Rigoletto*. More than forty years later audiences were still marveling at his magnificent portrayals of Philip II, Fiesco, Don Basilio, Baldassarre (*Favorita*), Don Giovanni and Roger in Verdi's opera *Jerusalem* (in a memorable performance at Parma in January 1986).

The most impressive of his vocal characteristics was the smooth, rich consistency of his timbre with a naturally dark color which resembled that of a *basso profondo*; it was a voice sustained by a faultless emission, flexible and light, based

The 1967-68 Opera Season in Parma: **Nicola Rossi-Lemeni** *had a personal success at the Regio in* Assassinio nella Cattedrale, *an opera written especially for him by Pizzetti in 1958. (Historic Archives of the Teatro Regio of Parma. Photo: Montacchini)*

The bass **Rossi-Lemeni** *in an opera little performed today but which was a favorite of many artists:* Il Piccolo Marat *by Mascagni. (Historic Archives of the San Carlo Opera Theater of Naples. Photo: Troncone)*

Cesare Siepi: a gentleman of the stage. The photo was taken in April, 1986, when Siepi performed Fiesco magnificently at the San Carlo. The low F sharp of the aria "Il lacerato spirito" resounded full and round, in a way that no one today can do. (Historic Archives of La Fenice Theater, Venice. Photo: L. Romano)

*In the early years of his career Ghiaurov frequently sang Don Giovanni, succeeding in creating an excellent portrayal, both vocally and dramatically. Here he is in a photo from 1964 together with the bass **Ganzarolli** (Leporello). (Historic Archives of the San Carlo Theater of Naples. Photo: Troncone)*

on a perfect breathing technique. His low notes were wide and resonant, of equal quality, reaching down to low C (a note which Siepi produced easily in the brief aria "Splendon più belle in ciel le stelle" from *La Favorita* and in Seneca's death scene from the *Incoronation of Poppea*).

Up until the late sixties, Siepi's high notes sounded well-placed and powerful, reaching up to g´. With the inexorable passing of time, however, this register began to show signs of strain and became a little wobbly, but this did not significantly compromise the splendor of a truly magnificent voice.

During the course of his extraordinary artistic career, Siepi sang at La Scala, Covent Garden (1950-62), the Metropolitan (succeeding Pinza from 1950 on), Vienna, Salzburg, and in all the major Italian theaters. Among his favorite roles were also Mefistofele, Padre Guardiano, Zaccaria in *Nabucco*, Ramfis, Silva and Sparafucile.

Nicolai Ghiaurov (Velimgrad 1929) was born in Bulgaria and gifted with a magnificent voice, which was to give new life and honor to the long line of Slavic basses. He began by studying violin and piano, then took his diploma in singing at Sofia, going on to complete a post-graduate course in Moscow. He made his debut in 1956 at Sofia, singing Don Basilio in *Barbiere*. It was immediately apparent

*Another of **Siepi's** famous characterizations: Ramfis in Aida. Parma, 1988. (Photo: Montacchini)*

"La calunnia è un venticello": **Ghiaurov** *often played the role of Don Basilio. (Photo: Archive Stinchelli)*

Principal singer of Attila ot the Staatsoper of Vienna, 1980 – a new triumph for **Nicolai Ghiaurov***. (Photo: V Claser, Vienna)*

to everybody just how unique Ghiaurov's talent was. The consistency and polish of his voice, its notable extension, the quality of his sound and his ability to color each one of his beautiful notes with a special expressive meaning made his singing always varied and interesting. He accompanied these gifts with an impressive physical appearance and good acting skills; and so Ghiaurov was soon enrolled by the world's major opera theaters to sing Boris, Méphistophélès (by both Boito and Gounod), Mosè, Philip II, Ramfis, Fiesco, Zaccaria, the Grand Inquisitor and Don Giovanni.

Thanks to constant study and practice throughout his exceptionally long-lasting career, Ghiaurov, even in the eighties and nineties, was still singing Boris, Philip II, Gremin, Don Basilio, Sparafucile and Colline, adding a magnificent performance of the Blind Man in Mascagni's *Iris* and of Dositej in *Kovantchina*.

An important Italian bass has emerged as one of the best prepared and gifted singers, though the Italian opera companies were somewhat late in discovering him. **Bonaldo Giaiotti** (Ziracco, Udine 1933) made his debut in Milan in 1958, but it was the Metropolitan that soon after took the initiative of assuring him a permanent engagement in the roles of Zaccaria, Fiesco, Basilio, Silva, Mefistofele, Ramfis,

Philip II, Oroveso and Alvise Badoero. His voice is rich, uniform, mellow and sustained by a professionalism and musicality that cannot be faulted. Perhaps it was precisely his introversion and an excessive scrupulousness that in the early years kept him out of big-time opera and the record industry and the major Italian theaters, especially La Scala. During the decade 1990-2000, he was still delighting audiences with superb performances of Baldassarre in *Favorita*, Mephistopheles in *Faust*, Zaccaria in *Nabucco* and his virtually unique Ramfis. He is unquestionably the last great Verdi bass of his generation.

To close this chapter, here are a number of other basses who, without being superstars, have nonetheless sustained the great Italian tradition with their artistic talent: **Giacomo Vaghi** (Como 1901 – Rome 1978); **Andrea Mongelli** (Bari 1901 – Rome 1970), who also sang as a baritone in the latter years of his career; **Nicola Moscona** (Athens 1907 – Philadelphia 1975); **Agostino Ferrin** (Piove di Sacco, Padua 1928 – Rome 1989); **Norman Treigle** (New Orleans 1927 – 1975); **Carlo Cava** (Ascoli Piceno 1928); **Raphael Ariè** (Sofia 1920 – Sankt Moriz 1988); **Paolo Washington** (Florence 1932); **Ivo Vinco** (Boscochiesanuova, Verona 1927); **Nicola Zaccaria** (Athens 1923); **Ezio Flagello** (New York 1931); **Giorgio Tozzi** (Chicago

1923) at the Met from 1955; **Robert Lloyd** (Andrew Lloyd, Southend-on-Sea 1940); **Gwynne Howell** (Richard Howell; Gorseinon, Wales 1938); and **Paul Plishka** (Old Forge, Pennsylvania 1941), all of whom were indispensable pillars of thousands of performances.

The most talented of the latest generation of Russian basses is without doubt **Yevgeny Nesterenko** (Moscow 1938), who made his debut in 1962 as Gremin in Tchaikovsky's *Eugene Onegin*, and has been on stage now for some forty years. It goes almost without saying that his repertoire includes all the main Russian operas, plus a vast selection of characters from the Italian repertory. His voice has a good texture, smooth and extended, even though he tends to sing the high notes in the throat (a fault, it must be said, common to many Russian and Slav basses).

Prominent among the following generation are **Ferruccio Furlanetto** (Sacile, Pordenone 1949), gifted with a deep, full voice, who is renowned for his performances in *Don Giovanni*, *Don Carlos*, *Vespri Siciliani*, *Nabucco* and *Attila* and has appeared in all the world's major opera houses; **Carlo Colombara** (Reggio Emilia 1964), equally involved in the main Verdi repertoire, endowed with interesting vocal characteristics but somewhat routine as a performer; **Paata Burchuladze** (Tbilisi, Georgia 1951), who made his debut in 1976 and has since performed in all the major international theaters, thanks to his powerful, attractively colored voice. The Russian **Askar Abdrazakov**, a singer of the latest generation, has a ductile, well-disciplined voice, well able to tackle both the Italian and Russian repertoires.

We must also mention two Italian singers, **Roberto Scandiuzzi** (Maserada, Treviso 1958) and **Francesco Ellero Artegna** (Ravascletto, Udine 1948), who have sung the Italian repertory (Philip II, Fiesco, Silva, Zaccaria) in the world's major opera houses.

THE *BASSO PROFONDO*

Representing the voice of baroque opera in the twentieth century is a restricted platoon of singers, all of whom more or less worthy of the title of *basso profondo*. Let us see who they are.

The flag bearer for this prestigious category is, without doubt, **José Mardones** (Fontecha, Alava 1869 – Madrid 1932) whose voice was unique for its volume and the beauty of its timbre. Between the end of the nineteenth century and 1926 he was much acclaimed, especially by the American public (he sang at the Met from 1911 to 1926), in roles such as Ramfis, Mephistopheles, Oroveso, Marcel in *Les Huguenots*, Pimen in *Boris Godunov* and Zaccaria. In his formidable performances, these characters became fantastic thunderbolts of sound.

Alexander Kipnis came from Russia (Zitomir, Ukraine 1891 – Westport, Connecticut 1978) to collect and later enhance Mardones' inheritance. He had made his debut in 1915 at Hamburg, and was very active in German and American theaters. What was amazing about Kipnis' vocal performances were his flexibility and the intelligence he applied to his interpretations. His voice spread easily over the entire range from the bottom of the stave (full, sonorous notes) to the high notes, with an extraordinary uniformity. He could also obtain all the shadings he wished from his compliant voice, from the most delicate *pianissimi* to *rinforzando* effects. Thus he was able to excel in a vast repertoire. Kipnis often sang Don Giovanni, but also Leporello, Sarastro, Osmin, Gurnemanz (*Parsifal*), an extraordinary Pogner in *The Mastersingers*, Fiesco, Philip II, Sparafucile, Boris, Gremin in *Eugene Onegin*, Rocco in *Fidelio*, Hagen, King Marke; and he was also a worthy Lieder singer, excelling in the Brahms repertory. He was a sensitive actor, moving well on stage, and he became irresistible in comic parts, where he showed a verve and musicality beyond comparison. Forced by Hitler to leave Germany, he settled in America, eventually becoming an American citizen.

Our account continues with **Juste Nivette** (1865), an unequalled Sarastro, Alvise in *La Gioconda* and Hagen at La Scala in 1901; the powerful **Mansueto Gaudio** (Vignale Borbera, Alessandria 1873 – Santiago, Chile 1941); **Giovanni Gravina** (Messina 1872 – Boston 1912), applauded as Ramfis and Sparafucile; **Wilhelm Strienz** (Stuttgart 1900 – Frankfurt 1981), famous above all as Sarastro; **Umberto Di Lelio** (Rome 1894 – 1945); **Emanuel List** (Vienna 1890 – 1967); **Luciano Neroni** (Ripa-

A cruel Mefistofele, that of **Giulio Neri**. The audience were awestruck by the terrible glares cast by his enormous blue eyes. (Historic Archives of the Rome Opera Theater. Photo: A. Villani)

Because of the strength and power of his voice **Neri** was able to tackle even the Wagner repertory without difficulty. Here he is in the role of Hagen in Götterdämmerung. (Historic Archives of the Rome Opera Theater. Photo: A. Villani)

transone, Ascoli Piceno 1909-1951), whose voice had the magnificent color of an authentic *basso scuro*.

"Ao! Ammaza che voce!" ("Oh! What a voice!") says Alberto Sordi to **Giulio Neri**, exhibiting his own unquestionable quality as a basso-profondo! The two were acting in the comedy film Mi permette, babbo? (Will you let me, Daddy?) in which they performed a memorable duet. (Historic Archives of the Rome Opera Theater)

The Neri Phenomenon

The last true *basso profondo* was **Giulio Neri** (Torrita di Siena 1909 – Rome 1958). There is universal agreement that it would be virtually impossible to describe his monumental voice in words: entire theaters, even open-air ones, would tremble under the sea of sound produced by Neri.

By 1938 he had established himself as leading bass at Rome's Teatro dell'Opera, and appeared there regularly until shortly before his death. His last performance was in *Norma* in 1958.

His timbre was naturally cavernous. Neri could sink down to C without losing any of the power and richness of his central notes, producing a unique "organ" effect. Between 1935 and the year of his premature death in 1958, he was unsurpassed as Sparafucile, Ramfis, the Grand Inquisitor, Mephistopheles, and in Wagner's operas, which he sang in the Italian version. Together with the Italian comic actor Alberto Sordi (who, having studied singing

Mariti Talvela *as Fafner (left) in* Das Rheingold, *with* **Karl Ridderbusch***, as Fasolt.*

before becoming an actor, could well have enjoyed a successful career as a bass, had he continued) Neri made a fun-filled movie entitled *Mi Permette, Babbo?* (Will you let me, Daddy?), where he sang a duet with the Roman actor, who was playing the part of an aspiring young *basso profondo* who, despite his ardent desire to emerge on the stage, was destined (as so often happens in real life) to remain an eternal student.

Martti Talvela (Hütola 1934 – 1989) and **Kurt Moll** (Buir 1938) had all the characteristics of the typical *basso profondo*, and were the only two singers who were able to perform the roles of Sarastro and Osmin with the appropriate style of interpretation.

Talvela, from Finland, a real giant in stature, first sang at Stockholm in 1961, and from then on his wide, resonant voice was to be heard in Wagner (Fasolt, Hunding, King Marke, Daland), Mozart (Sarastro, Osmin), and in Verdi's *Don Carlos*, where he played the part of the Grand Inquisitor with a fine vocal rendering. Sadly, he died of a sudden heart attack while still at the height of his career.

Kurt Moll sings in German and Austrian opera houses, with a repertoire including *Tristan und Isolde; The Mastersingers of Nuremberg* (Pogner); *Die Entfuhrung aus dem Serail* (Osmin), an opera in which he is able to perform the aria "Ach! Wie will Ich triumphieren" like a real virtuoso, singing the complicated *cadenza* in one breath and finishing with a well-emitted trill; *The Magic Flute, Parsifal* (Gurnemanz); *Der Freischutz* (Caspar); *The Flying Dutchman* (Daland) and *La Forza del Destino* (the Padre Guardiano).

THE COMIC BASS:
FUNNY BUT NOT FARCICAL

Many basses perform in the comic repertory, but few are truly great in it. Those few, however, are the rare singers who do not need to indulge in jokes and exaggerations to win the audience's favor. A real *buffo*, that is, a comedian, not a clown, should not be a failed *basso nobile*, or a flunked-out Philip II, to be more explicit. Quite the opposite. He must unite the vocal elegance of the *basso nobile* with a refined phrasing and acting skill. Fun-loving or grumpy, chasing after servant girls, youngsters, or whoever else happens to be passing by, he must never surpass the limits of correct, refined acting, never be vulgar.

Not many singers qualify for the title of comic bass. Few in the twentieth century were worthy of being called *buffi*, but one who did earn the title was **Antonio Pini-Corsi** (Zara 1858 – Milan 1918), the first Ford in *Falstaff*, chosen personally by Verdi for the historical *prima* at La Scala in 1893.

Verdi's choice leaves no doubt as to the extraordinary talent of this actor-singer. He could don the costume of Dandini in Rossini's *Cenerentola* (his debut opera in 1878 at Cremona) and with equal conviction that of Rigoletto, King Alfonso in *La Favorita* and Gérmont in *Traviata*. His favorite roles were those of Dulcamara (*Elisir d'Amore*), Don Pasquale, Don Bartolo and Taddeo (*Italiana in Algeri*), characters which he virtually transformed in his interpretations. After all this praise, in fairness we should also mention what the publisher Ricordi said about him after the opening night of *Falstaff*. He declared that Pini-Corsi was a third-rate singer, who hammed the part and was also anti-musical. And his recording of the aria "Udite, udite o rustici" actually confirms Ricordi's opinion.

Virgilio Lazzari (Assisi 1887 – Castel Gandolfo 1953) was one of the most acclaimed Leporellos, both in American theaters and at Salzburg. He had a clear voice, which was governed by a controlled and aristocratic manner. He was also a fine actor and sang with a repertory of some fifty-five operas. He studied in Rome with the famous Antonio Cotogni.

Vincenzo Bettoni (Melegnano 1881 – Milan 1954) alternated serious and comic repertories, making his debut as Silva in *Ernani* in Pinerolo in 1902. He often sang at La Scala (1926-40) and in England, covering a sizeable repertory (*Tristan und Isolde*, *Faust*, *Gioconda*, *Mignon*,

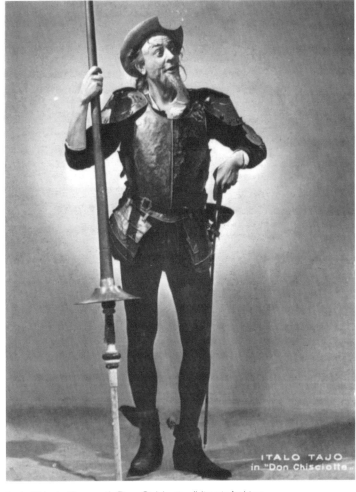

Italo Tajo in Massenet's Don Quichotte. *(Historic Archives of the Rome Opera Theater. Photo: A. Villani)*

Comte d'Ory, *Fra Diavolo*, *Barbiere di Siviglia*, *L'Italiana in Algeri*, *Cenerentola*), thanks to his flexible, well-extended voice.

Between 1922 and 1962 **Salvatore Baccaloni** (Rome 1900 – New York 1969) dominated the stage with his amiability, his sense of humor and his refined singing. It could not have been otherwise, considering the training he had. He was a boy singer in the Sistine Chapel and afterwards studied with Talli and Kaschmann. He was a perfect Don Pasquale, Bartolo, Don Magnifico, Taddeo, Mustafà, and even Osmin. After 1940 he performed almost exclusively at the New York Metropolitan Opera, where he was proclaimed the "new Lablache".

Andres Perello de Segurola (Valencia 1874 – Barcelona 1953) obtained a memorable success as Leporello at Salzburg in 1910. **Wilhelm Hesch** (Elbeteinitz, Czechoslovakia 1860 – Vienna 1908) was a remarkable *buffo*. **Vanni Marcoux** (Turin 1877 – Paris 1962) made an exceptional Don Quichotte in Massenet's opera and Gianni Schicchi, but he also performed in all the most important *basso nobile* parts during a career lasting over forty years. He had a repertory of two hundred and forty roles.

In later years, the most important comic basses included **Fernando Corena** (Geneva 1916 – Lugano 1984) and **Paolo Montarsolo** (Portici, Naples 1925), who both tended to exaggerate but had an irresistible sense of humor.

Everlasting Tajo

Italo Tajo (Pinerolo 1915 – Cincinnati, Ohio 1993) was one of those miraculous cases of artistic longevity that can only be explained by his rigid self-control, a correct and constant study, intelligence and sensitivity. Of course, we cannot limit his successes to the category of comic basses (the *buffi*). In fact, Tajo made his debut in 1935 at the Teatro Regio of Turin in the *basso profondo* role of Fafner in *Das Rheingold*. During the first part of his fifty-year-long career (Tajo was still singing in small parts such as that of the sacristan in *Tosca*, Alcindoro and Benoît in *La Bohème* and Simone in *Gianni Schicchi* throughout the eighties and into the early nineties), the Italian singer showed a marked inclination for the classic repertory of the *basso nobile*: Ramfis, Banquo, Don Giovanni, Méphistophélès in Gounod's *Faust*, Attila and Sparafucile. He did not give these parts mere vocal splendor, but added a psychological depth achieved by a variety of accents and a lively, vivid phrasing, always perfectly suited to the character.

Tajo's voice never had a particularly attractive timbre, nor was it powerful enough to stun. What was amazing was his ability to produce any shading he wished, starting from an almost inaudible trill in *pianissimo*; he also exhibited an elegant and incomparable acting style. So, together with his serious repertory, he gained a huge success in comic roles: from his legendary Dulcamara to Don Basilio, from Figaro (*Marriage of Figaro*) to Don Pasquale, and a wide selection of characters from the Neapolitan repertory of the eighteenth century, many of which have been preserved by the RAI recordings. He gave his farewell performance in 1991, at the Met, as the sacristan in *Tosca*.

Salvatore Baccaloni as Don Pasquale. From 1926-1940 he sang at La Scala, where Toscanini worked with him and suggested that he specialize in the comic roles of Italian opera, in which he enjoyed great success. He was one of the most famous and celebrated Met stars from 1940 to 1962.

"A Doctor of My Standing..." (*Barbiere di Siviglia*)

Enzo Dara (Mantua 1938) is the *basso buffo* of today. Few could ever imagine him as Ramfis or Monterone, Angelotti (*Tosca*) or Timur (*Turandot*), or even less as Klingsor in *Parsifal*; yet his first performances, from 1960 until 1966, were actually in these parts.

After having sung Bartolo and Dulcamara in 1967, Dara discovered that his real vocation lay in the comic field, and he dedicated himself entirely to it from then on. His best quality is that of vocal agility; in the fast vocalizing passages, and especially in the patter pieces, he enunciates so perfectly, despite the supersonic speed, that every word can be understood. (His "Signorina, un'altra volta..." by Don Bartolo, or his execution of Don Magnifico's demanding aria "Sia qualunque delle figlie", are unsurpassed).

To his gifts as a virtuoso, Dara adds a great natural sense of humor, never going over the top, never trying for easy laughs. Dandini, Don Pasquale, Geronimo in *Matrimonio Segreto*, Taddeo, Dulcamara, Don Magnifico, and the above-mentioned Don Bartolo are all roles from which the Italian bass has eliminated many of the bad habits which had accumulated in the bass tradition.

Wladimiro Ganzarolli (Piacenza d'Adige, Padua 1932) was a good Leporello and Mozart singer during the sixties and seventies; **Domenico Trimarchi** (Naples 1940) was often engaged by theaters to sing Don Bartolo, Dandini, Taddeo and Frà Melitone, with excellent results.

Among the most acclaimed young *buffi* we must mention **Simone Alaimo** (Villabate, Palermo 1946), who also sings Rossini's *opera seria*, and **Maurizio Picconi**. They are both complete artists with very good interpretative gifts but a limited repertory.

Enzo Dara in Il Barbiere di Siviglia (1996). *The most interesting characteristic of this comic bass from Mantua is the agility of his voice, both in vocalized singing and above all in rapid articulation. (Fondazione Arena di Verona. Photo: Gianfranco Fainello).*

FAMOUS BASS-BARITONES

We decided not to include the voices of **Mario Petri** (Perugia 1922 – Città della Pieve, Perugia 1985), **George London** (George Burnstein; Montreal 1919 – Armonk, New York 1985) and **Ruggero Raimondi** (Bologna 1941) in the *basso nobile* section because we believe them to be ideal examples of the ambiguous category of the bass baritone. They are voices which are well-extended, with an indefinable vocal color, always changing repertory by virtue of their ambivalent characteristics, varying over a wide number of roles.

Petri (whose real name was Mario Pezzetta) sang from 1948 until 1960, when he interrupted his operatic career to become an actor in sword fighting, swashbuckling films, and a pop singer. At the beginning of the seventies he returned to opera, this time as a baritone, but without great success. He was acclaimed in many performances of *Don Giovanni* and *The Marriage of Figaro* (as the Count), often under the guidance of Herbert von Karajan, who numbered him amongst his favorite singers. His voice was never very attractive, but it was extraordinarily

expressive, well-modulated, put to the service of a dynamic acting ability and an attractive physical appearance. Without exaggerating, singing with taste and style, Petri was also a good Don Magnifico and Mustafà in *L'Italiana in Algeri*.

Canadian born, but Austrian by adoption, George London was one of the most acclaimed bass-baritones between 1940 and 1960. He gave intense and vigorous performances of *Don Giovanni*, *The Flying Dutchman*, *Boris Godunov*, *Parsifal* (Amfortas), *Carmen* (Escamillo), *The Marriage of Figaro* (Figaro), *Aida* (Amonasro) and *Tosca* (Scarpia). His career was interrupted at the height of success after an unsuccessful operation on his vocal chords. Opera thus prematurely lost one of its most interesting and sensitive personalities. He began producing opera in 1971, with *The Magic Flute* at the Juilliard School, New York, and *The Ring* in Seattle and San Diego, 1973-75.

Ruggero Raimondi began at Spoleto as Colline in 1964. He immediately exhibited a smooth emission, and was able to cover the entire range fluently yet with considerable power, earning himself a place among the most gifted young *bassi nobili*. From 1965 to 1975 he sang in a vast repertory: *Vespri Siciliani, I Lombardi, Faust, Boris, The Marriage of Figaro, Simon Boccanegra, Ernani, Carmen* and *Don Carlos*. But he became inseparably associated with the role of Don Giovanni, and became immensely popular after he had starred in Losey's film of that opera in 1979. However, when he performed parts more strictly limited to a bass voice, his low register sounded artificial and unnatural, safeguarded only by his excellent technique.

He has no difficulty, however, in the high register (his a´ is effortless and penetrating), to the extent that he has ventured (though sometimes only on record) into the baritone repertory: Escamillo, Scarpia, Iago and Falstaff. His appearance as Don Profondo in Rossini's *Il Viaggio a Reims*, at Pesaro in 1984, was truly surprising. His agility was noteworthy and his rapid

Don Carlos: *"Nel posare sul mio capo la corona"* sings **Raimondi** (Philip II) *and so opens, very solemnly, the scene of the auto-da-fé. (Historic Archives of the Teatro Comunale of Bologna. Photo: R Ferrari)*

vocalization that of a true belcanto bass. However, these gifts were only partially confirmed by his following Rossini performances (*Turco in Italia* and *L'Italiana in Algeri*).

Raimondi moves with elegance on the stage, and he participates in the drama with the credibility of a great film actor, and for precisely this reason he is much in demand by the top opera directors and conductors, and also the film industry, which has captured on screen his interpretations of Don Giovanni, Boris and Escamillo (in Rosi's *Carmen*).

Other famous bass-baritones are **Jean-François Delmas** (Lyons 1861 – Saint Alban de Monthel 1933), very active in the Wagnerian and French repertories (he was the first Athanaël in Massenet's *Thaïs*); **Nikolai Schewelev** (1868 – Tiflis 1929), highly successful as Escamillo, Rigoletto, Hans Sach and the principal roles of the Russian repertory; **Arthur Endrèze** (Chicago 1893-1975), famous as Hamlet; and **Jaro Prohaska** (Vienna 1891 – Munich 1965), a Wotan and Baron Ochs of extraordinary effect.

In the following generations, some of the most famous names were **Alfred Jerger** (Brunn 1889 – Vienna 1976), the first Mandryka in *Arabella* in 1933 at Dresden and an acclaimed Mozart singer; **Gustav Neidlinger** (Mainz 1910 – Bad Ems 1991), a specialist in the role of Alberich in *The Ring*; **Ferdinand Frantz** (Kassel 1906 – Munich 1959), a noteworthy Wotan; **Herman Uhde** (Bremen 1914 – Copenhagen 1965), who worked in all the most important German theaters, Covent Garden, and at the Metropolitan, giving unforgettable performances of *Lohengrin, The Flying Dutchman, Tales of Hoffmann, Wozzek*, until his death in Copenhagen while he was singing Bentzon's *Faust III*; **Franz Crass** (Wippenfürth 1928), specialized in the roles of Sarastro and the Flying Dutchman; **Theo Adam** (Dresden 1926), who performed in a vast repertory, with a particular predilection for the parts of Jochanaan in *Salome*, Wozzek, and Pizzarro in *Fidelio*; **Tom Krause** (Helsinki 1934), active in the Mozart repertory and as a concert artist; **Roger Soyer** (Thiais, France 1939), a famous Don Giovanni; **Nicolai Ghiuselev** (Pawlilceni, Bulgaria 1936), really more of a bass than a baritone, despite his frequent ventures into an ambiguous repertory (Escamillo, Scarpia, Alfonso in *Lucrezia Borgia*); **Jules Bastin** (Brussels 1933 – 1996); **Simon Estes** (Centerville, Iowa 1938). Regarding **Justino Diaz** (San Juan, Puerto Rico 1940), despite the fact that the Kutsch-Riemens dictionary dares compare him with Ezio Pinza, we have always found him a singer of poor taste and mediocre technique.

Mario Petri, *at right, with two illustrious colleagues,* **Ferruccio Mazzoli**, *at left, and in the center,* **Boris Christoff**, *in Handel's Julius Caesar presented in Rome on December 26, 1956. The reading of the score was certainly not philological; but the audience was more than satisfied with the singing. (Historic Archives of the Rome Opera Theater)*

Mario Petri, *an exuberant Don Giovanni. In this role he was the favorite of von Karajan, who called him to his side in many performances. Petri was also a film actor. One remembers an amusing film made with the famous Neapolitan comedian, Totò (Totò Against the Black Pirate). (Historic Archives of the Rome Opera Theater. Photo: Villani)*

During the performance of Aida conducted by von Karajan at Salzburg in 1980, Ghiaurov was replaced in the role of Ramfis by **Ruggero Raimondi**. *Here he is, involved in this difficult and not very satisfying role for a bass. (Historic Archives of the Salzburg Festival. Photo: Rabanus)*

THE BELCANTO BASS: SAMUEL RAMEY

The Handel and Rossini renaissance was bound to have beneficial effects on the bass category, as has already been made evident in respect to Dara and Raimondi.

Samuel Ramey (Colby, Kansas 1942) is the best singer to emerge from this belcanto revival. He is a bass who traces an ideal *fil rouge* from the legendary Boschi, Montagnana and Galli (historic basses of the eighteenth and nineteenth centuries) through to the teachings of Pasero. From this last singer Ramey has borrowed the smooth singing style, his impeccable legato, varied phrasing, which is always expressive, and his capacity for vocal shadings. Since 1973, Ramey has been displaying these qualities in many operas which were also dear to Pasero, such as *Don Carlos*, *Mefistofele*, *Barbiere*, *Puritani*, *Rigoletto* and *Faust*.

Ramey's spectacular agility, his rare extension and his ability to add variety to his interpretation with taste and imagination, can be traced back to the eighteenth and nineteenth century basses mentioned previously. He is the only bass of the twentieth century to restore to song the force and incisiveness of an unequalled belcanto class, composed of head-spinning *roulades*, trills and interminable vocalizing and incredible *passaggi di*

Samuel Ramey wouldn't even be recognized by his own mother disguised like this! Looking at him he seems almost a painting, an ugly sketch – but instead it is Mefistofele ready to enter on stage and terrify the audience. (Giandonato Crico Collection)

Samuel Ramey, magnificent star of Maometto II. As a Rossini interpreter, the American bass has no equal in the current era. (Photographic Archive of the Rossini Opera Festival, Pesaro)

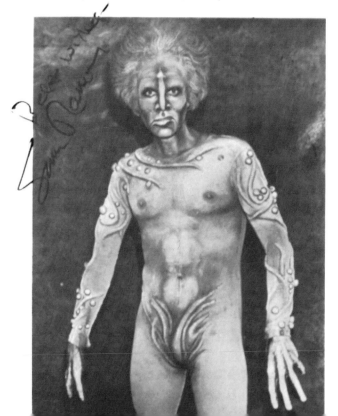

sbalzo, showing that he can jump easily from low D to high a´. His roles are Assur (*Semiramide*), Maometto (*Maometto II*), Mosè (in the double version of the opera, *Moïse* and *Mosè in Egitto*) and Argante (in Handel's opera *Rinaldo*). Thanks to these particular vocal qualities, Ramey is practically the singer-symbol of the Rossini Opera Festival of Pesaro. There, he is often the protagonist and star of the summer opera season (*L'Italiana in Algeri*, *La Donna del Lago*, *Edipo a Colono*, *Maometto II*, *Turco in Italia*, *Viaggio a Reims*, *La Gazza Ladra* and the *Stabat Mater*).

An amiable extrovert, Ramey moves with great ease on the stage, and is equally successful in comic roles, such as Don Giovanni, Mustafà (*Italiana in Algeri*), Selim (*Turco in Italia*), Figaro (*The Marriage of Figaro*) and Don Basilio.

*A moment from Rossini's Turco in Italia. At left, Donna Fiorilla (the soprano **Lella Cuberli**), kneeling, entreating is Don Geronio (**Luigi De Corato**); and at right, **Ramey**. (Photographic Archive of the Rossini Opera Festival, Pesaro)*

A perfect testimonial of Ramey's incredible voice is the following episode: in *L'Italiana in Algeri* the two *buffi*, Mustafà and Taddeo, compete with each other, by the use of their high notes, in the "Pappataci" duet. The first to pronounce the perilous "Pappataci Mustafà" is Taddeo, who then invites the naïve Pasha to repeat the vow: at that point Ramey launches his thunderous "Pa-ppa-taci Mustafà", two powerful high g´s, perfectly placed and as penetrating as that of any tenor. Of course, at this point, the audience never fails to utter a murmur of amazement and admiration.

Capable of equaling, even surpassing, the popularity of the best-loved tenors, Ramey best exploits his talent in belcanto, being less successful in the Verdi and, it might be added, "classical" repertoires, which he began to explore in the nineties. His performance of Philip II was not exactly unforgettable, nor was his Don Giovanni, however well-sung it may have been, but I would certainly number among his best the two performances of Mephistopheles (by Boito and Gounod), in which Ramey superbly combines his technical perfection and instinct for drama.

Following in the footsteps of Samuel Ramey and his phenomenal contribution to belcanto, many other basses have specialized in the Rossini and Handel repertoires, with good, sometimes excellent, results. The Italian singer **Michele Pertusi** (Parma 1965) has succeeded in exploiting to the best of his ability a voice that is not particularly strong but very well-prepared, and thus been able to tackle not only Rossini (Mustafà, Assur, Selim in *Turco in Italia*, Maometto, Mosé) but also Donizetti's *Lucrezia Borgia* and Verdi's *Oberto*. A good impression has been made, at the beginning of his career, by **Boris Martinovich** (1955), who studied with the same teacher as Ramey, and by **Ildebrando D'Arcangelo** (Montesilvano, Pescara 1969), an impressive figure on stage, well-suited to the roles of Don Giovanni or the Count in *Nozze di Figaro*, but who has pushed himself to the impossible heights of Assur in *Semiramide*.

Appendix

Glossary

Agility: An ease, lightness and flexibility of vocal execution, a special gift of the virtuoso singer.

Appoggiatura: An appoggiatura, or leaning note, is a vocal ornament mainly used by singers in the 1700s. It is an unharmonized auxiliary note which falls on the strong beat of a measure, a half tone above or below the essential note to which it is smoothly connected.

Aria: An air, song, melody or tune; often for solo voice, with accompaniment by an instrument or orchestra. Opera composers use the aria to enable singers to display their ability.

Belcanto: An Italian term for beautiful singing, now frequently used to imply a style of voice production especially suited to the operas of Rossini, Bellini, Donizetti, early Verdi, etc.

Bis: The Italian term for "encore".

Bravura: A striking display of ability and technique in a difficult passage.

Break: Place in the vocal range where the registers change. When a singer passes from one register to another there can be an abrupt change of vocal quality.

Breath: Air used in respiration. A singer inhales normally and exhales either with the glottis wide open and without producing vocal vibrations, that is, silently, or with the glottis closed, thus activating the vibratory action of the vocal chords.

Breath control: The mastery and correct use of the three breathing techniques used in opera singing. These techniques are breath renewal, breath retention and breath support; and their mastery enables the singer to conserve breath during phonation and to keep a well-regulated, continuous pressure for the production and projection of the voice.

Breathing: The act or process of drawing air into the lungs for oxygenating and purifying the blood, and its subsequent exhalation (Webster). This is a quote from *Human Physiology* by Starling: "The constant renewal of air in the lungs is brought about by rhythmical movements of the thorax or chest cavity which cause an alternate increase and diminution in their size. As the lungs swell up with each enlargement of the thorax, air (breath) is sucked in through the trachea or windpipe. This is the process called *inspiration*. As the thorax relaxes it contracts and its capacity is diminished causing an explosion of air and deflation of the lungs. This is *expiration*. The completed cycle of inspiration and expiration is called *respiration*. The frequency of respiratory movement varies with age, muscular effort, fatigue and emotional excitement. During full inspiration the thorax is enlarged in all dimensions, from above downwards by the contraction of the diaphragm (diaphragmatic breathing) and in its transverse diameters by the movements of the ribs (costal breathing)".
Breathing is important to the singer because normal voice production or phonation depends upon the presence of a steadily expiring stream of breath.

Buffo: The Italian word for comic or funny. It is used in opera, and particularly Italian opera: *basso buffo*, *tenore buffo*, but also *buffo* by itself, meaning a comic bass. We also find *opera buffa*, meaning comic opera.

Cabaletta: The word originates from the latin *copula*, coming from the Provençal *cobla*. A *cabaletta* is a verse, a brief opera aria with a simple rhythm and lively time, sometimes varied, placed at the end of a scene or a *concertato*. The term entered into common usage during the nineteenth century in Italian opera, especially in Verdi operas (the famous *cabaletta* "Di quella pira" from *Trovatore*, "Sempre libera" in *Traviata*, "Sì, vendetta" in *Rigoletto*).

Cadenza: Here we are referring to the vocal *cadenza*, that is to a series of ornaments performed, without instrumental accompaniment, before the end of the virtuoso aria. Initially, in the eighteenth century, the singers inserted *cadenze* (even three in 'da capo' arias) of their own invention, or even improvised. From Mozart on, the composers themselves included them in their works (celebrated *cadenze* are: the *cadenze* of Gilda, "Caro nome" in *Rigoletto,* and that of Lucia, the Mad Scene from *Lucia di Lammermoor,* which was written not by Donizetti but by the Ricci brothers). Singers, however, continued (and continue) to insert their own *cadenze:* the famous *cadenza* added by Titta Ruffo in the "toast" from Ambroise Thomas' *Hamlet;* and Roberto Stagno's final, additional, trill for the "Brindisi" of Turiddu; or the *roulade* with a high c˝ sharp which Lauri Volpi executed at the end of "La donna è mobile," sending Toscanini into a frenzy. Today, baritones such as Sherrill Milnes and Leo Nucci are in the habit of adding brief *cadenze* in the arias of *Trovatore, Barbiere di Siviglia, Ballo in Maschera,* not to show off their agility (as did Galvany or Battistini) but to display their power and extension in the high register. The reinstatement of the amazing, at times even excessive, nineteenth century *cadenze* is due to singers such as Sutherland, Sills, Horne, the bass Ramey and the tenors Merritt and Blake, specialists in vocal arabesques in the operas of Rossini, recently revived in philological style.

Cavatina: Diminutive of *cavata.* A short aria in one or two sections (not like the classical 'da capo' aria in three sections) often preceded by a recitative, which has the purpose of presenting the character. Some famous cavatinas are those by Figaro in *Barbiere di Siviglia,* "Largo al factotum"; by Dulcamara "Udite, udite, o rustici" from *Elisir d'Amore;* the "Casta diva" by Norma.

Claque: A French term used to signify a group of people paid by a singer or theater (or even sometimes without any financial reward) to be present at a performance to applaud this or that singer (irrespective of the quality of the performance) and, vice versa, the "anti-claque" to whistle and boo a performer. The claques have always operated in favor of one artist or against another, so much so as to encourage famous rivalries (Banti and Morichello, or Cuzzoni and Durasanti in the eighteenth century; Callas and Tebaldi, Caballé and Gencer, and Domingo and Pavarotti in the modern era). Berlioz has left an unforgettable essay on the claque, describing its members, their ways of applauding or disapproving, penetrating the psychology of this particular category of music maniac. To a special category belong the so-called *Vedovi* (Widows), nostalgic supporters of Maria Callas, ready to whistle any artist who dares to sing "her" operas.

Coloratura: Brilliant vocalizations, such as florid ornaments, arabesques, runs, trills, rapid scale passages. Thus we get the coloratura soprano, a specialist in music that requires a virtuoso rendition.

Color: The quality or timbre of the voice; the various shades of vowel quality. Color refers to the features of a particular voice which give it a character or individuality of its own, and give life and imaginative intensity to the expression. It is a composite of gradations in tonal quality and dynamics which vividly renders the text of the song or aria.

Colpo di glottide, Coup de glotte, Glottal stroke: A little trick used by some singers to assist in attacking a note. The vocal chords are put into rapid vibration by a tiny, almost imperceptible movement resembling a cough, which, closing the larynx orifice, provokes the attack of the sound. It is a very useful technique, in fact even fundamental for producing staccato sounds; the famous *picchettati,* even *colpi di glottide,* hiccup style, of Leyla Gencer are famous, almost proverbial.

Concertato: A musical interval placed at the end of a scene or act of an opera, with the participation of the solo voices, the orchestra and often the choir. Celebrated *concertati* are: those which close the first act of *Barbiere,* "Mi par d'esser con la testa" (Rossini); the final acts of *Don Giovanni* (Mozart) and Bellini's *Norma.*

Corona or Punto Coronato: A graphic sign which, placed above a note or a pause, prolongs *ad libitum* its duration. In use since the 1400s, in the eighteenth century it served to indicate the start of a *cadenza* or, when the corona was placed at the start of an *aria di portamento,* to indicate the possibility of performing a *messa di voce* closed by a trill. The interpretative tradition of the nineteenth century has inserted *corone* where the composer never dreamed of putting them; thus we have the high a´ of "Sacerdote, io resto a te" in the version by the tenor De Muro or by Del Monaco, which seem unending; and also the phrase of Don José in *Carmen* "Dragon d'Alcalà," sung back-stage; or the "Amami Alfredo" of Violetta Valéry.

Critical edition: A musical edition prepared on the basis of strictly philological criteria, in absolute respect of the original text and related documents. They can be about a composer's global production (*opera omnia*), or about different composers of the same period and background (*monumenti musicali*).

The main critical editions of recent times relate to the *opera omnia* of Rossini (care of the Rossini Foundation of Pesaro, since 1969) and of Verdi (care of Ricordi and the Chicago University Press), undertaken on the basis of reasonably valid criteria and with praiseworthy intentions. However, the musicologists entrusted (and our comments essentially regard Verdi) with this work often forget, in the impetus of their philological enthusiasm, to pay attention to the philology of tradition, failing to integrate the primary source of the text with an accurate choice of the principal ornamentations, of the *cadenze* and of the *puntature* added, right from the first performances, by the great singers. As a result we have, for example, the philological *Rigoletto* presented at Vienna by Riccardo Muti: gone are the high notes, modified is the tempo in some passages, gone are the soprano ornaments; the original score was absolutely respected, but the end result was disappointing. Even Verdi himself, and perhaps with few misgivings, accepted the virtuosity of his singers, fully aware that, thanks to them, the opera would be a success. He even asked his friend Donizetti to write the *puntature* for the singers in his opera *Ernani*.

Da capo: Repeat from the beginning. A 'da capo' aria, often used by Handel, is one in which the first section is repeated after a contrasting section.

Diapason: In the music of ancient Greece it was the name which indicated an octave; a basic sound, usually the A, used for establishing the pitch of all the other notes and for tuning instruments. The placement of the sound is fixed at 440Hz, or double vibrations, a second; but for centuries the diapason varied from region to region.

Only in 1700 was there an effort to resolve the problem, studying a method to uniform the tuning and pitch of the instruments; however, the congresses and conferences organized by acoustic physicists during the Romantic period failed to establish an identical diapason for everyone; also because there was a tendency (especially in string instruments) to increase the pitch, little by little, as the lute-makers strove to give their instruments an ever more brilliant and incisive sound. The present measure was established in 1939 at a congress in London, with a later decision in 1971 by the Council of Europe to confirm the frequency of 440Hz. Despite all this, from Bach to our time, the A has passed from 563Hz to 377Hz a second, that is to say that it has grown by more than a semitone: Duprez's mythical high c´´ in chest voice would correspond today to a b´, or even a b´ flat. This does not authorize certain singers, however, to lower the pitch of the most difficult arias: the tenor Penno sang the "Pira" in B flat major; Pavarotti today performs "La gelida manina" and the duet "O soave fanciulla" (*Bohème*) a half tone under; Frederica von Stade adjusted to her own pleasure the arias of *Sonnambula* in San Francisco. These habits have always existed in the theatrical world. The same things were done by Malibran, Garcia, Pasta and Alboni.

Diaphragm: A partition consisting of muscles and tendons which separates the chest from the abdominal cavity. The diaphragm is convex upwards and flattens on contraction, thus increasing the capacity of the chest or thorax. The diaphragm is a most important factor in the breathing process, especially for opera singers.

Diction: The manner of enunciation in speaking or singing. Good diction requires clear and accurate formation, production and projection of the elementary sounds of a language, subsequently combining them into fluent patterns which are suited to the expression of the words and music of a song or aria.

Diva: The term originates from the Latin word for goddess. It is used to denote a great or especially gifted female singer.

Dynamics: The variation and control of the force or power radiated into space. The term can be broken down into loudness and intensity.

Encore: A French word used in English (but not in French) to mean "Perform it once more." An encore is a repetition or extra piece performed in response to such a demand. The word "bis" has the same meaning and is used in Europe.

Enunciation: A projective, energizing or dynamic process whereby vocal sound, audibility and distinctiveness are applied to the vowels and consonants being articulated.

Falsetto/Falsettone: A singing technique which uses the resonance cavities of the head. The voice which results is penetrating, high, sweet if well-emitted, otherwise querulous and chirping. With the use of the chest resonance cavities, one can obtain a mixed sound, the reinforced *falsettone* with which the tenors of the early 1800s pushed their voices up to high e´´ flat, f´´ and g´´ (David, Rubini, Nourrit).

Fila di voce/Filatura: Literally, to draw the voice out into a mere thread of sound.

Flautato: The so-called *attacco flautato* (fluted attack) of a note is, in imitation of the flute, the abrupt passing from one note to another, without intermediate passages or *portamenti*. Some singers prefer to reach their notes using this type of effect; while others (Corelli, for example) adopt a technique of *portamento*.

The Gods: Term used in English-speaking countries to indicate gallery seats high up in the theater.

Habanera: A Cuban rhythm (the word derives from the name of the city, Havana), originating from Spain, in moderate 2/4 time, similar to the tango. *Habaneras* were composed by Ravel, Debussy, Albèniz, but the most famous of all is that of Bizet, "L'amour est un oiseau rebelle," which marks Carmen's entrance in his opera. The motif did not originate with Bizet, but with the Spanish musician Sebastian Yradier (1809-1865) who wrote the celebrated melody for his opera *El Arreglito*. The entrance of Carmen was very difficult; the first Carmen, Célestine Galli-Marié, obliged poor Bizet to write thirteen different versions, and she was only satisfied with the present *habanera*. As compensation for so much trouble, after Bizet's early death, the singer collected the funds necessary build a fine monument dedicated to the composer.

Heldentenor: A German term signifying, literally, a hero-tenor. A Heldentenor uses his strong voice for singing the heavy tenor parts in Wagner operas or other operas of similar type.

Inflexion: Variations of the voice in pitch.

Intonation: Singing in tune.

Legato singing: A passage marked as legato should be sung smoothly, without noticeable breaks between the notes.

Lied/Lieder: A German word meaning aria, song or melody. It comes from medieval times, when it emerged in the soloist verse form of the troubadours and *Minnesänger*. In the thirteenth and fourteenth centuries the Lieder underwent a polyphonic elaboration, transforming into *conductus, rondeaux, Diskantlied, Tenorlied*, always acquiring more poetic and expressive value.

With the seventeenth century production of the accompanied solo, the Lied rapidly spread, often using more than one voice with an accompaniment of *basso continuo*. In the eighteenth century many odes and Lieder verses were published and used in *Singspiele*.

The pre-Romantic Lied has its roots in *Volkslied*, simple and inspired, reaching the height of its popularity in the late eighteenth century. The *Kunstlied* developed with the support of the classic composers (Haydn, Mozart, Beethoven) and reached its peak with Schubert, Schumann, Brahms and Wolf. Words and music integrated perfectly, as did the solo voice and piano accompaniment. Lieder are often grouped together in song cycles: *Die Schöne Müllerin, Winterreise* (Schubert), *Dichterliebe* (Schumann); or are presented with sumptuous orchestral accompaniment, *Lied von der Erde* (Mahler). In the twentieth century the *Kunstlied* was neglected by composers, with the exception of those of the New School of Vienna: Schönberg, Berg, Webern.

Singers from Germanic countries specialize in Lieder, be they tenors, sopranos, basses, mezzo-sopranos, or baritones, whereas the Italian school has always ignored Lied, with the exception of some lullabies, *Ave Maria*, or a few other melodies often sung as encores by Gigli, Schipa and other colleagues, at the end of their recitals. Latin singers have stubbornly disregarded the formidable patrimony of German Lieder, despite its being musically fundamental and an excellent form of voice training.

Loggionismo: (derives from Italian "loggione"=the gods). This Italian word relates principally to a favorable or critical attitude towards the singers performing the opera. The term derives from the time in which the first real divas of the opera stage appeared, and is comparable to the fanaticism of some football supporters, or political or religious bigots.

Loggionismo comes from the word *loggione*, or gallery, generally destined to those opera lovers who cannot afford the exorbitant prices of seats in the stalls. However, apart from the limited view of the stage (both in height and depth), the *loggione* is the best place to follow an opera and every music critic should be seated there! *"Le son monte,"* say the French, and in fact, the best acoustics are found right there, up in the "gods," where the voices are perfectly amalgamated with the sound of the orchestra; in addition, the critic who sits in the *loggione* escapes the perilous proximity of relatives and close friends of the singer who are decidedly more annoying than the most exuberant *loggionisti*; moreover, perched up in the "gods", the critic also avoids the venomous gossiping with theater managers, artistic directors and theatrical agents.

Loggionismo is on the one hand fun and folkloristic, on the other detrimental. For decades the world capital of *loggionismo* was Parma. In the small bars scattered around the Teatro Regio the regular *log-*

gionisti would gather. The backstage *loggionisti* in particular had the dreadful habit of stuffing themselves with the local red wine, ham and chocolate while waiting for the tenor or prima donna to sing a famous aria. And they were unmerciful. The tenor who didn't please them was insulted, even under his hotel windows, and it was not unknown for the railway porter to refuse to load his luggage onto the train. Carlo Bergonzi, who was born at Vidalenzo, near Parma and therefore a local glory, was vehemently berated for having sung in *pianissimo* the b´ flat of "Celeste Aida". Cornell MacNeil was so exasperated that he threw an inkwell while screaming at the audience "That's enough, you idiots!". Elena Mauti Nunziata was forced to interrupt her performance of *Traviata* (with Maestro Previtali conducting) because of the disapproving whistles and jeers.

Today, times have changed and Parma's opera lovers are content with the good and not so good, as is the case in most Italian opera theaters. The anger and the enthusiasm of the *loggionisti* have dissipated, even if every now and again you still hear an "old-style" objection. One of the most recent incidents was the interruption of the Genoa-staged *Traviata* during "Parigi o cara", where Joan Sutherland was forced to withdraw from the performance, the innocent victim of the inadequacies of the tenor. Other incidents have occurred, for example during *Lucia di Lammermoor* at La Scala when the audience booed Pavarotti; at the even worse performance of *Lucia* at the opening of the 1988-89 season of the San Carlo of Naples; the ugly version of *Luisa Miller* at La Scala with Katia Ricciarelli in 1989, which culminated with the diva cursing the audience; and the *Vespri Siciliani* which inaugurated the 1989-90 season at Milan, severely criticized by the audience on opening night.

In conclusion, a note about the different forms of protest which differ from country to country. In Italy the "boo" and a protest whistle are the norm, together with picturesque insults in cases of more extreme disapproval (sometimes even programs, or vegetables are thrown onto the stage). "Hissing" is reserved for less serious cases, such as a poorly-sung aria. In Austria the "boo" is used but not the protest whistle, and in serious cases the *loggionisti* (who occupy the *Stehplätze*, or standing places) hurl insults, sneeze, or laugh during an aria. In American theaters the whistle is a sign of approval and vast enthusiasm, as is the stamping of feet; dissension is rare and is limited to shouts and a few isolated "boos". In France, disapproval is shown with "Uh! Uh!". In the Soviet Union you just don't applaud, and the same is true in England. In China you always applaud.

Mask: The hollow bone cavities of the skull found behind the eyes and the back of the nose. In singing, the words "placing the voice in the mask" or "in the facial mask" are technical terms which refer to the obvious use of these cavities in the emission and projection of sound.

Melisma/Melismatic: The word originates from the Greek meaning "song". It is used to signify the extension and prolongation of a single vowel or syllable into an expressive but non-florid vocalisation.

Messa di voce: In vocal technique this consists in gradually swelling the sound from a *pianissimo* to a *fortissimo* and vice versa, all in one breath; a technique also known as *filare il suono*, that is "to thread the sound". In belcanto the *messa di voce* had great importance because it allowed a singer to exhibit the length of a breath, the fullness of his/her sound and technical ability. On the scores a composer would mark where to execute a *messa di voce* with a *punto coronato* at the beginning of an *aria di portamento*. (In some Handel arias, and in the Malcolm aria in Rossini's *La Donna del Lago*, Marilyn Horne gives a perfect example of the *messa di voce* as it should be executed, with a final trill as well!)

Mezzavoce: The sound is emitted very, very softly or with a muffled tone. The true *mezzavoce* requires a quantity of breath equal to, if not more than, that used for a high note as well as a perfect positioning of the sound in the facial mask. Only the greatest singers know how to correctly use the *mezzavoce* (Pertile, Schipa, Kipnis, Pinza, Callas, Kraus); others willingly substitute the *falsettone rinforzato* (Gigli, Lauri Volpi, Tagliavini) if not the falsetto (Carreras, Di Stefano, Domingo), which is the easiest way of tackling the problem without too much trouble.

A correct use of *mezzavoce* assures a varied interpretation and the observation of the text's expressive demands. Verdi wanted the entire prologue of *Simon Boccanegra* to be performed with *mezzevoci*, and likewise the entrance of Nabucco "Tremin gli insani" (sung by the baritones at the top of their voices), and the attack for "Sì, vendetta," far more effective and logical if murmured by the baritone; not to mention the "Sogno" sung by Iago or the difficult "Parmi vedere le lagrime" by the Duke of Mantua.

The agilities of Rossini's score, on the other hand, should be performed with strength, according to the precise instructions of the composer; a rule always respected by Horne and Valentini-Terrani, but ignored by Caballé and Gasdia, who tend to perform the more complex Rossini melismatic passages with an out-of-place use of *mezzavoce*.

Mezzofiato: A virtuoso effect obtained with a sort of interruption and immediate release of the flow of air on a held note without resorting to any intake of breath. Today this technique has almost completely fallen into disuse; but it was often adapted in the Liberty period by Mattia Battistini, and the tenors Anselmi, Schipa, Gigli, and Pertile, who placed it, often excessively, in the middle of an aria or in the *cadenza* of the aria.

Oratorio: A composition, usually for solo voices, choir and orchestra, based on a sacred text, and usually performed in concert form, often in a church, without acting, scenery or costumes.

Ornament: A term used to describe the vocal, melodic decorations which were not written into the score by the composer but were improvised by the performer according to his or her personal taste. Many of these ornaments have become traditional and are often believed to be an integral part of the score. Audiences may excpect and even demand their inclusion.

We must distinguish between the improvised or Italian ornaments, not indicated in the score and entrusted to the taste and fantasy of the interpreter, and the fundamental or French ornaments, marked in the score by specific symbols and placed in precise points of the melody, respecting both pitch and rhythm. Among the principal fundamental ornaments are the *acciaccatura*, the *appoggiatura*, the *arpeggio*, the double *cadenza* or *gruppetto*, the *mordente*, the *tremolo*, the trill, and the vibrato.

Opera critic: An expert in "antique" voices, an avid collector of dusty old recordings, of vintage static and crackle, of dates, quotes, relics of every kind, lists of names, addresses, certificates of birth and death; ready to describe the voices of David or of Malibran with a precision and self-assurance which the same critic would be incapable of using to describe a performance of Pavarotti heard the evening before.

Passaggio: As a technical term used in voice production, it refers to the break between the various vocal registers, e.g. from low to middle register, from middle register to high register.

Phonation: When vocal sound is produced in the larynx or glottis this process is called phonation, that is, the vibratory activity of the vocal chords producing pulsations sufficiently rapid to create the sensation of tone. When these tones are sustained, they form the singing voice.

Phrasing: The use of vocal patterns and expressive technique that are appropriate to the musical thought in a song. Phrasing needs to be the result of genuine feeling and not a cold analysis of the musical structure. Unobtrusive phrasing, clearly and correctly applied to the piece, constitutes one of the greatest refinements in a performance.

Picchettato: In vocal technique, the term refers to the quick emission of staccato notes, often in the high register. It is a type of virtuosity especially used by coloratura sopranos; and the absolute champion of this skill was Maria Galvany, who sang at the beginning of the twentieth century.

Pitch: The degree of acuteness or graveness of tone. The greater the number of vibrations per second the higher the pitch.

Portamento (French, *port de voix*): The *portamento* is usually indicated by a slur mark connecting two notes of different pitch; the *portamento* is characterized by passing from one note to another by sliding rapidly over all the intermediate notes. Some singers make excessive use of this vocal technique, with the intention of facilitating their rise to the high notes, or more simply, from bad habit (Gigli, Corelli, Bergonzi, Tebaldi).

Prima donna: This Italian term meaning "first lady" refers to the leading lady in an opera company. The term comes from the early years of opera, in the seventeenth century, when the term *primo uomo* was also used, but then it was applied to the *castrati*. In our time the title *prima donna* is often given to a female vocalist of high reputation and vast earning ability; as a result the term *prima donna assoluta* (the absolute first lady) has arisen to satisfy the vanity of certain eminent singers.

Projection: The act of transmitting the voice through the atmosphere from singer to listener.

Puntatura: The substitution of a note with another (usually higher) by a singer, for the purpose of better showing his or her ability. The *puntature acute* (high points) by now have become part of the tradition of certain operas (the c″ of the "Pira" in *Trovatore*, the e‴ flat of *Traviata*, the a′ flat in the Prologue of *I Pagliacci*) and should not be considered a whim of the lead singer. The composers were conscious that the success of a super-high note could determine the success of the entire opera, and were more than willing to meet the requests of their singers. During a concert recital at Rome, the soprano Editha Gruberova used a score of the aria "Ebben ne andrò lontana" (Catalani's *La Wally*) which ended with a high e‴, that is, a traditional *puntatura*.

Range: The pitch range of the singing voice. See "Tessitura".

Recitative: A type of singing in which the words are delivered in a declamatory way with the intention of emphasizing the natural inflections of speech. Another name is *musica parlante*, speaking music. In opera and oratorio recitative commonly serves for dialogue or narrative. Recitative is divided into various types, the principal ones being *recitativo secco* (dry) which is a quick patter, with a simple accompaniment of chords, and *recitativo strumentato* (instrumented) which has an orchestral accompaniment and was brought to its apex by Wagner.

Roulade: A French term meaning a fast-vocalized passage, as found especially in Rossini and bel-canto composers.

Smorzatura: A gradual dying away of the sound.

Sprechgesang: German, meaning "spoken song". The term was used for the first time by Schönberg in *Pierrot Lunaire* (1912) and then by other composers of the New School of Vienna, to indicate a form of declamation which synthesizes the values of singing and acting, while fully respecting the rhythm. The intonation oscillates in a continuous *crescendo, glissando, diminuendo* (Italian terms commonly used in music and meaning "growing," "sliding," and "diminishing") without ever remaining fixed (or if so, only for a fraction) on any one note. The word is particularly suitable to describe the recitative used by Wagner and especially the type used by Richard Strauss in his operas.

Staccato: The word means "detached," and in singing, the staccato sign requires a disconnected attack for each note or tone, each of which is cut short or separated from the next note by infinitesimal gaps of silence. There are two ways, in singing, of attacking and releasing a staccato note. These are: diaphragmatic action, such as we use when we laugh; or glottal attack, similar to the mechanism used when coughing.

Stecca: A familiar term amongst opera singers, especially those of the Italian school, to indicate a vocal "accident", that is, a singer's mistake. It may be an off-key note, hoarseness, a break, a sob, a yell, a scream or a flop; also a note simply not sung, but rather "eaten". The *stecca* of the tenor Gayarre in *The Pearl Fishers* is famous; it happened during the performance on December 8, 1899 at Madrid: after having failed the first high note in the aria "Mi par d'udir ancor" (worth translating, as it says, "I seem to hear again!") he repeated the aria at the end of the opera, but, alas, he failed again. He then turned to the audience and said *"Esto ce acabò"* (It is finished!). Shortly afterwards he died of consumption.

Style/Stylistic: In opera these words refer to the particular way in which a singer performs, his or her own special characteristics.

Tessitura: A term used to indicate the approximate extension of a musical piece in relation to the voice for which it has been written. The tessitura is, therefore, the ambit of sounds, from the low to the high, in which a singer is most at ease. It is not to be confused with "extension" (or range), which regards the complete orbit of sounds possible for a certain voice. In the following table we have listed the tessitura and extension or various categories of voices.

	Tessitura	Extension
Tenor	g–g´	c-d´´
Soprano	g´-g´´	b flat-g´´´
Baritone	d-d´	G-a´
Mezzo-soprano	e´-e´´	g-b´´
Contralto	b-b´	e-g´´
Basso	B-b	C-f´ sharp

Timbre: Timbre is the tone quality or tone-color which distinguishes, for example, the note sung by a boy soprano from that same note sung by a tenor or by a mezzo-soprano. It is the special resonance quality of a tone which distinguishes it from other notes of the same intensity and pitch.

Timbre is determined by the form of the sound wave being emitted by the singer and the relative frequencies and intensities of its harmonic parts and overtones. It is the identifying quality of a vocal tone which is established in the main by the resonant properties of the singer's facial mask.

Transposition: The changing of the pitch of a composition, without making other changes, in order to make it more suited to a particular singer's vocal range.

Travesti Roles: "Trouser" or "Pants" Roles: As can be guessed by looking carefully at both words, these terms refer to roles which are written for a female mezzo-soprano when the character being portrayed is male (Octavian in *Der Rosenkavalier*). There are a few, but rare, *travesti* roles for men, in Wolf-Ferrari's *Il Campiello*, two old women are played by tenors.

Tremolo: In singing, the *tremolo* is an uncontrollable unsteadiness or faulty trembling of the pitch. It is caused by an inability to maintain stability in the laryngeal mechanism during phonation, which frequently results from muscular weakness, or nerves and tension. The *tremolo* must not be confused with vocal vibrato. The vibrato varies within a semitone interval whereas the *tremolo* varies more than a semitone.

Trill: Not to be confused with vibrato or *tremolo*. In singing, the trill is the controlled rapid alternation of two distinct pitches in the musical interval of a semitone, a third or a whole tone. Joan Sutherland and Selma Kurz are two singers famous for their trill.

Verismo/Verist School: The term describes a style of Italian opera composed mainly in the late nineteenth and early twentieth centuries which presented "real-life" situations instead of the rather idealized subjects and characters of operas written before this date. Composers of the Verist school include Leoncavallo, Puccini, and Mascagni. Some singers have specialized in Verist roles (Magda Olivero).

Vibrato: The vocal vibrato is a regular periodic oscillation of vocal tone above and below its normal pitch level and always within a semitone interval. In vibrato the concept of interval is completely missing; vibrato is not to be confused with *tremolo* or trill. The vibrato adds life to and enriches a tone, but it is never exaggerated.

Voice: To reproduce the sound of the human voice (phonation) the following are needed: a) the respiratory muscles of the thorax closed in the rib cage with the lungs functioning as bellows (capacity of approx. 3500-6700 cm3 of air); b) the vocal chords (four) functioning as source of the vibrations; and c) the cavities of the forehead, nose, mouth, trachea and lungs serving as resonators. The highness of a sound depends on the tension and length of the vocal chords. The shorter the larynx, the higher the voice, and vice versa. This is why basses are, generally, men of tall stature.

The timbre of the voice is conditioned by the resonance cavities (the trachea and lung cavities below the larynx, and above the larynx the oral cavity, the nasal fossae, the forehead cavities and the vibrations of the facial bones).

The quality of the voice depends on the number of harmonic frequencies (below 9 frequencies it is opaque, and above 14 it is shrill). These frequencies can be augmented with a good breathing technique. The sound can be very powerful and penetrating using only, and exclusively, the right pressure of air flow on the vocal chords, thus exploiting the principle of resonance without using any other energy form.

Volume: Fullness or quantity of tone.

Zarzuela: An idiomatic Spanish opera with spoken dialogue.

A LESSON IN SINGING: A. KRAUS

High-Class Master Class

The following transcription includes the major points discussed by tenor Alfredo Kraus in a two-hour Master Class held in Rome at the Brancaccio Theater, on May 22, 1990. This Master Lesson offers a full discussion of singing technique, a fount of valuable information and insight for professionals and non-professionals alike.

The audience, formed by young singing students and singing teachers, listens and comments. Many have their eyes, and ears, opened for the first time while others are undecided what to think. Numerous questions arise. "But what about the roundness of the sound?" "Don't you risk singing in the nose?" "My teachers always told me to cover during the break, to darken the sound!" "I have always breathed pulling my stomach in during the expulsion of breath!" and so on. Kraus never loses one bit of his proverbial calm. It is the outlook of a person who is sure of what he is affirming. He knows that any misunderstanding or unresolved doubt could be fatal for many budding talents, so he repeats for the fourth time his explanation of how to breathe, indicating his abdomen, making the students touch it when on the stage, singing with them the most difficult phrases and sailing up to any high note with no effort at all.

Initial explanation and the concept of voice placement

Thank you for your warm welcome. I am pleased to see that so many of you have joined us for our friendly chat this afternoon.

I must first say that the voice is a mystery. It is not tangible. It is a sound and not at all material. We cannot even hear how it really sounds, because our ears perceive at the same time both an external and internal sound; this is its mystery. It is the most fascinating musical instrument that exists, because we ourselves are the instrument, and we control it by means of internal sensations.

Why do we always hear people talking about voice placement without their ever offering an explanation? We say "Putting the voice in the mask" and the reason for this term is that placing the voice correctly we use the internal cavities behind our facial bones (the so-called "mask") as a natural amplifier, because in the throat we have none. On the contrary, the area that surrounds the vocal chords tends to absorb sounds as it is made of soft mucous tissue and flesh. It is up to us to project our voice as close to the listener as possible, as "forward" as possible, using a column of air that passes through the vocal chords. The further forward the sound is placed, the closer it is to the listener's ear, and it is also better sustained in the mask. The more it is sustained in the mask, the better we use the facial amplifiers (i.e. the cavities we were speaking of before: the frontal sinuses, the nasal sinuses, etc.).

Why do we say "voice in the mask"? We say so because a very intelligent person discovered that there is one sound that is naturally placed in the facial amplifiers: it is the Latin sounding vowel "i" (as in "igloo"). It is also the least tiring vowel to sing on. When we say "i" the sound is already there, forward, and correctly placed in the mask; when we say "e" (as in "excellent") we notice that in respect to the "i" it is further back; as for the "a" (as in "arrive") we may as well wave it good-bye, for the sound sinks completely into the throat. However, when we talk we can mostly get away with this, even if many people have to seek the assistance of voice specialists (phoniatritians) because they speak badly. If we could manage to put all the sounds in the position of the "i" simply while talking, there would be no work for these doctors.

The "I" vowel opens the throat

There is a real obsession in most schools of singing: that of darkening the voice. But why should I darken my voice if it is naturally clear? It is nature who decides if a voice is clear and bright or dark and rich; we cannot make it become so by artificial coloring. Many of my colleagues (even famous ones), when they come to a Latin "i" tend to sing a French "ü"; or when they come to a Latin "e" they pronounce it "ö" (as in "earth"); instead of "a" they say "o". This is all mistaken. It is wrong to think that this darkening of the sound helps technique and rests the voice: this method sends the voice backwards into the throat, making it lose color and sonority. Up until a short time ago all that I am saying was mere theory (put to practical use by those singers who have a correct technique; unfortunately they are hard to come by).

Now, thanks to new studies, and to a video made by Professor Tapia of the Santandér University in Spain, we are able to actually see the movements of the vocal chords and the surrounding area during the emission of the voice. The revelations are amazing. It can be clearly seen that the vowel that most widens the cavities (the famous "open throat") is the "i," the "weakest" vowel. They have also measured the sound frequencies, and the results show that the "i" has the largest number of frequencies. How can we explain this? Simple: the "i" may seem small but it has the right resonance; it is sustained in the natural amplifiers and therefore has a larger number of frequencies, so you can hear it better. Volume doesn't count. The sound must vibrate correctly and carry well, reaching every listener in an auditorium.

As you can see, studying singing simply becomes a matter of placing the voice in the natural position of the "i". That is all. Seems easy, doesn't it?

I am no genius, nor am I a freak: if I am able to do it, so is anyone else. The problem is that very few people have talked about this until now.

It has become a technique in disuse. When I debuted at the Rome Opera a Spanish friend of mine introduced me to Giacomo Lauri Volpi. Lauri Volpi himself accompanied me at the piano as I sang "Questa o quella" and "La donna è mobile". He exclaimed straight away: "This is the right technique. These days nobody sings like this anymore". He also told me to be careful in my choice of repertory, because if I kept to a correct repertory I would be able to continue singing for a long time. Lauri Volpi knew what he was talking about!

Everybody has their virtues and their defects. I think that Lauri Volpi, apart from the style and taste of his time, had an excellent technique. He sang a bit of everything, this is true… he, who had told me not to step outside my natural repertory. On the other hand, it was customary to do so then. He was, in my opinion, a "heroic" tenor, but he also sang light lyric roles with the aid of a reinforced falsetto. Today this may be questionable, but then it was perfectly acceptable. I think that both Lauri Volpi and Gigli modified their natural voices when they used this reinforced falsetto. They also changed the style, giving the impression of a strange, artificial lightness. Aside from this, Lauri Volpi had a good technique, based on the principles I have just explained to you, and what's more, his breathing was excellent.

Intercostal-diaphragmatic breathing

Lauri Volpi confirmed that the right breathing method is "intercostal-diaphragmatic". When we open our ribs as widely as possible the elastic membrane we call the diaphragm is completely flattened. In this way it is able to sustain the column of air that is needed to sing. This is very important: when breathing in, the ribs widen; then you must sustain the sound and as you gradually emit it, continue to push the diaphragm outwards, so that it remains as tight as possible during the whole process. It is wrong to pull in your stomach while exhaling. I'm sorry if some of you disagrees. By pulling in your stomach the membrane loses tension and can no longer sustain the sound. Therefore, to sustain the sound, the diaphragm must remain tense and as flat as possible, and during the emission of breath you must push outwards. This is essential. Of course, there are many small tricks and techniques to think about as you study. They may seem stupid, but are often very useful. To understand singing we need a special language, and also a lot of imagination. It cannot be explained in any other way. It is not like the piano that has keys we see and touch. A person with little imagination will always have difficulty in studying singing. Great difficulty.

The mobility of the facial muscles

An example: let's imagine that there is a small hole in our forehead, between our eyes, and that it is from this opening that the sound passes. This hole is always the same size; it will never change. If this opening is the right size for the "i" ("igloo") which can pass through it perfectly (and it would seem so), how can the "e" ("excellent") which is larger, and the "a" ("arrive") larger still ever pass through it? Of course, if I had a magic power that automatically reduced the larger vowels making them lighter and higher they would be able to pass easily. But instead it seems almost impossible to put the "e" and "a" sounds into the same opening as that of the "i". To do this we must be assisted by our facial muscles. The heavier and the larger the vowel is, the more we must lift it by raising our cheek muscles, lightening the sound as we ascend towards the high notes. Many singers pronounce "ü" (as in "soon") and "eu" (as in "earth") with their mouths tightly pursed, or open in an O-shape, without moving their facial muscles at all. It would be best to remember that in singing neither "u" (as in "book") or "o" (as in "octopus") exist, even if we are sometimes obliged to sing them. The "u" is the most difficult of all, as the "o" we may pronounce like a French "a". For example the word "amore" correctly becomes "am-a-re" as if you were saying the Italian verb "amare" and not the noun "amore". The "u," however, has hardly any frequencies so we have to make do by putting it as near as possible to the "i" in the cavities surrounding the nose. Be careful, do not put it *in* the nose; many people tend to confuse the two things.

People who are used to hearing voices placed in the throat, when they hear a correctly placed voice, they are likely to exclaim: "He's singing in his nose". It is true that we are close to the nose, but we are not actually in the nose. I can easily block my nose and continue to sing or speak when my voice is sustained in the "mask". There are people who have difficulty in understanding this difference because they are used to hearing a guttural or backward-placed voice. But that's their problem. We must go ahead and forget about the people who don't want to understand. Another useful example is to consider the length of piano strings: the low notes have long strings, the high ones have short strings. Let us pretend that our vocal chords are not in our throat, where we cannot control them, but between the eyes, where we can manipulate them thanks to the air pressure exerted by the diaphragm. Now let us imagine that we are singing normally and climbing towards the high notes. As we increase the pressure, pushing the diaphragm outwards, the vocal chords are shortened, and the sound becomes higher and more resonant. It is like a river that is at first wide and calm, but when the banks tighten it begins to flow faster and with more force.

Avoid an "O"-shaped mouth

Another thing to avoid is the "O"-shaped mouth that so many singing teachers recommend: a round mouth with the chin lowered. One must articulate logically, using the upper jaw, and not the lower one. If you lower the chin the sound becomes closed, but using the upper jaw and keeping the lower one still, gives much more space and sonority to the voice. A few days ago I was watching the Callas Competition on television, and I was particularly struck by the mezzo-sopranos who were among the finalists. It was easy to understand that their teachers had always told them: "You must cover, darken the sound, for you are a mezzo-soprano" (it would be interesting to see if they actually were mezzo-sopranos). The poor girls kept darkening, losing both color and sonority, and sending the voice backwards. Then, when they reached the high notes, they were physiologically forced to open their mouths wide and lift their cheeks in order to make the sound become more brilliant.

This is the basis of singing. Each singer has his/her own individual vocal instrument, which is the same for everyone; true, each with different characteristics, but there is only one technique. The fact that many people manage to sing with other techniques does not mean a thing; there are voices that are as strong as iron, and can survive any sort of treatment. However, they all have their faults, and serious ones at that. How many tenors fail the "To-o-sca, sei tu" passage from Mario Cavaradossi's first aria! This is because they almost all say "Tu-u-scou" strangling the high b′ flat and sending the voice backwards. Instead you must forget the "o" and think of a dark "a". The audience will hear a clear, easy "To-o-sca," but you have really said "Ta-a-sca." These seem like silly little tricks, perhaps they are, but there is no escaping from them.

Q: Can you explain how to approach a note?
You must forget about the throat and attack the note from the top to the bottom, as though it were coming from above your head. In this way the note will be perfectly clean from the beginning, and stylistically correct, without those awful *portamenti* that rise up from below, that touch the throat, or those hiccups. Think of those little balls that balance on top of water shoots in village fairs: the pressure must be

always maintained otherwise the ball falls off. It is the same sort of mechanism that works for the breath in sound production. You must maintain a constant air pressure, and sustain every note, including the descending ones, always keeping the position high. The notes preceding a high note are particularly important, because they function like the steps of a ladder.

The *passaggio?* Where's the problem?

I never think about the *passaggio* (or the so called "break" between the registers). The further I climb the more I increase the pressure, raise the position, and widen the sound. It almost feels as if your very head is widening to give more space to the voice. Like when I want to call to a friend standing on the other side of the street, I don't shout "üüüü!", which is a tight and closed sound, instead I shout "aeeee!", which is open and wide. Almost all students are taught by their teachers to close, cover or turn the sound, and some even vomit it. This is not the right way to do things.

Q: I would like to ask you to explain breathing again, because singing teachers are very often so confusing on the subject. Did you say that during expiration we must push downwards?

No, not at all. Not downwards, outwards! When I widen my ribs as much as possible and begin to emit the sound, I feel as if there are external forces that pull my diaphragm, extending it always further. These forces are, of course, not external but inside my own body. It is I who push outwards.

Q: But doesn't the stomach have to be pulled in during the process of exhalation?

No, never.

Singing is the simplest thing in the world, but many people seem to want to complicate it. I never talk about the "*passaggio*". There are various changes of registers (a low register, a middle register and a high register), but there is no change in position. We do not have various throats in different parts of our body, but only one, and one position in which we can control it. Why create such problems over the *passaggio?* Many people make a sort of vomiting sound when they make the *passaggio*, a sort of "augh!", which instead of opening the throat closes it. The point of resonance is the same for every sound, chest voice and head voice. Women produce with ease the chest notes, but they too have a high placement. We use technique to render similar all the notes in our range, without the need of so-called "breaks" or *passaggi*. If

a singer has a problem on their high or low notes what should they do? What *passaggio* should they look for? Should they pass over a bridge, or through a tunnel perhaps?

Q: You criticized the reinforced falsetto used by Lauri Volpi and Gigli, but I find the mezzavoce *used by Gigli sublime. Is the* mezzavoce *out of fashion as well?*

The *mezzavoce* is out of fashion because nobody knows how to produce it. However, I was not referring to *mezzavoce*, I was referring to reinforced falsetto. They abused this falsetto, while *mezzavoce* is quite another thing.

Once we have asserted that the "i" vowel is the most open and free of all, we can do little else other than attempt to put all the other vowels in the same position.

It is obvious that there are other parts of our phoniatrical apparatus that participate in forming the sound. They are the mouth, the larynx, the pharyngeal cavities, etc., but we cannot control them consciously. We can only manipulate the voice once it is in the facial amplifiers, so you must start from the "i," which has the highest position and, therefore, is the most distant from the throat.

Q: In 1964 I was very impressed by Luciano Pavarotti singing La Traviata *at the Rome Opera, even after having heard Franco Tagliavini, who at the time had the more robust voice of the two. Pavarotti was amazing for the uniformity of his voice, even though it was quite small. Today his voice has become stronger and he has changed repertory. Do you think this is a correct evolution?*

Let's forget about Pavarotti. I think that a correct technique allows a voice to maintain its best features intact throughout the years...

Q: Excuse me, but I have always heard that a voice becomes more robust as time goes by.

Look, Gigli started his career singing the repertory of a light lyric without being one, this doesn't mean a thing. Juan Oncina, one of my colleagues, always sang parts for a light tenor. Once upon a time, thanks to a frequent use of falsetto or *mezzavoce*, you could sing the light lyric repertory and at the same time many works of the *verismo* school. Caruso did so at the beginning of his career, but he did not really have a light voice. Why should a voice change? Our basic features don't change, do they? It is clear that with time we grow older, but our height remains the same. I may put on three kilos of weight, or loose five kilos, but I won't change that much. Technique must help preserve the voice as much as possible over the years. Of course, there will always be some slight change as time goes by, the voice might darken slightly, or might gain sonority in the low notes, but mainly the vocal features remain the same. Certain tenors begin their career singing the "gelida manina" in the original key, and only five years later they have to lower it by half a tone. Does this seem right to you? What has happened? Quite simply, they have made their voices heavy, pushing on the middle register and losing the high notes. It's unnatural. Any respectable tenor must have a high c´´.

Q: Could you please explain, once again, the correct method of breathing?

You haven't understood it yet?

I have heard different theories on this subject, but I only have one. The breathing method is intercostal-diaphragmatic. You don't push your stomach out, or pull it in. You must widen your ribs, thus flattening the diaphragm. Once the diaphragm is completely flat all the way around, you emit the voice while pushing outwards. We must continue to make the note "travel" until the end. For example, when I emit an "a" it is not only one "a" but millions of "a's", like machine gun fire.

Q: Maestro, I would like to ask you about vocal agility. There are many singers with light voices who should have no problems with it, but instead have many. What would you advise them to do?

It is a question of practice. You must make sure that every note is part of a single flow and are all sung legato without that awful "ha-ha-ha" sound. We Latins have the habit of adding a sort of "h" before each note. It is a dangerous habit, because it breaks the continuity of the sound and increases the risk of compromising the support. The secret for singing well is that of singing legato. This will also give you the necessary agility.

Q: Without discussing the specific virtues of your colleagues, I would like to ask you what the difference is between the open method of singing (like Di Stefano) and the rounded method (like Bergonzi)?

I cannot talk about singing methods. For me there exists only one method for singing, only one technique. You must pardon my presumption, but I insist that the correct technique is the one I use myself. The fact that some manage to sing well by virtue of their natural gifts alone, is neither here nor there. As I said before there are the so-called "iron voices," that can survive any sort of treatment. You must know how to listen accurately, to hear if a "round" voice can really resolve the high notes, or if a voice placed in the throat can resolve them at all. Most listeners know nothing of these terms. They only want to listen to a beautiful voice, especially one that screams a lot.

Q: You mean as in the case of some much publicized voices?

Exactly.

Q: Can you explain how to perform the mezza-voce?

This is one of the many contradictions of singing. To diminish the sound we must increase the pressure and decrease the volume, that is, we must compress the diaphragm further while reducing the weight of the sound, lifting it ever higher and lightening it. This is not easy. We cannot solve this problem in five minutes. However, it is the only way to reduce the sound, keeping the same position, without having to use falsetto. The facial muscles are very helpful in this as well. We must train them to be elastic and mobile.

Q: When you talk about the sustainment of the voice, you make a vertical gesture. How can the widening of the ribs horizontally have anything to do with this vertical pressure?

Of course, singing is full of these contradictions. If I breathe pulling my stomach in, the diaphragm would lose tension. How could I sustain the voice then?

Q: So we must keep a constant pressure, pushing outwards along the whole circumference of our abdomen?

That's right. On all sides. Thus the diaphragm remains as tense as possible.

Q: When you talk about tension of the diaphragm, I don't understand what you mean. Can you explain yourself better please?

The diaphragm is an elastic membrane. When it is relaxed, in its normal position, it is not completely horizontal. If I keep it horizontal during expiration, by pushing outwards, I can support the column of air needed to sing. Otherwise where could I sustain it to be able to project it forwards? Take a trampoline artist, for example. From where does he project himself when he jumps? He is sustained by something that resists his pressure, then he jumps. Have you ever watched a small baby crying naked on a bed? What does it move? The ribs. And where does the baby sustain the sound? In the facial mask. You can be sure that the baby will never lose his or her voice. The parents might be tempted to jump out of the window from sheer desperation, but the baby will cry for days on end without losing its voice. This happens because the baby is using a physiologically perfect technique, breathing naturally, widening the ribs to extend the diaphragm and projecting the column of air into the facial amplifiers. I am afraid I cannot be any clearer than that.

Conclusion

I believe above all that there is no lack of voices, but a great lack of voice teachers. Plenty of voices arrive, albeit periodically. Probably, the only reason why there are no more dramatic sopranos or tenors or mezzo-sopranos is because they are ruined by the conservatoriums, the singing teachers, and schools. Then there is another phenomenon: those voices that manage to survive even the worst training and the worst teachers. These singers have such natural gifts that they can sing anyway and, if they know how to manage themselves, can expect to have a successful career, despite their faults. The teacher is important only to a certain extent. The teacher can give advice, some clues, some indications of technique, but if the student is as stubborn as a donkey it is all to no avail. The student must have natural talent before he or she decides to become a singer. The teacher is important in recognizing the student who has no problems, or faults, or the student who starts off straight away with many doubts and mistakes.

Yes, today we have a crisis situation – but it's not all the fault of the singers.

INDEX OF NAMES

This is an index of the singers cited in the book. The page numbers in italics refer to singers' picture captions.

Abbreviations:

s   soprano
t   tenor
ms   mezzo-soprano
bt   baritone
bs   bass
c   contralto

GREMESE
Cinema / Performing Arts / Entertainment

Matilde Hochkofler
MARCELLO MASTROIANNI
The Fun of Cinema
192 pages   US$ 29.95 – GB£ 19.95
A lavishly illustrated biography enriched by casts and credits. Here the enthralling story of Fellini's favorite actor.

Stefano Masi – Enrico Lancia
SOPHIA
224 pages   US$ 29.95 – GB£ 19.95
A tribute to the greatest Italian Diva of all times. The Authors tell us about the debuts, the fears, the films and the world stardom of this beautiful actress.

Cinzia Romani
TAINTED GODDESSES
Female Film Stars of the Third Reich
182 pages   US$19.95 – GB£ 12.95
"The Author explores this sinister, unknown territory with deft characterization and scrupulous attention to detail. An authentic revelation!" John H. Davis

Stefano Masi
ROBERTO BENIGNI
80 pages   US$ 12.95 – GB£ 7.99
Sensitivity, intelligence and pure comedy have led Benigni to be dubbed the new Chaplin. His spirit is captured in this book on his life and films (including Life Is Beautiful*).*

Grazioso Cecchetti
CLASSICAL DANCE (vol 1 and 2)
192 and 144 pages   US$ 24.95 – GB£15.95
This is the only existing diretc testimony of the famous Cecchetti method of classical dance. It includes over 700 original sketches and painstakingly compiled explanations and exercises.

Claudio G. Fava
ALBERTO SORDI
An American in Rome
190 pages   US$ 39.95 – GB£ 19.95
The first book on Sordi's life and career, richly illustrated with beautiful black and white stills.

Lorenzo Cuccu
PAOLO AND VITTORIO TAVIANI
Nature, Culture and History Revealed by Two Tuscan Masters
160 pages   US$ 29.95 – GB£ 19.95
An invaluable mirror of the personal and professional development of two worthy masters of cinema's great neorealistic tradition.

Oreste De Fornari
SERGIO LEONE
The Great Italian Dream of Legendary America
184 pages   US$ 39.95 – GB£ 24.95
The great American Western would never be the same after Sergio Leone's spaghetti western revolution... and Americans love it.

Jean A. Gili
ITALIAN FILMMAKERS
Self Portraits: A Selection of Interviews
192 pages   US$ 24.95 – GB£ 15.95
Careers, lives and artistic creations of ten of Italy's most famous post-War filmmakers through their own voices. A selection of unique interviews and photos.

Stefano Masi – Enrico Lancia
ITALIAN MOVIE GODDESSES
Over 80 of the Greatest Women of Italian Cinema
226 pages   US$ 29.95 – GB£ 19.95
A dazzling bouquet of more than 80 of Italy's most famous divas from the 1930s to the present day, with historical commentaries and a treasure of collector's photos.

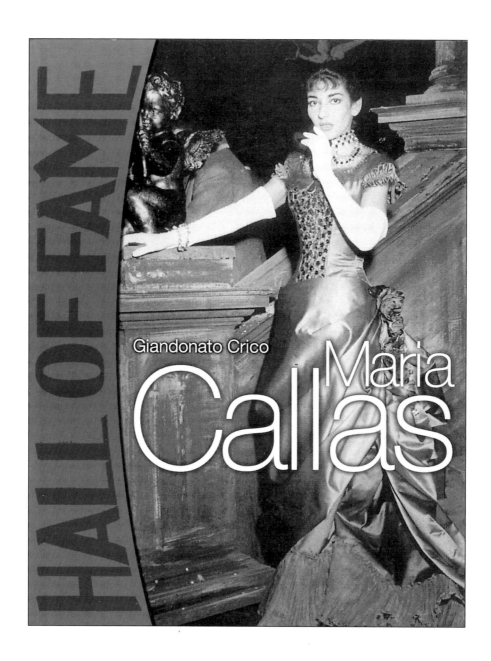

HALL OF FAME

Giandonato Crico

Maria Callas

The Author portrays the life and brilliant career of this opera singer from the inside. The book contains a selection of pithy quotes by Maria Callas herself and photos never seen before. Love affairs, friends, scandals and temper tantrums form the base of the Callas myth. Her story is worth knowing.

80 pages   US$ 12.95 – GB£ 7.99